Google™ Analytics 2.0

Jerri Ledford
and Mary E. Tyler

Wiley Publishing, Inc.

Google Analytics™ 2.0

Published by
Wiley Publishing, Inc.
10475 Crosspoint Boulevard
Indianapolis, IN 46256
www.wiley.com

Published simultaneously in Canada

ISBN: 978-0-470-17501-9

Manufactured in the United States of America

10 9 8 7 6 5 4 3 2

Library of Congress Cataloging-in-Publication Data

Ledford, Jerri L.

 Google Analytics 2.0 / Jerri Ledford and Mary E. Tyler.

   p. cm.

 ISBN 978-0-470-17501-9 (paper/website)

 1. Google Analytics. 2. Internet searching--Statistical services. 3. Web usage mining--Computer programs. 4. Internet users--Statistics--Data processing. I. Tyler, Mary E., 1970- II. Title.

 TK5105.885.G66T95 2007

 658.8'7202854678--dc22

                        2007026265

To all of my friends who think I'm famous, who are more excited about each new book than I am, and who support me in ways that few writers (or technologists) ever experience. I'm not famous, but without you, I couldn't do it. I love you all. Thank you!

— Jerri

To Jim Roberts of Carnegie Mellon University, who taught me to teach. To Lorrie Kim, who said, "This is too good to keep to yourself." To Jerri Ledford, my coauthor and mentor, who said, "You can do this." Again. And again. And again. And for Mom, because there aren't enough words.

— Mary

About the Authors

Jerri Ledford has been a freelance business-technology writer for more than 10 years, with more than 750 articles, profiles, news stories, and reports online and in print. Her publishing credits include: *Intelligent Enterprise, Network World, Information Security Magazine, DCM Magazine, CRM Magazine,* and *IT Manager's Journal.* She has also written a number of books. When not writing, she divides her time between Alabama, Mississippi, and Tennessee, hiking, gardening, playing with electronic gadgets, and spending time with friends and family, who refer to her fondly as "tech support."

Mary E. Tyler is a professional technology journalist and a former software and web developer. She specializes in open source, enterprise software, intellectual property, motorcycles, and anything Macintosh. Tyler has three daughters, four cats, one small, fluffy lapdog, and a spouse in the career military.

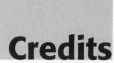

Credits

Acquisitions Editor
Katie Mohr

Development Editor
William Bridges

Technical Editor
Todd Meister

Production Editor
Elizabeth Ginns Britten

Copy Editor
Nancy E. Rapoport

Editorial Manager
Mary Beth Wakefield

Production Manager
Tim Tate

**Vice President
and Executive Group Publisher**
Richard Swadley

Vice President and Publisher
Joseph B. Wikert

Project Coordinator
Adrienne Martinez

Compositor
Laurie Stewart,
Happenstance Type-O-Rama

Proofreading
Sossity Smith

Indexing
Jack Lewis

Anniversary Logo Design
Richard Pacifico

Contents

Acknowledgments

From Mary: First, thanks to my stellar agent, Laura Lewin, who sold this book, and Neil Salkind, who negotiated the second edition, and to the staff at Studio B. They're good folks. Thanks to Bill Bridges, our development editor; Katie Mohr, who acquired this book for the publisher; and everyone else at Wiley who made it printable. Thanks, also, to the engineers at Google who answered our questions and to the cool staff of Browsercam.

Endless gratitude to my fellow writers online, who gave me community, advice, and various kicks in the pants as needed. There are too many to name, but they all hang out at The Writing Mother and Jay's Writers' World. I'm sure there are others I should thank. Apologies to anyone I forgot.

From Jerri: Mary, your vision on the first edition turned into an amazing reality. It's been a wild ride, girl! You're a phenomenal writer, and I've learned much along the way. Thank you!

We couldn't have created the book without the help of some very dedicated "Googlites." To David Salinas, Brett Crosby, Christina Powell, Michael Mayzel, and Brandon McCormick, thanks for all your help and for pointing us in the right direction. And thanks to my very own "Google Guy," Alex Ortiz. Your passion for and belief in Google Analytics comes through, my friend. I am more appreciative than you'll ever know for your answers and your efforts in ensuring that there are great screenshots for our readers to see.

There's also an entire team of people at Wiley who helped make the book possible. Mary has mentioned several, and I'll add my thanks to Todd Meister, our amazing (and super-patient) tech editor, Katie Mohr, and Mary Beth Wakefield (wonderful, helpful people), and Bill Bridges, who deals with my writerly eccentricities as if they were normal! Thanks to all of you (and to anyone I may have overlooked).

Introduction

In late 2005, Internet behemoth Google purchased leading web analytics firm Urchin and began offering the service free of charge to certain well-placed technology publications' web sites. Not long after that, Google launched the Google Analytics service based on the Urchin software, offering it to the general public as a completely free service. Response was incredible — overwhelming — and a quarter of a million new accounts were created overnight, with an estimated half to three-quarters of a million web sites tracked.

All of this caught Google unprepared, and people had to be turned away because there weren't enough resources to support everyone who wanted an account. Google began taking e-mail addresses for interested webmasters who couldn't be accommodated at launch.

How did this happen? How did Google so grossly underestimate the demand for Google Analytics? After all, at $200/month, Urchin did only well — it had good software and a relatively low price point for the industry, but it wasn't exactly inundated with clamoring customers.

Apparently, assessments based on Urchin's sales weren't exactly accurate. The demand for real analytics is huge, and the price tag of "free" is exactly the price tag that draws in the masses.

But what are analytics? Most webmasters know enough to realize that they need analytics. But do they know how to read them? How to use them? Are analytics just "site stats on steroids," or can they be used by the average webmaster, who is a layman and not a professional, to improve the performance of a web site?

The answer is that, with Google Analytics, the average webmaster can use analytics to improve the performance of a site. And well over a half-million users have figured this out, using Google Analytics. So many users have turned to Google Analytics and begun to make suggestions about the program that the design team at Google decided it was time to implement some new features and make the application easier to use. And that's how the Google Analytics 2.0 application was born.

The purpose of this book, *Google Analytics 2.0*, is to explain the concepts behind analytics and to show how to set up Google Analytics, choose goals and filters, read Google Analytics reports and graphs, and use that information to improve your web site performance. Advanced information about topics such as filtering, goal setting, and e-commerce tracking, and more in-depth explanations of some of the theories of analytics, are among the new features added. We provide numerous examples of the ways companies use these reports to do business better to illustrate how some of the functions of Google Analytics work. We have even included examples (although sometimes not flattering) of our own sites and usage patterns to help you understand the value of the reports and capabilities available through Google Analytics 2.0.

Overview of the Book and Technology

Google Analytics 2.0 is a powerful tool for measuring the success of your web site, your marketing efforts, and your products and services. With that in mind, we strive to give you all of the tools you'll need to begin using the program immediately if you've never used it before. That includes explanations of how to get started using Google Analytics, as well as chapters on how to find and use reports.

We've also tried to explain what each of the reports means, in the grand scope of your business. Where it's appropriate, we tell you how these reports apply to our personal web sites; and where it's not, you'll find both fictional examples and examples of real companies that use Google Analytics.

What's new in this book is the advanced material that you'll find here. We include information that takes you beyond just getting into Google Analytics 2.0. Of course, you'll learn all about what's new with the program, but more important, you learn how to use the application for more in-depth analysis of your web site statistics. Using the advanced techniques and tips provided throughout the book, you'll be able to drill down deeper, find more specific information, and use information in ways that you never have before when using Google Analytics. There's even an entire chapter of advanced material to help you gain still more value from your Google Analytics application.

How This Book Is Organized

The book is divided into several parts. Each part corresponds with a section on the Google Analytics user interface. Here's a quick map of what each part contains:

- **Part One: Basic Analytics** — This part contains three chapters. Chapter 1 introduces you to the concept of analytics and the reasons why you should use Google Analytics 2.0. And then, in Chapters 2 and 3, we compare Google Analytics to a program with which you may already be familiar — AWStats. The purpose of the comparison is to familiarize you with basic analytics and web statistics concepts you will need to understand Google Analytics 2.0.

- **Part Two: Setting Up Google Analytics** — Google Analytics can be a little intimidating when you first see the program. But when set up properly, it is a very powerful program that helps you improve your web site effectiveness. To that end, this section walks you through getting started in six quick chapters. Chapter 4 gives you the basics on signing up for Google Analytics and navigating the user interface. Chapter 5 gets you started setting the program up. In Chapter 6, we try to demystify filters and filtering, and then we take that a step further by explaining goals and goal setting in Chapter 7. The next chapter in this section, Chapter 8, covers integrating Google Analytics with Google's AdWords. Finally, Chapter 9 provides guidance for some of the more advanced features of Google Analytics.

- **Part Three: Dashboards** — We begin to get into the meat of Google Analytics in the two chapters in Part Three. These chapters help you get control of Google Analytics 2.0. In Chapter 10, you learn how to access and customize the dashboards, and Chapter 11 covers everything you need to know about setting date ranges.

- **Part Four: All Reports: Visitors** — You'll find most of the information on the reports in Google Analytics 2.0 in the "All Reports" sections of the book. Each of these chapters follows the structure of the reports. Part Four contains six chapters that cover all of the Visitor reports, including an overview, trending reports, loyalty reports, browser capabilities, network properties, and user-defined reports.

- **Part Five: All Reports: Traffic Sources** — This part includes three chapters that detail the Traffic Sources reports. The Traffic Sources overview, AdWords, and additional traffic reports are covered here.

- **Part Six: All Reports: Content** — Part Six contains only one chapter, but that chapter contains information on all the content reports in Google Analytics 2.0.

- **Part Seven: All Reports: Goals** — Like the previous part, Part Seven contains only one chapter. This chapter covers all of the goals-specific reports in Google Analytics 2.0.

- **Part Eight: All Reports: E-Commerce** — The e-commerce reports help you to better understand your e-commerce sales. This part of the book contains three chapters that detail the e-commerce reports available to you. Chapter 23 is an e-commerce overview. Chapter 24 includes product performance reports. And Chapter 25 explains additional e-commerce reports that are available.

We suggest that whether you're interested in Google Analytics for marketing, content optimization, or e-commerce, you should skim through the whole book first. Even if you don't want to know which of the pages on your site sells the most gadgets, there is value to be found in these reports, and we show you where to find it.

Once you've read through the book, keep it near your computer to use to refresh your memory on how to use a report or where to find it.

One thing you may notice is that each report is in a section of the book that corresponds with a section in Google Analytics 2.0. We've tried to maintain a structure similar to that of Google Analytics 2.0 to make it easier for you to find everything. If you don't know where something is located in the program, look at the illustrations in the book. They'll show you exactly where we found it.

One more note about the illustrations you'll find here. You may notice that some of them have no data. We've done this on purpose. Chances are that there will be areas of Google Analytics where data is not yet being collected. This is because you have to set up your web site and some of the reports and then give them time to collect data. We're leaving these blank figures just so you can see what they might look like before you have data in them. In the majority of illustrations, however, you'll find varying amounts of data. In some cases, examples of micro-businesses are used, and in others we've included examples of larger businesses. Again, this is to help you understand the varying levels with which Google Analytics 2.0 can be used to improve the effectiveness of your site.

Who Should Read this Book

Do you have a web site or blog that you'd like to track? Can you edit the HTML on that site? Are you web savvy but not an analytics expert? If that's you, you've got the right book. We tried to explain everything in the following pages in the context of how small-business owners and micro-business owners might need to use it. These concepts apply to home-business owners as well. There is a wide audience for Google Analytics 2.0. Our aim is to help the beginning and intermediate users become experts, so you'll find information in these pages that runs the gamut from very basic to quite advanced.

Depending on where you are with your Google Analytics account, you might be able to skim over certain sections of the book. For example, if you've already set up a Google account and your Analytics account, you can glance at Chapter 1 without paying too much attention to detail. If you haven't completed one or both of those actions, however, you probably shouldn't skip that chapter.

We do recommend that everyone read Chapters 5–7. The information included in those chapters is relevant to nearly everyone who uses Google Analytics 2.0.

If you want, you can even skim through the whole book first and then come back and focus on only the sections that apply directly to your needs at this time. The great thing about *Google Analytics 2.0* is that it's designed to be a lasting resource. You can always pick the book up later if your needs change.

Tools You Will Need

As with any report that you create, there are a few supplies that you'll need along the way. With Google Analytics, it's fairly simple. First, you need a web site to track. It can be your own web site, your company web site, or even a blog site, so long as you have access to the HTML code for that site. You have to have access to the code because you need to alter the code so that Google can track your site.

In addition to your site, you'll also need access to the Google Analytics program. Signing up for Google Analytics is easy; you'll learn all about it in Chapter 4.

You may also want a Google AdWords account. It's not essential to have, but part of the true power in Google Analytics lies in its integration with Google AdWords. If you don't have an account and haven't even considered using one, read through Chapter 8 and then go ahead and sign up for the account if you think it will be useful. It takes only a minute, and you can deactivate your AdWords campaigns at any time.

Finally, throughout the book you'll find references to books on certain topics. These are not requirements, just suggestions that you may find useful if you want to know more about that specific topic. The books recommended here can be found through Amazon.com or any local bookstore. We've tried not to include anything obscure or hard to find.

Moving On

Enough. We've covered everything you're likely to want to know about using the book, so it's time to move on. Well, everything except the blog. If you have questions while you're reading the book, or if you just want to learn what's new or changed with Google Analytics, check out our blog at `www.google-analytics-blog.com`. You'll find all kinds of up-to-date and extra information about the program there, and even some tutorials that include advanced information and uses for Google Analytics.

Now it's time to get going. Have fun, and thanks for reading!

One
Basic Analytics

Having web site statistics is one thing. Understanding what they mean and what you should do with them is another thing altogether. If what you want is to get into the nitty-gritty, reams of information are available to you. If, however, what you're really looking for is a quick, easy-to-understand explanation of analytics and why you should care, read on.

This part of the book gives you the working knowledge you need to understand the importance of analytics, all in three short chapters. When you've finished reading these first three chapters, you'll understand basic web measurements, how they apply to your web site, and the difference between site statistics and analytics. Then you'll be ready to tackle Google Analytics.

Why Analytics?

Short Answer (for underlings)

Because.

Slightly Longer Short Answer (for your boss)

Because it's there and it's free, and web-page counters are *so 1997*.

Long Answer (for you)

First there were log files and only people who bought really expensive software could figure out what the heck the half-million lines of incomprehensible gobbledygook really meant. The rest of us used web-page counters. Anyone could see how many people had come to a page. As long as the counter didn't crash, or corrupt its storage, or overflow and start again at zero, there would be a nifty little graphic of numbers that looked like roller skates (or pool balls or stadium scoreboard numbers or whatnot).

Around 1998, the arbiters of taste on the Internet (i.e., everybody) decided that page counters were *so 1997* and that there must be a better way.

And also about that time, web site statistics packages or "stats" came into common use — not common use by huge businesses that could afford thousands of dollars for software but common use by us peons who rent our web space from hosting companies for as little as $5 a month. Stats packages basically collect data but leave you to analyze that data. So they tell you what happens; they just don't put what happens into any type of business context.

If you have Windows-based hosting, you may have a Windows-specific stats package, or your host may use the Windows version of one of the open source stats packages. If you have hosting on a Linux web server running Apache (and about 60 percent of web servers run Linux and Apache), you'll most likely have Analog, Webalizer, or AWStats, and you may have all three. These software packages are open source under various versions of the GNU Public License (GPL). This neatly explains their ubiquity.

They're free as in freedom, but more important to this particular purpose, they're free as in beer. Free as in beer is a large attractant to bottom line–conscious ISPs and web hosts. While a good site-stats package will provide numerous important metrics to help you measure traffic and fine-tune your web site's performance, there are a few key things that site stats just won't tell you. We'll get into that later.

Where stats packages leave off is where analytics come in. Comparing what a good analytics package does to what a good site-stats package does is like having Mark McGwire bat right before the Little League's MVP. One could be kind and say it's a Major League to Little League comparison, or like putting a man next to a boy, but the truth is that analytics are like site stats on steroids. The long answer to "Why analytics?" is almost as short as the slightly longer short answer: web analytics are site stats on steroids (and page counters are *so 1997*). Stats give you numbers. Analytics give you information.

If Analytics Are So Great, Why Don't We Have Them?

The short and simple answer to this is that medium and large companies that can afford analytics do have them. There are many analytics software packages that cost money, among them WebTrends, HitBox Professional, and Manticore Technology's Virtual Touchstone. The low-end price for web analytics is $200 per month. The high-end price? A couple grand a month is not unusual. To the microsite, the small site, the web merchant on a shoestring, the mom-and-pop site, the struggling e-zine, the blogger who aspires to be Wonkette but isn't yet — that is, to most of the sites on the web — two hundred bucks a month sounds like a lot of money!

Then, in mid-2005, Google rocked the boat, buying a small company called Urchin. Urchin was no Oliver Twist. It was, in fact, a runner-up for the 2004 ClickZ Marketing Excellence Award for Best Small Business Analytics Tool. Its product, Urchin Analytics, had a monthly cost on the low end of the market — about $200 a month — and was designed for small businesses.

Six months later, Google did something completely unprecedented. It rebranded Urchin's service as Google Analytics with the intention of releasing it as a free application. Google prelaunched it to a number of large web publications (among them NewsForge.com, where Mary Tyler is a contributing editor). And shortly after that, Google opened it to the public, apparently completely underestimating the rush of people who would sign up — a quarter of a million in two days.

Google quickly limited the number of sites that registrants could manage to three, although if you knew HTML at all, the limitation was pathetically easy to bypass. Google also initiated a sign-up list for people who were interested, which eventually morphed into an invitation system reminiscent of the controlled launch of Google's Gmail. The moral of this story is, "Don't underestimate the attraction of *free*."

Now That We Have Analytics, What Do We Do With Them?

What do you want your web site to do better?

Analytics is software that generates metrics. Metrics are measurements. There are all sorts of possible web site metrics — measurements you can take — about how many times files are accessed, how many unique IP addresses access the site, how many pages are served, and so on. Analytics can calculate the most popular pages, how long the typical person stays on the typical page, the percentage of people who "bounce" or leave the site from a particular page, and thus the percentage of people who explore the site more deeply.

Ad nauseam.

Yes, you can look at a zillion different metrics until it makes you dizzy, sick, and hopeless. Fortunately, some metrics have more impact on your site than others. Which metrics matter? That depends on what your site is. If your site is content, there's one set of metrics that matters. If your site sells things, a whole different set of metrics matters.

The point here is that you have to figure out your web site's purpose. For content businesses, it might be how much time the visitors spend, how deep visitors dig, and how often visitors return. For a business concerned mainly with selling things, it might be average time to sale, rate of shopping-cart abandonment, and profit, profit, profit. Once you know what metrics are meaningful for your web site, you can use those metrics to improve the site's performance. What do you do with analytics?

You improve your bottom line.

Here's a scenario for you. Mark owns a small rug store. It's nothing fancy, but the store does have the best prices in a three-state area, so it stays pretty busy.

Mark's wife, Anna, is his official webmaster. Anna doesn't have any formal training in web site design, but through trial and error she has managed to put up an attractive site. The problem is, attractive doesn't necessarily translate into effective, and Mark and Anna want to know how effective the site is.

That's where Google Analytics comes in. When Anna first activates her Google Analytics account, she just watches it for a few weeks to see how much traffic the site gets, where it comes from, and what pages visitors spend the most time on.

After a few weeks, Google Analytics has given Anna enough information that she knows the planning pages of the web site are the ones that customers spend the most time on. She can also see that the majority of her visitors come from a link on their local Better Business Bureau site.

These facts help Anna and Mark make some decisions about their marketing budget. Being small means that marketing needs to be effective because there's less budget for it than a larger company might have.

Based on what they've learned from Google Analytics, Anna decides to create a monthly newsletter for the company, which includes tips for planning where and how to place a rug and effective decorating tips for using rugs. They also agree to try AdWords for a few months to see how an AdWords campaign would improve the business.

To track all of this, Anna sets up filters and goals in Google Analytics. Using the metrics returned by these filters and goals, she'll be able to see if her decision to build on the strengths of the web site actually turns into more sales.

Anna and Mark aren't real. They're (unpaid) performers in this little skit, but their story illustrates how you can use Google Analytics to improve your marketing, which in turn will improve your business. Your specifics might be different. But if you use Google Analytics as a tool to monitor and build marketing efforts, you'll find there are many benefits to knowing the who, what, when, why, and where of web site traffic.

What Analytics Is Not

The short answer is: Google Analytics is not magic. It's not some mystical force that will automatically generate traffic to your web site. Nor is it the flashing neon sign that says, "Hey, you really should be doing this instead of that." And it's most certainly not the answer to all your web site traffic problems. No, analytics is none of those things.

What analytics *is* is a tool for you to use to understand how visitors behave when they visit your web site. What you do with that information is up to you. If you simply look at it and keep doing what you're doing, you're going to keep getting what you're getting.

You wouldn't place a screw driver on the hood of a car and expect it to fix the engine. So don't enable Google Analytics on your site and expect the application to create miracles. Use it as the tool that helps you figure out *how* to achieve those goals.

Analytics and AWStats

AWStats

AWStats (Advanced Web Statistics) is an open source log analyzer written in Perl that can use a variety of log formats and runs on a variety of operating systems. The official documentation of AWStats is mostly targeted to system administrators rather than to owners of web site businesses. In short, it's not much help in figuring out what the statistics mean.

Wait a minute!

This is a book about Google Analytics, so why the heck are we talking about some open source stats program? Because the thing about analytics is that to make any sense, there needs to be some data. It's going to take at least a couple days to get **any** data into Google Analytics. It'll be months before there's enough data to make any sense. But you may already have a wealth of historical data right there in AWStats. Never looked at it, you say?

Thought so.

That data you've probably got in AWStats, which maybe you never really understood because there's no in-depth documentation on it, are still valuable. This is your past. For some things, bigger and newer isn't necessarily better. Google Analytics and AWStats have different features with different strengths and weaknesses. For some things — many things — Google Analytics blows

AWStats out of the water. For other things, Google Analytics uses a different methodology, with its own limitations.

There are two main differences between Google Analytics and AWStats. First, AWStats is primarily a site statistics program. AWStats counts more than it calculates. It has far fewer metrics and capabilities than Google Analytics. It's intended to be a simpler sort of program — nothing wrong with that. Google Analytics is intended from the get-go to be a business strength program. It calculates as much as counts and gives you metrics that, as a business person, you'll want.

Second, AWStats is a log analyzer. Google Analytics relies on cookies and JavaScript (referred to as "scripting" from here on out). This has several far-ranging implications.

For example, to a log analyzer, all traffic coming from a single IP address is one "user." When using scripting, you set a cookie on an individual user's machine, or even in a particular account profile. Then, if five computers share an outside IP on a local area network, and there are three user accounts on each computer, you "see" 15 users, not one.

On the other hand, if users turn off cookies, or don't allow "third-party" cookies, you may not be able to track them at all with Google Analytics. At best, you may be able to track them for a particular session, but a half-hour later (or the next day), they will look like brand-new visitors.

Another excellent example is tracking search engine visits (see the section "Robots and Spiders" in Chapter 3). A log analyzer has to identify search engines from lists of known spiders, by the spider's identifying itself, or by a wild guess. Some small percentage of a log analyzer's traffic may be misidentified as a real person when it's not.

On the other hand, most spiders, robots, and search engines, by default, don't execute JavaScript code. Google Analytics won't misidentify these sorts of false visitors. Of course, Google Analytics won't pick up real visitors who have JavaScript turned off, either.

Just as you can argue Mac vs. PC or football vs. figure skating, you can argue script-based tracking vs. log analysis. I'm not going to say one is intrinsically better than the other. There are tradeoffs with either methodology. As long as you know what those tradeoffs are, and what effect they may have on your metrics, you can allow for any ambiguity that might arise.

At some point, no matter how you gather data, you're going to have to plow into the nit-picky little boring stuff: log analysis vs. scripts, nobodies vs. people, pages that are pages vs. pages that really aren't. So because we work hard and play hard — and you note which comes first — we're going to dig in and go through some of the details, the basic concepts that will make what you see in Google Analytics mean something.

That is why we're here, after all.

CASE STUDY: SKATEFIC.COM

SkateFic.com **is Mary's web site. Mary's company, Private Ice, publishes figure-skating fiction, humor, essays, and poetry both as free online content and for sale as both a paperback and an e-book. The site is relatively simple in structure and execution and does not require any special intervention to force the metrics to make sense. There is content for the sake of content, content for the sake of advertising, and products for sale, without any of those things being overly complex. It makes a good overview, and we'll refer to** SkateFic.com **from time to time to compare and contrast both Google Analytics and other case studies.**

We're starting out with AWStats for a couple of reasons. First, if you have a web site, you're very likely to have AWStats already. Rather than trying to extrapolate from our case study to your web site's likely results, you'll be able to look at your own web site's information populating the AWStats reports. AWStats is also a bit less complex a tool than Google Analytics. It's easier to explain basic concepts without having to deal with all the complexity.

AWStats Browser

We're going to get under way by taking a look at the AWStats window (http://awstats.sourceforge.net/) shown in Figure 2-1.

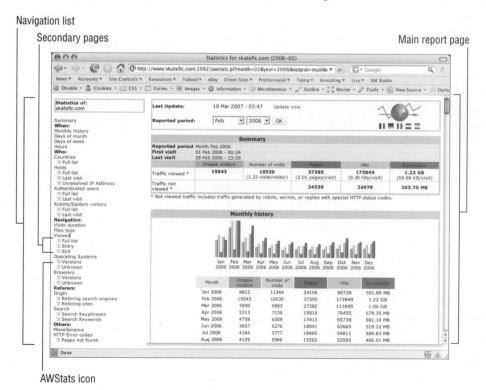

Figure 2-1: AWStats browser window in Firefox

The AWStats window has a left-hand and a right-hand frame. The right-hand frame shows the reports. The left-hand frame shows the domain name for the site statistics you're viewing followed by a text link navigation list. You can go directly to sections of the main report from any flush-left link. Secondary reports, left-indented with a tiny AWStats icon, replace the main report in the right-hand frame when you click the navigation link.

AWStats Dashboard

AWStats doesn't have many controls on the dashboard (shown in Figure 2-2). Much of what can be configured is set by your web host at install time. The dashboard appears at the top of the main report. AWStats notes the time of the last update. Most web hosts update in the middle of the night. The time listed is on the server's time zone and is not necessarily your time zone. You can force an update by clicking the Update Now link.

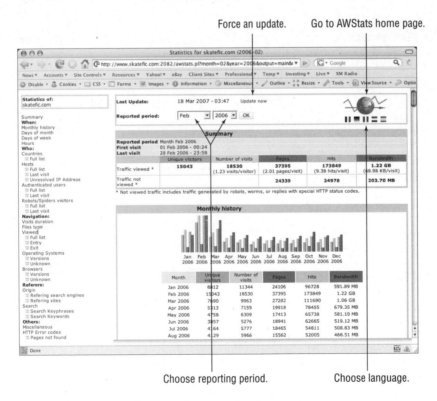

Figure 2-2: AWStats dashboard at top of main report

If you need up-to-the-minute results, or if your site is very busy during a specific part of the day, it's probably smart to force an update before you look at the stats. If you're updating results for a couple days, the update can take some serious time — upwards of a half-hour — depending on how busy your web site is. If your site is not very busy, or if it has been only a couple of hours since the last update, you might have the same overhead as a normal page reload.

Use the drop-down menus to change the month and year. To view a whole year, choose Year from the month menu and then the year from the year menu. Click the globe to go to AWStats home page at `SourceForge.net`. Click the flags below the globe to change the reporting language. Available languages depend on which ones your web host has installed. In this screenshot, French, German, Italian, Dutch, and Spanish are installed, as well as the English default.

Summary

In Figure 2-3, the first three lines of the summary tell you what period the summary covers and the first and last visits during that period.

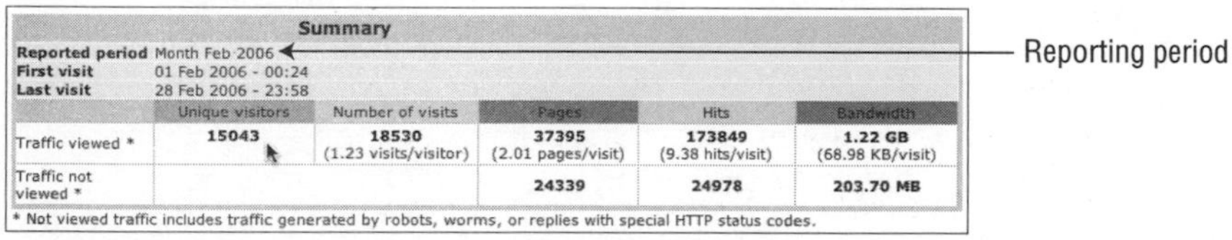

Figure 2-3: AWStats summary showing reporting period

The rest of the summary is a two-line table. One would think the captions are pretty self-explanatory. Nope. No such luck.

People and Not People

First off, there's the difference between Traffic Viewed and Traffic Not Viewed. In general terms, Traffic Viewed is generated by people. This isn't a completely sure thing, but it's close enough for most purposes. Traffic Not Viewed is generally generated by things that are not people. This includes robots, worms, or replies with special HTTP status codes.

LIVING ON SERVER TIME

AWStats shows server time, not necessarily your time, not necessarily your time zone. For example, when reading times in AWStats reports, it's important to remember that the server might be in Central Time while you might be in Eastern Time.

Don't know *when* your server is?

There are two solutions:

■ **If you have shell access to your server:** Open a terminal program, ssh to your web server and log in, and run the date command at the prompt. The output from date lists the time zone, as shown in the figure that follows. Note that this data may not appear exactly the same on your program because your time zone may differ. In fact, many servers outside the United States will use GMT (Greenwich Mean Time).

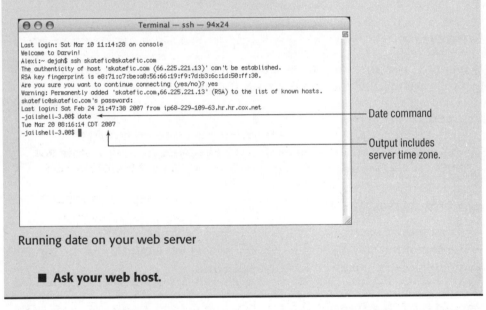

Running date on your web server

■ **Ask your web host.**

Robots are software programs that access web pages for their own purposes. Search-engine crawlers (also known as spiders) are robots that index web pages for inclusion in their search results. There are other spiders with less savory purposes such as harvesting e-mail addresses for use by spammers. Worms attack your web server, either to shut the server down (a denial-of-service attack) or to break into the server. Either way, worms can create a large amount of traffic that is of no interest beyond making sure it doesn't overwhelm your server completely. We'll get into "special status" HTTP requests a bit later. But in general, these are "noncontent" responses that redirect the visitor to another page or inform the user that the page cannot be found.

CASE STUDY: A VERY ROUGH ESTIMATE

Information useful in dealing with bandwidth and pages is shown in the figure that follows.

Summary					
Reported period	Month Feb 2006				
First visit	01 Feb 2006 - 00:24				
Last visit	28 Feb 2006 - 23:58				
	Unique visitors	Number of visits	Pages	Hits	Bandwidth
Traffic viewed *	15043	18530 (1.23 visits/visitor)	37395 (2.01 pages/visit)	173849 (9.38 hits/visit)	1.22 GB (68.98 KB/visit)
Traffic not viewed *			24339	24978	203.70 MB
* Not viewed traffic includes traffic generated by robots, worms, or replies with special HTTP status codes.					

Pages   Bandwidth

Pages and bandwidth from February 2006

To get a rough idea of how much bandwidth each page takes, divide the bandwidth per visit by the pages per visit. Strictly speaking, this is very inaccurate, but the purpose here is not to get hard, fast numbers. The purpose here is to get a very rough idea of whether you have a problem with download times or not.

68.98KB/visit ÷ 2.01 pages/visits = 34.31KB/page

Kbps means kilobits per second, not kilobytes per second. There are 8 bits in a byte. So:

34.31KB/page x 8 bits/Byte ÷ 56KB/second = 4.9 seconds/page

As far as this analysis goes, there's not a big problem on average. Does that mean there's not a problem with specific pages? No. Does this mean you can forget about download times from here on? No.

Be aware that when you (or your designer) dream up a fantastic looking page, that if no one bothers to wait to download it, the net effect on your business will be negative, not positive. Balance your desire for bells and whistles with the reality that only a little more than 2 percent of world population has broadband.

AWStats records only Bandwidth Used, Hits, and Pages for Traffic Not Viewed. For the most part, you can ignore those statistics. If your web site is even remotely busy, most of the Traffic Not Viewed is search engines crawling your site. As Martha Stewart would say, "This is a Good Thing." Don't fret about it. In a bit, we'll discuss how to tell if you're suffering from an infestation of worms or another malady. Sit tight.

People

Now, on to Traffic Viewed. In AWStats, Traffic Viewed is, to the best AWStats can guess, traffic generated by people. Why guess? Because AWStats is a log analyzer. Every time your web server sends out a message to a client — any client — it logs that action. There's no real way to tell from the log if an access is really a person. It could be a person. It could be a proxy server. It could be 35 people sharing a web connection on a local area network (LAN). There could be people reloading pages from a cache (a page stored on their computer) downloaded the day before. When using any log analyzer, there's a fudge factor. That's the nature of the beast.

Bandwidth

The bandwidth measurement is a webmaster's first lesson in the importance of collecting useful metrics as opposed to useless ones. With the exception of knowing whether a site is nearing or over its bandwidth limits, there is pretty much no useful business purpose to a measurement of bandwidth. Most web sites don't benefit from knowing the size of the average download.

With one small exception. Here in the United States, we tend to think of everyone as having high-speed Internet. The fact is that broadband penetration is less than 50 percent in the United States. According to the Organization for Economic Co-operation and Development (www.oecd.org) only 137 million people have high-speed access worldwide. Such figures could mean that half of the people who visit your web site are using dial-up at 56 Kbps or less.

At 56 Kbps, loading time for pages and other content such as multimedia is a big issue. It used to be that you had about 10 seconds for your page to load before a user would abandon the page. Now you have about two seconds. You can use the average bandwidth per visit along with the average pages per visit to get a very rough estimate of how much data your average visitor is downloading and how much time it takes.

Hits

For the first few years that we had web sites, we all quoted the number of "hits." It wasn't until 1997 that we realized hits are another meaningless metric. Why? To a web server, any access of any document — a page, a script, a multimedia file, an image, and so on — is a hit. Because one page or site may have lots of images, and another may be mostly all text, hits become a particularly poor measure of a site's performance and an even worse measure of how a site performs in comparison to other sites.

Pages

Finally, we've reached a meaningful metric — pages, also known as page views or page hits, the subject of Figure 2-4.

Back in the dark ages of 1997, when we were all using page counters, page views were what we were actually trying to count. In AWStats, the Pages metric is the aggregate of page *requests*.

Pages: The aggregate of page requests

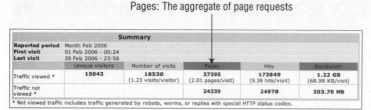

Summary					
Reported period	Month Feb 2006				
First visit	01 Feb 2006 - 00:24				
Last visit	28 Feb 2006 - 23:58				
	Unique visitors	Number of visits	Pages	Hits	Bandwidth
Traffic viewed *	15043	18530 (1.23 visits/visitor)	37395 (2.01 pages/visit)	173849 (9.38 hits/visit)	1.22 GB (68.98 KB/visit)
Traffic not viewed *			24339	24978	203.70 MB
* Not viewed traffic includes traffic generated by robots, worms, or replies with special HTTP status codes.					

Figure 2-4: A meaningful metric

HOW MANY HITS?

On the `SkateFic.com` **home page, there are 12 images. What's more, the page is dynamic, made of five files stitched together by the server. And then there's one hit for the page itself, so a single visit would yield the following:**

> **12 images**
> **5 component images**
> **1 page**
> **---------------------------**
> **18 hits**

Hits aren't very helpful, are they? You can see it graphically in the following figure.

Each of these 12 images is a separate hit.   Header file (1 hit)

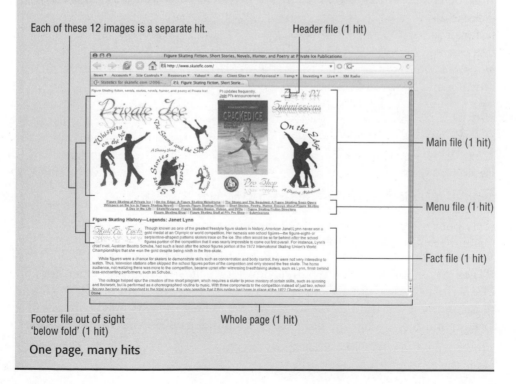

Main file (1 hit)

Menu file (1 hit)

Fact file (1 hit)

Footer file out of sight 'below fold' (1 hit)

Whole page (1 hit)

One page, many hits

CAVEAT WEBMASTER: REQUESTS

A request means only that the web browser asked the web server for the page. It does not mean the page was actually delivered or viewed. The user may have clicked the Back button because the page was loading too slowly. The user could have gotten up from the computer, allowed the page to load, and then come back later and closed the window without looking at it.

This is one of the caveats of using a log analyzer such as AWStats for web metrics. You see only what the server sees. You don't see what the user actually does. It's a limitation of the software and the Internet experience.

In Google Analytics, whether a page view is counted on or not depends on whether the script code runs or not. Google advises that you place your JavaScript code at the bottom of the page so that it executes last. This way, you know the whole page has loaded. If you have a long page, where the only important content is located at the top, you might want to place the script code mid-page. It's up to you.

Either way, caveat webmaster.

AWStats counts all pages, static and dynamic, plus requests for CGI scripts and a few other kinds of files. This specifically does not include requests for images or cascading style sheets, although it may include files that you wouldn't think of as pages in the strictest sense, a possibility illustrated by Figure 2-5.

Page views

Files type		Hits	Percent	Bandwidth	Percent
jpg	Image	76599	44.1 %	372.41 MB	29.8 %
css	Cascading Style Sheet file	33154	19 %	89.75 MB	7.1 %
gif	Image	26601	15.3 %	88.76 MB	7.1 %
html	HTML or XML static page	19037	10.9 %	531.61 MB	42.5 %
php	Dynamic Html page or Script file	18330	10.5 %	165.72 MB	13.2 %
cgi	Dynamic Html page or Script file	27	0 %	25.60 KB	0 %
- com		1	0 %	10.45 KB	0 %

The com file: Is it really a page?

Figure 2-5: "Page" doesn't always mean what you think.

Still looking at the summary on the main page, scroll down to (or click the navigation link for) Files Type. The Pages total, 37,395, includes 19,037 static HTML page views, 18,330 dynamic views for pages with a .php extension, 27 CGI script accesses, and 1 "com" page, which has no description. You wouldn't be a dummy if you didn't even know what that file type was. As it happens, it's a command file, a program, but exactly what it does is beyond our scope here.

ASS-U-ME NOTHING

You know the old joke about assuming things. Assuming makes an ass of you and me. But the truth is, every analytics package — every software package of any sort — makes assumptions. What is a page? How long is a visit? How long should the idle period between visits be? There are assumptions about any number of other aspects of data collection and processing as well. Most of these assumptions are neither right nor wrong. They're just assumptions. It's important to know what assumptions a particular analytics package is making if you want to be able to construe what your data really mean. We'll cover assumptions made by the software as we go.

Is that com file a page? Why? A program can output a page. Not always, but that's one of the caveats of analytics software — assumptions. AWStats makes the assumption that a com file is a program that outputs a page, and it counts an access of that com file as a page.

Is it a page for business purposes? Unless you have a com file that you specifically know produces a viewable page, it probably isn't. And that means, for business purposes, that this portion of the Pages metric is meaningless. Only pages that are pages should count. If you have a lot of pages that are not pages counting, it's a problem. If it's only a few, a small percentage of your total, you're probably safe to ignore the pages that are not pages.

Number of Visits

The Number of Visits a web site receives should be straightforward. That would be nice and easy, wouldn't it? Of course, it would.

No such luck, as Figure 2-6 indicates.

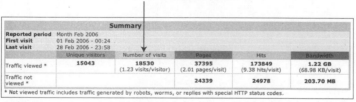

Figure 2-6: Number of Visits is almost but not quite what it seems.

Like Pages, Number of Visits has two key assumptions: How long a visit is and how much time has to pass between page loads to make one person have two visits? Fortunately, there are industry standards — after all, this isn't 1997.

A visit is as long as it is. As long as the visitor keeps clicking from page to page, it's still one visit. However, when the user stops clicking for 30 minutes, the visit ends. If the user starts clicking again, it's a new visit. Thirty minutes is the industry-standard timeout for visits.

So, say a user toddles into `SkateFic.com` at 9:00 a.m., and between 9:00 and 9:30 she clicks from page to page, reading her favorite serial fiction. At 9:30 she gets a phone call. For the next 28 minutes, she talks on the phone. When she hangs up at 9:58, she finishes reading the page she left to answer the call and loads the next page at 9:59. That's one visit, because the break between page loads was less than 30 minutes.

Now, say the same user is having a Grand Central Terminal sort of day. The phone rings again at 10:00 a.m. This time the user talks for 31 minutes. When she goes back to reading and loads a new page, she's initiating a second visit as far as AWStats is concerned. Same person, same day — and, if you asked the user, same visit — but for pretty much every stats and analytics package, it's two different visits.

The average of 1.23 visits per visitor varies in meaningfulness. For a site that gets a lot of returning visitors, it might have some meaning. For a site where 90 percent of visitors never return, the average doesn't mean much, because it is dragged down by the vast bulk of people who never return. You could have 10 people who average three visits per month and 90 people who come once and never come back. Average visits will be 1.2, but it won't be a very useful metric, except to tell you that most of your visitors don't return after the first visit.

Unique Visitors

The big problem with counting unique visitors is that it's impossible to figure out from server logs who's unique and who's a visitor. Figure 2-7 deals with this problem.

"Unique visitors" aren't always what they seem.

Summary					
Reported period	Month Feb 2006				
First visit	01 Feb 2006 - 00:24				
Last visit	28 Feb 2006 - 23:58				
	Unique visitors	Number of visits	Pages	Hits	Bandwidth
Traffic viewed *	15043	18530 (1.23 visits/visitor)	37395 (2.01 pages/visit)	173849 (9.38 hits/visit)	1.22 GB (68.98 KB/visit)
Traffic not viewed *			24339	24978	203.70 MB
* Not viewed traffic includes traffic generated by robots, worms, or replies with special HTTP status codes.					

Figure 2-7: When is a unique visitor neither unique nor a visitor?

There are caveats aplenty here because you're counting visits from unique IP addresses, not actual people:

■ Any sort of local area network connected by a single Internet gateway may have several users with the same apparent IP address.

■ A proxy server owned by an ISP that caches frequently accessed pages will show up as one unique visitor even though it represents hundreds, if not thousands, of users. You can put a no-cache directive on your pages, but it works only if the proxy pays attention to it. And using such a directive may slow your site for some users.

■ In the home, it is very common to have more than one person using the same computer. You may have three different people visiting from one IP address.

■ People visit from different places: from home, work, school, or from a laptop at the coffee shop. What looks like four unique visitors may actually be only one.

■ People on dial-up change IP addresses almost every time they log in. If a person visits every day from a different IP, that person looks like 20 or 30 people, depending on how the ISP assigns IP addresses.

There isn't much you can do about these issues. It's the nature of the beast — and log analyzers. Google Analytics is script-based, so it does not have many of these problems, but it has a series of issues of its own. The bottom line is that you can't measure unique visitors with complete accuracy. You measure unique visitors as well as you can and you make sure to compare apples to apples. As far as the technology goes, AWStats Unique Visitors is the number of unique IP addresses that made requests to your web server. It's the best measurement a log analyzer can provide of how many people visited.

Yearly Summary

AWStats calculates its metrics on a monthly basis. To produce yearly metrics, it adds the results from all months, with the warning shown in Figure 2-8.

Summary					
Reported period	Year 2005				
First visit	01 Jan 2005 - 00:06				
Last visit	31 Dec 2005 - 23:58				
	Unique visitors	Number of visits	Pages	Hits	Bandwidth
Traffic viewed *	<= 42960 Exact value not available in 'Year' view	65382 (1.52 visits/visitor)	167257 (2.55 pages/visit)	525524 (8.03 hits/visit)	3.84 GB (61.57 KB/visit)
Traffic not viewed *			194580	197127	1.73 GB
* Not viewed traffic includes traffic generated by robots, worms, or replies with special HTTP status codes.					

AWStats methodology yields a bogus number here.

Figure 2-8: The yearly summary warns that "unique visitors" is not an exact metric.

While this strategy doesn't affect the other metrics, it also doesn't produce an accurate number of unique visitors. If a particular IP appeared in January, March, and July, it would add three unique visitors rather than just one. It's not practical to save all the logs and run the analysis on one huge lump every time the user wants a year-to-date. Suffice it to say that the AWStats unique-visitors metric is not accurate in the aggregate.

In Summary

That wasn't so bad, now was it?

CHAPTER 3

Yes! More AWStats!

Yes, There's More

So you made it through Chapter 2 okay? Good. If you want only the very basics before you jump into Google Analytics, you can probably skip this chapter. So why are we writing it? Good question. In this chapter, we're going to cover some of the caveats that make collecting and analyzing site traffic so fraught with pitfalls. We're still going to use AWStats as the prime example, and we still expect you to look at your own data if you have them. You'll also see some of the things that AWStats can do that Google Analytics can't.

Now, we think this stuff is scintillating reading, but you might find it a little less exciting than Chapter 2. Nothing can be done about that. Cope. And now let's go to Monthly History, as shown in Figure 3-1.

> **NOTE** Our screen shots have been taken in AWStats 6.4. If you have a different version — version information is printed at the bottom of the reports frame — what you see may vary significantly from what we shot.

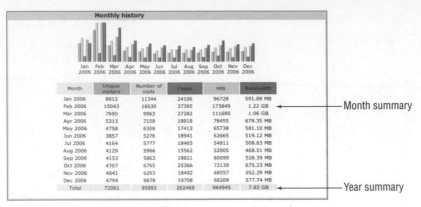

Figure 3-1: Monthly History has values from each month's Summary.

Monthly History

The Monthly History has two parts: a bar chart and a table of values. The values in the chart and the numbers in the table correspond to the Summary information for each month. Each column of the chart has a total at the bottom that appears on the earlier –Year– Summary. As with the –Year– Summary, the total of Unique Visitors is not accurate. (This is the problem discussed near the end of Chapter 2.)

In the bar chart, each colored bar is in proportion to other bars of that color. However, there is no correlation between different colored bars. In Figure 3-1, the tallest yellow bar and the tallest turquoise bar are the same height. But the tallest yellow bar is 18,530 visits, whereas the tallest turquoise bar is 173,849 hits.

The Monthly History has a simple purpose. It exists solely so that you can compare traffic numbers from month to month. Why did traffic double in February? Why did it drop off in March?

These questions are as much business related as site related. In the specific case at SkateFic.com, the 2006 Winter Olympics were in February, driving interest in figure skating through the roof for a short period. But then, despite TV coverage of the world championships in March, traffic fell as casual fans went back to their regularly scheduled programs. With eight years of historical data behind us, it's easy to see that the pattern of activity was the same during the 1998 and 2002 Olympics.

This is another benefit of having metrics. You can discern both short-term and long-term patterns, sometimes just by looking. Does your web site peak in August every year? Did editorial coverage in a major magazine spike traffic in January? Do you get a lot of traffic around a particular real-world event? What are the long-term and short-term trends?

Another way of looking at traffic, by days and hours, is shown in Figure 3-2.

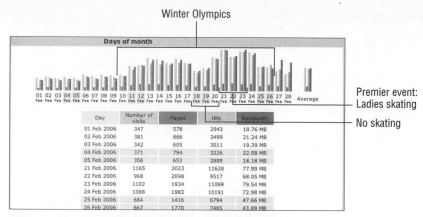

Figure 3-2: Days of Month shows traffic for each day.

Days and Hours

The Days of Month, plus Days of Week and Hours reports (see Figure 3-3), all answer the same basic questions: "Is traffic to the web site cyclical?" and "Did any special events influence traffic?" Days of Month gives you a daily breakdown, lets you compare against the average, and shows how AWStats arrived at the Summary numbers.

From a business standpoint, comparing monthly reports shows that SkateFic has a much stronger showing in the winter, during the figure-skating season — duh. The 2006 Olympics also boosted traffic considerably in February 2006. There aren't any particular intramonthly trends, even when comparing across months.

Too bad that the Days of Week and Hours reports aren't as useful. In the Days of Week report, averaging tends to even out both anomalous bumps and meaningful anomalies. The Hours chart, unlike the Days of Week chart, gives you aggregate numbers where averages would be more meaningful. The Hours graph is the saving grace, showing peak hours around 8:00 a.m., 2:00 p.m. to 3:00 p.m., and 9:00 p.m. (remember those are Central Time).

What does it mean in a business sense? The Days of Week chart means absolutely nothing because averaging kills any bumps that might have meant something. The Hours chart shows that SkateFic is busy before work, after school, and after the nightly news. Most visitors are probably from the continental U.S. because the site is busiest during the U.S. day. There's a significant population of night owls and people from the Eastern Hemisphere because there is a base line of traffic even while westerners are sound asleep. This raises the geographical question shown in Figure 3-4.

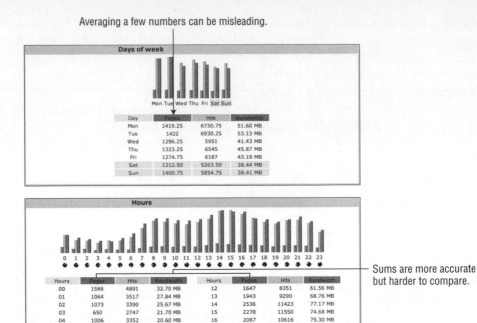

Averaging a few numbers can be misleading.

Days of week

Day	Pages	Hits	Bandwidth
Mon	1419.25	6730.75	51.60 MB
Tue	1422	6930.25	53.13 MB
Wed	1296.25	5951	41.43 MB
Thu	1323.25	6545	45.87 MB
Fri	1274.75	6187	43.19 MB
Sat	1212.50	5263.50	38.44 MB
Sun	1400.75	5854.75	38.41 MB

Hours

0 1 2 3 4 5 6 7 8 9 10 11 12 13 14 15 16 17 18 19 20 21 22 23

Sums are more accurate but harder to compare.

Hours	Pages	Hits	Bandwidth	Hours	Pages	Hits	Bandwidth
00	1588	4891	32.70 MB	12	1647	8351	61.56 MB
01	1064	3517	27.84 MB	13	1943	9290	68.76 MB
02	1073	3390	25.67 MB	14	2536	11423	77.17 MB
03	650	2747	21.70 MB	15	2278	11550	74.68 MB
04	1006	3352	20.60 MB	16	2087	10616	75.30 MB
05	800	3392	27.43 MB	17	1948	9510	61.89 MB

Figure 3-3: Traffic for Days and Hours

Countries (Top 25) ▾ Full list

Countries		Pages	Hits	Bandwidth	
United States	us	26370	134239	935.18 MB	
Unknown	ip	5152	9711	71.03 MB	
Canada	ca	1928	10936	77.66 MB	
Great Britain	gb	966	4306	56.65 MB	
European Union	eu	633	3189	28.30 MB	
Netherlands	nl	362	785	7.80 MB	
Australia	au	346	2310	14.82 MB	
Japan	jp	174	1113	8.58 MB	
Switzerland	ch	142	203	1.33 MB	
Germany	de	128	422	3.85 MB	
Sweden	se	112	449	3.22 MB	
China	cn	88	334	2.01 MB	
Russian Federation	ru	60	355	1.68 MB	
Italy	it	58	382	3.14 MB	
Finland	fi	50	286	1.86 MB	
Singapore	sg	49	279	1.59 MB	

Figure 3-4: Think your visitors are all American? Think again.

Countries

Americans have a terribly bad habit of being Amero-centric. AWStats uses a reverse domain name system (DNS) to figure out where site visitors are coming from. The top 25 countries of origin are listed on the main page in order from most traffic to least. Usually, there are a significant number of incoming IP addresses that cannot be resolved. These are listed as "Unknown."

By clicking the **Full List** link, you can see all the countries that showed up in the logs. Would you think that people in 96 countries — including Iran, Bermuda, Nigeria, Mongolia — would be interested in figure-skating fiction? That seems to surprise everyone who isn't still laughing over the idea that figure-skating fiction actually exists.

Your site may have a much greater reach than you realize. Knowing this can influence decisions about content and e-commerce. Would your site strategy change if you knew that 35 percent of your traffic was coming from the European Union?

We thought so.

Hosts

The hosts list (see Figure 3-5) offers several different views of the same information: the host names and IP addresses of visitors. This is the same information used to tell which country visitors hail from.

On the main page of AWStats, the first line after the title bar gives an overview of how many known and unknown/unresolved hosts there were, as well as how many unique visitors this represents. Then the main report starts with the host who requested the most pages, listing hosts in descending order from most traffic to least.

In Figure 3-5, you should note two interesting points. First, unlike the other reports that show only "people," the hosts list shows both "people" and "not people." Spiders and other robots are not second-class citizens on the hosts list. Second, Google spiders have the top five wrapped up. What does this mean? Well, Google indexes the site for new content at least once a week, sometimes twice. For a small site, this is very good news. It means that the 800-pound gorilla of search engines has taken notice and indexes regularly. New content will not languish in obscurity.

ISP proxy caches

Google spiders

Hosts (Top 25) · Full list · Last visit · Unresolved IP Address				
Hosts : 17198 Known, 2854 Unknown (unresolved ip) 15043 Unique visitors	Pages	Hits	Bandwidth	Last visit
crawl-66-249-65-48.googlebot.com	950	950	7.55 MB	15 Feb 2006 - 19:52
crawl-66-249-65-231.googlebot.com	897	897	7.40 MB	21 Feb 2006 - 15:49
crawl-66-249-66-108.googlebot.com	604	604	4.88 MB	25 Feb 2006 - 12:08
crawl-66-249-72-66.googlebot.com	551	551	6.70 MB	28 Feb 2006 - 17:44
crawl-66-249-66-241.googlebot.com	507	507	3.85 MB	09 Feb 2006 - 20:16
66-215-117-37.dhcp.mrba.ca.charter.com	493	986	399.19 KB	26 Feb 2006 - 15:52
cpe-66-1-252-195.co.sprintbbd.net	404	807	323.45 KB	12 Feb 2006 - 04:43
c-71-197-56-228.hsd1.co.comcast.net	358	358	4.67 MB	28 Feb 2006 - 17:58

Figure 3-5: All hosts welcome

In the title bar of the report are three links. Full List goes to a list of all hosts, with the highest-traffic hosts first. Last Visit loads a list of the last 1,000 hosts to visit your site, organized by the time of their last visit. Unresolved IP Address goes to a list of the top 1,000 hosts who could not be found by name, listed from highest traffic to lowest.

Robots and Spiders

In Chapter 2, we talked about visitors who are people and visitors who are not people. One particularly important kind of visitor that is not a person is an indexing spider or web crawler. The Robots/Spiders report (see Figure 3-6) lists the various named and unnamed but identified web crawlers that have run their sticky little legs all over your pages.

Not all spiders are "known."

Robots/Spiders visitors (Top 25) ▪ Full list ▪ Last visit			
15 different robots*	Hits	Bandwidth	Last visit
Inktomi Slurp	6719+1799	47.98 MB	28 Feb 2006 - 23:54
Googlebot	4799+98	52.25 MB	28 Feb 2006 - 23:58
MSNBot	3970+426	62.75 MB	28 Feb 2006 - 23:20
WISENutbot	1088+7	10.17 MB	28 Feb 2006 - 23:58
Unknown robot (identified by 'spider')	873+185	14.88 MB	28 Feb 2006 - 19:26
Unknown robot (identified by 'crawl')	598+114	9.21 MB	28 Feb 2006 - 20:12
Unknown robot (identified by hit on 'robots.txt')	0+278	89.35 KB	28 Feb 2006 - 22:31
Unknown robot (identified by 'robot')	225+9	1.75 MB	28 Feb 2006 - 01:58
AskJeeves	100+49	828.09 KB	28 Feb 2006 - 22:11
Voila	3+78	53.86 KB	28 Feb 2006 - 09:36
Voyager	69+8	1.15 MB	28 Feb 2006 - 18:05
Scooter	17+8	207.10 KB	27 Feb 2006 - 05:38
Lycos	15+9	210.00 KB	17 Feb 2006 - 12:02
Alexa (IA Archiver)	0+17	2.74 KB	28 Feb 2006 - 08:20
Fast-Webcrawler	3	263.97 KB	27 Feb 2006 - 22:42
* Robots shown here gave hits or traffic "not viewed" by visitors, so they are not included in other charts. Numbers after + are successful hits on "robots.txt" files			

Figure 3-6: Get indexed. Get found.

Named spiders are known robots from known entities: Google, Inktomi, MSN, Yahoo, and so forth. Other spiders are not known, but when they hit a special file on the top level of the web site called robots.txt, the server marks them as spiders. Robots.txt tells spiders where they are allowed to go and what they are allowed to index. For example, if you didn't want the pictures on your web site indexed, you could put a line in your robots.txt to make the whole images directory off limits to spiders. Most good spiders pay attention to these directives, but there's no money-back guarantee.

Hits from spiders are reported a little differently from hits by other entities. For each spider, the first number under Hits is the number of requests the spider made. Then there's a plus sign and the number of times the spider successfully "saw" the robots.txt file. As you can see from Figure 3-7, different spiders hit the robots.txt file in greatly varying numbers. Those numbers could mean anything from lots of spider visits to very inefficient spidering methods. In general, spiders are good. Being indexed is good. Being found is even better.

Sad truth: Most visitors bail before they read even a single page.

Visits duration		
Number of visits: 18530 - Average: 153 s	Number of visits	Percent
0s-30s	15773	85.1 %
30s-2mn	842	4.5 %
2mn-5mn	515	2.7 %
5mn-15mn	547	2.9 %
15mn-30mn	303	1.6 %
30mn-1h	306	1.6 %
1h+	244	1.3 %

On the other hand, more than 2,000 hang out.

Figure 3-7: A cringe-worthy report on the length of visits

SQUASH INVADING SPIDERS

Creating a robots.txt file isn't very difficult. Here are some resources that will help you create such a file if you don't have one:

How to Set Up a robots.txt to Control Search Engine Spiders: The how and the why of setting up a robots.txt file.
`www.thesitewizard.com/archive/robotstxt.shtml`

Robots.txt Validator: Make sure your robots.txt file is correct with this nifty tool.
`http://tool.motoricerca.info/robots-checker.phtml`

Robots.txt file Creator: An online tool that will create a robots.txt file for you. You still have to understand the settings, but the creator will handle the syntax.
`www.123promotion.co.uk/tools/robotstxtgenerator.php`

Remember that the robots.txt file goes at the top of your web site directory structure — the same directory as your home page.

CAVEAT WEBMASTER: COUNTING SPIDERS IN GOOGLE ANALYTICS

It's very important to note that Google Analytics deals with spiders completely differently than AWStats. AWStats identifies spiders if the spider says, "I'm a spider" or if it hits robots.txt, or if it shares the name of a known spider. Often as not, in Google Analytics, spiders don't execute the JavaScript code that says, "Hey, I'm here!" Google Analytics may not count spider visits at all — or it may, depending on whether the spider runs that script code or not.
Caveat Webmaster.

Visits Duration

Why does this report make us cringe — okay, just Mary, it's her web site after all. The Visits Duration report shows how long visits were. The average visit is about 2.5 minutes. That's not too bad. But then, you look at the numbers that went into those 2.5 minutes. Fewer than 2,000 people stayed more than two minutes. Only 15 percent stayed more than 30 seconds! For a content site, that's enough to shake an editor to her soul.

One of the measures of a successful content web site is how "sticky" that site is. Stickiness is about whether visitors bounce in and then bounce out just as fast. Apparently, lots of people do. Either they find what they want and leave, or they don't find what they want and leave. Either way, they leave before they get deeper into the site.

This observation in itself is valuable. But where did most of these people come from? How did they encounter the site? Did they leave immediately, or did they try to load another page? Did they find what they wanted and leave? Or didn't they look? Those last two are very different things.

AWStats can't tell us. While AWStats provides the raw data of "who came, how many, where?" it can't say "who came and left immediately, how many dug in deeper, and where did they go?" For that, you need Google Analytics. This is one park where the Little Leaguer, good as he is, can't hit a homer.

Pages-URL

The Pages-URL report (see Figure 3-8) lists the top 25 URLs by the number of times that page was viewed. Links across the title bar will take you to the Full List of all URLs recorded for your site.

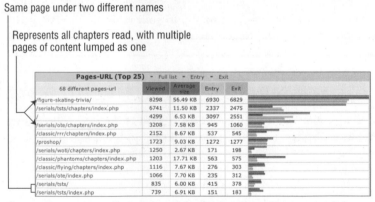

Figure 3-8: AWStats's most popular Page URLs tells you much but not everything.

The Entry and Exit links (see Figure 3-9) go to pages showing the full list of URLs sorted by the most entries and most exits, respectively.

The Entry and Exit lists, as with many of the secondary pages, allow you to filter the list with Regular Expressions. A Regular Expression (abbreviated RegEx) matches patterns using a special syntax that we'll discuss in more depth in Chapter 6. Also in Figure 3-9, the RegEx `.*/serials/.*` matches all the URLs that contain the directory `/serials/`. At `SkateFic.com`, the serials directory contains all the currently running serial novels. From a business standpoint, knowing how to filter the Pages-URL list gives you the ability to look at different sections of your web site — that is, if your web site is structured so that different sectors of your business correspond to different structural parts of your site.

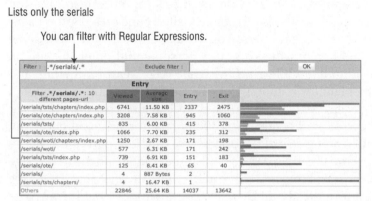

Figure 3-9: Entry and Exit lists let you filter results with Regular Expressions.

What if they don't? What if you use variables to steer people to different parts of your site? For example, in Figure 3-9, the top two URLs are for `/chapters/index.php`. While not immediately apparent, those two URLs can represent hundreds of individual chapters, because each of them comes with a variable such as: `/chapters/index.php?Chapter=23` for Chapter 23 of the serial.

A business with an online catalogue might have one catalogue page that uses an item number to pull item descriptions from a database. A site that uses a content management system (CMS) may have very few actual pages and may only differentiate pages by a series of variables in the URL. See any of those variables in the URLs that AWStats shows? Nope?

We don't either.

This is another one of those things that AWStats doesn't do that you'll find you need. It's great to know how many people read chapters of one serial or another (or read articles or visit the catalogue). But it's not as helpful as knowing that 2,000 people read the newest chapter (or article) and that 337 people read 10 other chapters or that 1,500 people looked at the week's sale item and that 1,800 people looked at a bunch of other catalogue items.

Here's another important piece of information that you both need and don't. Take a look at Figure 3-10.

Trivia page   Entries and exits are unrelated.

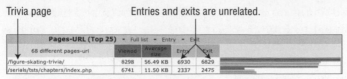

Figure 3-10: Is Figure Skating Trivia a good draw or not?

The /figure-skating-trivia/ directory contains a single page with numerous short biographies of figure skaters. It has turned out to be a top search term for SkateFic.com. It's also the most visited page on a regular basis.

Look at the Entry and Exit numbers. You would think they'd have some relationship to one another, but they don't. A person could enter the site on another page, poke around a while, find the trivia page, read for a while and then leave for another site (or a cuppa joe) — no entry, one exit, one view. A person could do the reverse, enter at the trivia page, exit elsewhere — one entry, no exit, one view. A person could enter on a different page, read some, check out the trivia, and end up reading one of the poems in a different part of the site — no entry, no exit, one view. Finally, a person could enter the site on the trivia page and leave immediately — a "bounce" — one entry, one exit, one view. That's the person we want to know more about! Do we know anything about them? No.

The trivia page is only a draw insomuch as it lures people further into the site. The trivia page on SkateFic.com is like a controversial article on a content site or a sale item on an e-commerce site. It's all well and good that people look at that page, but what you really want is people to be pulled further into the site. It's that supercheap sale item at the grocery store, a loss leader. How effective your loss leader is depends on how many people get further into your site from that page.

AWStats can't tell you that. It can say how many people viewed a page. It can say how many people entered there. It can say how many people exited. What it doesn't say is how many people saw that page and only that page. That particular analytical association is a crucial one.

Operating Systems and Browsers

If you're a Mac or Linux person, how many times have you heard what amounts to "We only care about Windows users"? Certain designers and even web site owners want to design sites only for the very newest Windows version, the very newest Internet Explorer browser. Cross-platform compatibility be damned! "So few people use Mac or Linux (or Netscape or FireFox or visit from their PDA or mobile phone) that we don't need to support it."

But is that really true?

Is it really true that all you need to support is the newest IE and the newest Windows? According to Figure 3-11, it would indeed seem that 87.4 percent of hits come from Windows machines and 75 percent from IE.

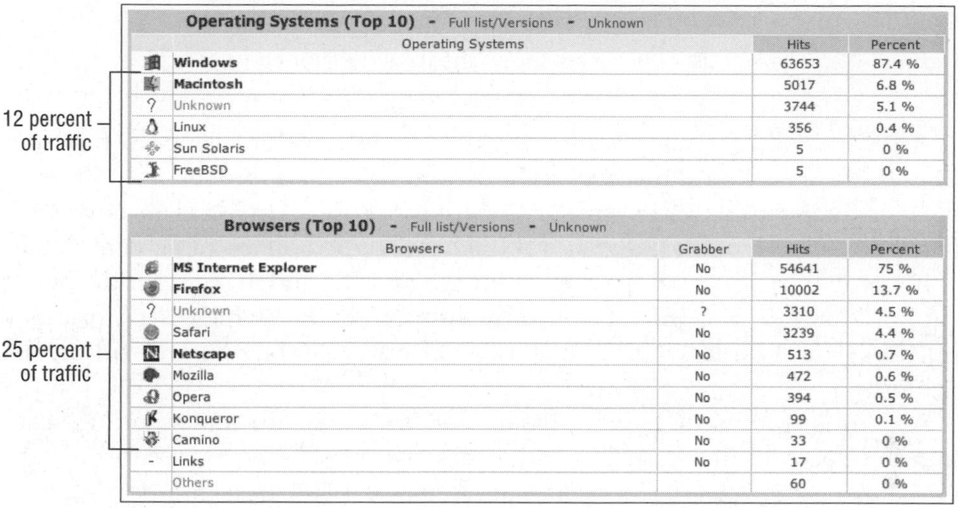

Operating Systems (Top 10) - Full list/Versions - Unknown		
Operating Systems	**Hits**	**Percent**
Windows	63653	87.4 %
Macintosh	5017	6.8 %
Unknown	3744	5.1 %
Linux	356	0.4 %
Sun Solaris	5	0 %
FreeBSD	5	0 %

12 percent of traffic

Browsers (Top 10) - Full list/Versions - Unknown			
Browsers	**Grabber**	**Hits**	**Percent**
MS Internet Explorer	No	54641	75 %
Firefox	No	10002	13.7 %
Unknown	?	3310	4.5 %
Safari	No	3239	4.4 %
Netscape	No	513	0.7 %
Mozilla	No	472	0.6 %
Opera	No	394	0.5 %
Konqueror	No	99	0.1 %
Camino	No	33	0 %
Links	No	17	0 %
Others		60	0 %

25 percent of traffic

Figure 3-11: Why "we only care about Windows XP users" is bad business.

It's not as exact as it would be if AWStats gave us pages or unique visitors, but it's the best we've got. Looks like a lot of Windows users. It might lead you to decide that the right thing to do is to support the newest IE 7 and the newest Windows Vista.

And you would be dead wrong.

Let's do some estimates. The earlier examples and screenshots show February 2006 (so don't get confused), but in February 2007, there were 5,749 unique visitors and 72,780 hits. That's 12.65 hits per visitor. The 63,653 hits from Windows machines work out to about 5,000 visitors. The other 750 odd visitors are on Mac or another OS. Maybe 12 percent doesn't seem like much, but are you willing to turn away more than 750 potential readers and customers? Mary doesn't happen to be, so even if she weren't a Mac-hack-from-way-back, she'd be putting the extra time and dollars into cross-platform compatibility. It's good business.

But say you're willing to sacrifice 12 percent of possible customers. You're sticking to the major-OS/major-browser strategy to save money. Saving money is good business. Are you sure you're saving money only supporting the most recent IE version?

Take a look at Figure 3-12 to see who's using IE 7. Certainly not the majority.

Top browser is not the newest one.

Browsers				
Versions	Grabber	Hits	Percent	
MSIE		**54641**	**75 %**	
Msie 7.0	No	19307	26.5 %	
Msie 6.1	No	1	0 %	
Msie 6.0	No	34244	47 %	
Msie 5.5	No	359	0.4 %	
Msie 5.23	No	178	0.2 %	

Figure 3-12: The Full List of browsers shows the flaw in major-browser strategy.

An estimated 2,700 visitors are using IE 6. About 1,500 are using IE7 (up from 14 in the first edition of this book). On the flip side, the approximately 400 people using versions of IE5 in February 2006 have dropped to 78 in February 2007. IE4 has dropped to single digits, and IE3 has dropped off the radar completely.

It's probably time to drop support for IE3 and IE4 and to consider dropping support for IE5. But IE7? If you only supported IE7 (which is notoriously finicky), you'd be leaving the majority of your visitors who are still on IE6 behind.

And other browsers: FireFox, Safari, Netscape, Mozilla and so on? A scant hundred fewer visitors use those browsers than use IE7. So in an effort to support 1,500 users, a whole lot of sites are ignoring 1,400 users. Supporting only the latest and greatest is starting to look foolhardy indeed, isn't it?

What's more, Mozilla, FireFox, Netscape, and Camino are all related, as are Safari and Konqueror. Support FireFox and Safari and you're likely to support Netscape, Mozilla, Camino, and Konqueror as well, with little extra effort. It's a six-for-the-price-of-two sale!

Now what exactly does "Unknown" mean? Many of those "unknown" browsers are not as unknown as you might think. Being book authors distinctly lacking in curiosity, no one here ever clicked that **Unknown** link in the title bar to find what you now see in Figure 3-13.

Unidentified spider

Blackberry browser

SBIder/0.8-dev_(SBIder;_http://www.sitesell.com/sbider.html;_http://support.sitesell.com/contact-support.html)	26 Feb 2006 - 21:25
RtpcjaorjvsgnqlRwcckR	26 Feb 2006 - 17:23
BlackBerry6280/4.0.0_Profile/MIDP-2.0_Configuration/CLDC-1.1	26 Feb 2006 - 16:39

Figure 3-13: Unknown does not always mean unknowable.

Lots of nonsense . . . and a gem. Those unknown browsers happen to be important if you're considering whether to support mobile technologies. Mary always avoided the subject of making SkateFic mobile-friendly, thinking, "Mobile surfers don't visit SkateFic." As it turns out, they do. Among the unidentified spiders, site-capture programs, and obvious gobbledygook promulgated by the truly paranoid are PDA browsers and the Blackberry browser. Which just goes to show that even when you know enough to write a book, there's always something to learn.

Maybe it's time to start supporting mobile surfers.

Connect to Site from . . .

The "Connect to site from" report has two sections: top and bottom. Figure 3-14 shows the upper part of the top section.

Typed URLs   Accurate

Connect to site from				
Origin	Pages	Percent	Hits	Percent
Direct address / Bookmarks	12188	43.6 %	19405	39.1 %
Links from a NewsGroup				
Links from an Internet Search Engine - Full list	13932	49.9 %	14238	28.7 %
- Google	10526 10537			
- MSN	1169 1201			
- Yahoo	651 675			
- Google (Images)	539 773			
- AOL	318 319			
- Ask Jeeves	281 281			
- Unknown search engines	151 154			

Not accurate

Figure 3-14: If you ever doubted Google was the 800-pound gorilla of search . . .

First is the traffic (pages and hits) coming from people who type your URL — direct addresses — or use a bookmark. These are your regular customers or readers, your core traffic. They know where your site is from memory or they have your site bookmarked. Chances are, they'll be back because they know you have what they want.

The second line of the upper section is for people coming in from newsgroups. Newsgroups are one of the more ancient forms of Internet communication, the killer app of 1991. Newsgroups, which tend to be very uncontrolled and egalitarian, are falling by the wayside, whereas conduits where content can be controlled (such as mailing lists and web forums) are on the rise. There was no incoming traffic from newsgroups. If there had been, it would have indicated that there was some word of mouth about your site and that people were visiting based on recommendations from other visitors.

The rest of the upper section lists search engine activity. Google tends to rule this list, with five times more traffic than everyone else put together. The first line has numbers for the aggregate of all search engines. The rest of the lines have names of individual search engines with two unlabeled numbers. Those numbers should be labeled, from left to right, Pages and Hits.

The bottom section of the table lists the external URLs that drive the most traffic. The top URL in Figure 3-15 is a Google AdWords ad. Fourteen (of 25) other URLs in the top-external-links list are either ad forms that repurpose

Google results or are AdWords-for-content placements from third-party web sites using the Google AdSense program.

All Google AdWords all the time   An image used on author's blog

Links from an external page (other web sites except search engines) - Full list			1768	6.3 %	15828	31.9 %
- http://pagead2.googlesyndication.com/pagead/ads	271	271				
- http://www.figure-skating-blog.com	163	9959				
- http://www.frogsonice.com/skateweb/fans.shtml	100	100				
- http://www.sportsfics.com	80	80				
- http://www.latimes.com/includes/google-adsense-content.html	50	50				
- http://www.comcast.net/qry/websearch/	45	45				
- http://users.tellurian.com/lizwoolf/skatefic.html	29	29				
- http://www.comcast.net/qry/websearch	28	28				
- http://www.bomis.com/rings/michellekwan/	24	24				
- http://www.googleadservices.com/pagead/adclick	23	33				
- http://apps5.oingo.com/apps/domainpark/domainpark.cgi	23	23				

Figure 3-15: AdWords traffic masquerading as external links

Clicking **Full List** will give you a full list of all external URLs. On SkateFic .com, the vast majority of those URLs are AdWords-for-content placements. But you have to know what to look for. You can't count on AWStats to tell the difference between a real external link and yet another AdWords placement or search engine result.

You can, however, filter the full list results. Figure 3-16 shows only the results that explicitly come from Google (there will be others that come from Google but don't say so). It's worthwhile to note that the percentages given on a filtered full list refer to the percentage of that filtered data set, not to the overall full list of external links. So the 63.1 percent of all the ads that reference Google comes directly from AdWords placement on Google's own web site.

Filtering with Regular Expressions can show who owns up to Google AdSense.

Filter :	.*google.*	Exclude filter :		OK

Links from an external page (other web sites except search engines)				
Filter .*google.*: 31 different pages-url	Paged	Percent	Hits	Percent
http://pagead2.googlesyndication.com/pagead/ads	271	63.1 %	271	61.7 %
http://www.latimes.com/includes/google-adsense-content.html	50	11.6 %	50	11.3 %
http://www.googleadservices.com/pagead/adclick	23	5.3 %	33	7.5 %
http://www.charter.net/google/index.php	14	3.2 %	14	3.1 %
http://www.chicagotribune.com/includes/google-adsense-content.ht...	13	3 %	13	2.9 %
http://www.baltimoresun.com/includes/google-adsense-content.html	9	2 %	9	2 %
http://www.sun-sentinel.com/includes/google-adsense-content.html	9	2 %	9	2 %
http://www.tesco.net/google/searchresults.asp	5	1.1 %	5	1.1 %

Figure 3-16: Filtering shows just how many "external links" come from Google.

So what does this all mean? Should you be concerned with the raw numbers or only with the percentages? How should your percentages of direct-address, search engine, and external-link traffic compare?

> **LINKS THAT DON'T ACTUALLY LINK AND OTHER ANOMALIES**
>
> Occasionally, you'll find a URL in the list that has no links to your site. This is actually a form of spam. The idea is to get webmasters clicking the URLs to find out where the link is to their site. If you are finding a lot of those spam URLs, ask your web host how to block an IP or domain and then block them.
>
> For another interesting anomaly, look at the second entry in the external links list of Figure 3-15. The hits number is huge, while the pages number is comparatively small. When this happens, it's because the external site is hitting a nonpage element, such as an image. `Figure-Skating-Blog.com` happens to be Mary's blog, so it's not a big deal. But if a site you don't own is hitting a nonpage item hard, it is stealing your bandwidth. You should check carefully for what it is using and then block it from using that resource. Many web sites allow you to block everyone from directly linking to nonpage elements while also allowing you to make exceptions for sites like your own blog.

It's like this: You want to keep current readers and customers coming back. You also want new readers and customers to find you. A very low percentage of direct addresses may indicate that people are not returning after their first visit or that your offline promotional efforts are not effective. This means that your site is not sufficiently sticky, or that people get to your site and don't find what they need. It means you're not building a core audience.

A low percentage of search engine-driven traffic can mean that your site is not well optimized for search engines and people are not finding it. About two years ago, Mary overhauled `SkateFic.com` with search engine optimization (SEO) in mind. The percentage of traffic driven by search engines doubled, as did total traffic.

If the external links aren't bringing in the traffic, you need to be concerned about word of mouth and viral marketing. This is especially so if most of your external-link traffic is coming from repurposed Google searches, small search engines, and AdWords placements. It means that you don't have a lot of sites that spontaneously link to yours.

So how is `SkateFic.com` doing? Search engine traffic is about 50 percent — not too shabby. Bringing in that many new people every month is growing the core readership by hundreds of eyes every month. Direct-address traffic is about 43 percent, which means `SkateFic.com` has a happy and returning fan base and is a healthy content site. But with only 6.3 percent of page views coming from external links, and many of them from small search engines and AdWords, `SkateFic.com` isn't doing very well as far as word of mouth. Putting more effort into getting links from other sites, especially figure skating–related sites, could pay off handsomely in the long run. Independent external links are a crucial part of an SEO strategy and would improve search-engine results, bringing in more, better-targeted traffic.

Key Words and Key Phrases

Speaking of targeted traffic, if you want to know what people are searching for in those search engines, look no further than the Keywords and Keyphrases tables in Figure 3-17.

Odd chance can bring in traffic for content that isn't.

Unless you're huge, single keywords don't mean much.

Search Keyphrases (Top 10) Full list			Search Keywords (Top 25) Full list		
8325 different keyphrases	Search	Percent	3697 different keywords	Search	Percent
figure skating facts	237	1.8 %	skating	6128	10.7 %
michelle kwan	154	1.2 %	figure	5586	9.8 %
figure skating	135	1 %	ice	2511	4.4 %
kristina cousins ice skater	113	0.8 %	skater	1355	2.3 %
figure skating history	79	0.6 %	skaters	950	1.6 %
kristina lenko	73	0.5 %	of	862	1.5 %
sandra bezic	69	0.5 %	kristina	856	1.5 %
figure skating poems	49	0.3 %	olympic	829	1.4 %
facts about figure skating	48	0.3 %	the	767	1.3 %
jef billings	46	0.3 %	facts	704	1.2 %
Other phrases	11664	92 %	history	666	1.1 %

Figure 3-17: Why are people coming here?

These search terms are bringing visitors to your site. Unless you're an 800-pound gorilla yourself, the Keywords table won't mean a whole lot, except that having your best keywords appear the most is desirable. See how "figure" appears 5,586 times and "skating" clocks in at 6,128, but "figure skating" brings in only 135? That's what we mean. SkateFic is ranked so far down in the search for "figure skating" that it seldom gets found. The traffic you do see in the table is actually brought in by AdWords.

For the most part, however, SkateFic's key-phrase performance is pretty good. There are only two anomalies (Kristina Lenko and Kristina Cousins), which bring people in but don't actually appear anywhere on the site. The rest of the key phrases are on topic and likely point to relevant content. By clicking **Full List**, one would see that "figure skating" appears in roughly half the searches, meaning people are generally interested in the subject matter SkateFic offers. This is important. Years ago, the two top searches were "Tina Wild," a porn star, and "hockey wives" — don't ask, we don't know either. Obviously, those searches did not bring in people who were interested in what SkateFic had to offer: a skating serial chapter that mentioned hockey players' wives and where the main character Tina had a wild-hair day.

Miscellaneous

At present, as shown on Figures 3-18 and 3-19, the only part of the Miscellaneous table that's working is the tally of bookmarks.

These 709 people plan to come back.

Miscellaneous		
Miscellaneous		
Add to favorites (estimated)	709 / 15043 Visitors	4.7 %
Javascript disabled	-	
Browsers with Java support	-	
Browsers with Macromedia Director Support	-	
Browsers with Flash Support	-	
Browsers with Real audio playing support	-	
Browsers with Quictime audio playing support	-	
Browsers with Windows Media audio playing support	-	
Browsers with PDF support	-	

Figure 3-18: Y'all come back now, y'hear?

Over time, this metric gives an indication of "stickiness."

Miscellaneous		
Miscellaneous		
Add to favorites (estimated)	2156 / 5749 Visitors	37.5 %
Javascript disabled	-	
Browsers with Java support	-	
Browsers with Macromedia Director Support	-	
Browsers with Flash Support	-	
Browsers with Real audio playing support	-	
Browsers with Quictime audio playing support	-	
Browsers with Windows Media audio playing support	-	
Browsers with PDF support	-	

Figure 3-19: "Stickiness" can change over time.

The measures of "favorite" bookmarking in the two figures above are important for at least two reasons. First, they tell you how many people liked your site enough to bookmark it — meaning that they plan to return again and again. They may never actually return, but some do. This is called "stickiness." You want your site to be sticky. The "favorites" metric helps you keep tabs on how big your core audience is — the people who intend to come back.

Second, if you follow this over the months, you can see whether your content is becoming more compelling or less — are more or fewer people intending to come back? SkateFic.com ran at 4.7 percent bookmarks for the five years or so before February 2006, as recorded cumulatively in Figure 3-18, Figure 3-19, covering February 2006 to February 2007, shows a big change. Not only did a healthy 5,749 enter the site during that year, but 2,156 bookmarked it — 37.5 percent compared to the average of 4.7 percent for previous years. One could explore the reasons for this, but Google Analytics records only effects; it won't tell you why. What it does give you are hard numbers showing that the stickiness of SkateFic.com more than tripled in a year, from 709 to 2,156. The site has gotten stickier, and it's doing better at attracting an audience interested in figure-skating fiction.

Error Codes

We want to add a quick word about error codes and here it is, with the help of Figure 3-20.

Click here for the full list of "not found" pages.

HTTP Error codes				
HTTP Error codes*		Hits	Percent	Bandwidth
301	Moved permanently (redirect)	1539	45 %	689.34 KB
404	Document Not Found	1470	43 %	938.29 KB
403	Forbidden	267	7.8 %	0
206	Partial Content	130	3.8 %	354.42 KB
302	Moved temporarily (redirect)	7	0.2 %	5.31 KB
400	Bad Request	1	0 %	372 Bytes
* Codes shown here gave hits or traffic "not viewed" by visitors, so they are not included in other charts.				

Figure 3-20: Where was that again?

It's worth noting that Google Analytics, by its nature, doesn't collect information on HTTP errors. Those errors are part of the log file, and Google Analytics doesn't look at logs. The only real point of interest is the 404 "not found" errors. If you click the 404 link, it'll take you to a page such as Figure 3-21 that lists all the URLs for the pages visitors requested that could not be found.

PayPal looking for code that isn't there, or possible break-in attempts

Required but not found URLs (HTTP code 404)		
URL (288)	Error Hits	Referers
/proshop/IPV_validate.php	84	-
/ssph/	63	http://www.sportsfics.com/
/submissions/unfinished	41	-
/ssph/shortstories/ICQ/	26	-
/ssph/humor/RR/	24	-
/function.main	21	-
/ssph/poetry/chang/	20	-
/ssph/humor/QXQ/chapters/index.php	19	-
/classic/phantoms/chapters/%22../images/Phantomshrule.gif%22	19	http://www.skatefic.com/classic/phantoms/chapters/index.php
/ssph/poetry/kao/	19	-
/classic/phantoms/chapters/\"../images/Phantomshrule.gif\"	19	-
/ssph/poetry/ckeeta/	19	-
/www/show.php3	18	-
/srials/ote/	18	http://www.skatefic.com/figure-skating-ssph/short-story-stories/
/_vti_bin/owssvr.dll	16	-
/MSOffice/cltreq.asp	16	-
/ssph/shortstories/CG/	13	http://www.sportsfics.com/
/function.include	11	-
/ssph/humor/QXQ/	11	http://www.sportsfics.com/
/ssph/humor/RR/chapters/index.php	9	-

Possible break-in attempts

Errors in SkateFic.com's HTML. Fix them!

Figure 3-21: Checking 404 errors can show you problems you'd otherwise miss.

The web server will know where to send visitors looking for those pages. If the URL is pointing to an old name that no longer exists, or shows that there's a misspelling in your HTML, you can fix it. On the other hand, it may be an attack on your web server if the URL isn't familiar (especially if it contains funny characters like \x05), or if the URL has a long, long string of nonsense after it, or if it contains things like admin or .dll, which you don't have on your web site. But unless those attacks are successful or overwhelming in number, you're probably safe in ignoring them.

We're Done!

We made it! Now that we've tied up all the loose ends and, we hope, taught you all the basics, it's time to move on to Google Analytics. You'll see, as you go on, more of what Google Analytics can do that AWStats can't, but you'll also see that what you've learned about AWStats is valuable in itself.

Onward!

Setting Up Google Analytics

The average professional analytics package is eminently flexible and powerful. It can track every detail, every goal, and every bounce on your web site. Unfortunately, that also means you have to be a propeller-head — or hire one — to set up and use the average professional analytics package. You'll spend a lot of dough getting every last detail exactly right, and it'll take more time than you have.

Google Analytics is not your average professional analytics package. Yes, it's slightly less flexible, but it's every bit as powerful. What sets Google Analytics apart is that it's intuitive — easy to use — even if you want to integrate Google Analytics with your AdWords campaigns. You won't even need a propeller on your hat, much less one implanted in your skull.

Still, there are some steps in the Google Analytics setup that could be a bit tricky. Part II includes everything you need to know about setting up Google Analytics, including how to integrate it with AdWords. Each chapter walks you through a different aspect of setting up Google Analytics. No propellers required.

If you really want more advanced information, however, you can find that elsewhere in the book. Chapter 9 covers some of the advanced functionality of Analytics. These real-world examples will have you using analytics in ways you may not have even dreamed were possible.

Getting Started

When Google purchased Urchin on Demand, industry analysts predicted that the merging of Google's technology with Urchin's capabilities would be a great relationship. Chalk one up for the analysts because it truly has turned out to be a marriage made in analytics heaven. Sure, there were some growing pains in the beginning, but combining a successful analytics program like Urchin with the power and simplicity of Google's technology has created an application that anyone can use.

It's not all roses and champagne, however. Even paradise has bugs, and Google Analytics isn't immune to them. Fortunately, the bugs have been pretty minor. You should have a minimum of frustration setting up Google Analytics. You could encounter a few issues, but we're going to walk you through those to make this as painless as possible.

First, You Need a Google Account

If you don't have an account with Google, signing up for one is easy. The amount of information required is minimal, just your e-mail address and physical location. In Figure 4-1, you can see the information required to create an account with Google.

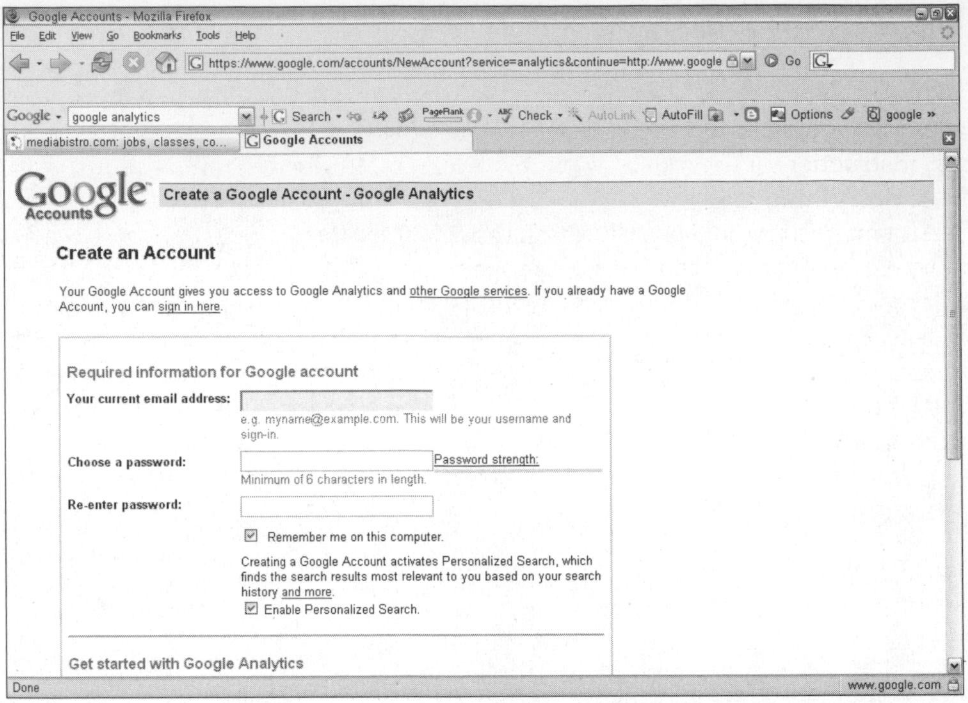

Figure 4-1: Google wants your e-mail address and a password to create an account.

You can sign up for a Google account through the main Google web page. Go to www.google.com and click the **Sign In** link in the top right-hand corner of the page.

On the page that appears, you'll see a sign-in dialog box where you can enter your username and password. You won't have that information yet. Instead, click the link below this box that says **Create an account now**.

On the next page, you'll enter your sign-up information. You'll be asked for your e-mail address, password, location, and a verification word. Once you've entered that information, read and accept the terms of service, and then click **I Accept. Create my Account**.

Google sends out confirmation e-mails for new accounts to prevent spam-bots from creating bogus e-mail accounts. Within a few minutes you should receive a confirmation e-mail. When you do, click through the link in the e-mail to activate your account. Once that's complete you'll have an active Google account.

Signing Up for Google Analytics

When you're ready to get started with Google Analytics, the first thing you need is a Google account. If you're a Gmail or AdWords user, or if you followed the instructions mentioned previously for creating a Google account, you have everything you need.

All you need to do is sign in, using the account information that you already have. Google Analytics is not in beta anymore. It's open to the public. Just enter your Google Account name and password as shown in Figure 4-2 and click **Sign in**. If you prefer for Google Analytics to be in another language, the program supports 17 languages including Queen's English, Russian, French, and Chinese. You can select your preferred encoding from a menu in the upper right-hand corner before you sign in.

You'll land on a splash page like the one in Figure 4-3. Click **Sign Up** to continue.

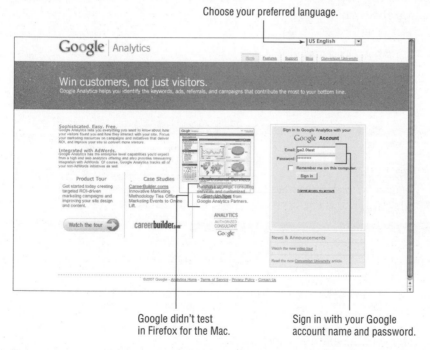

Choose your preferred language.

Google didn't test
in Firefox for the Mac.

Sign in with your Google
account name and password.

Figure 4-2: To sign up, enter your Google Account name and password.

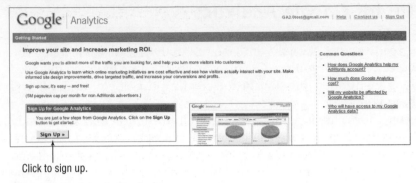

Click to sign up.

Figure 4-3: A typical splash page

Now, to the meat of the sign-up process. From the page shown in Figure 4-4, choose http:// or https:// from the menu, depending on whether your site is on a secure server or not. Then enter your site's URL. In this case, we'll be tracking the web site for Mary's mother's rental house (Mary is already tracking every other site she owns).

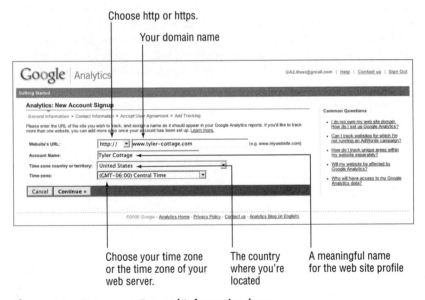

Choose http or https.

Your domain name

Choose your time zone or the time zone of your web server.

The country where you're located

A meaningful name for the web site profile

Figure 4-4: Enter your General Information here.

Give the site a name, although Google Analytics will automatically enter the domain name for you. Choose the country where you're located. This sets the time zone menu to show only the correct time zones for your country, so don't choose France when you need Fiji. Next click **Continue**.

PRIVACY, GOOGLE, AND YOUR DATA

Over the last year, we've fielded many questions about what Google may or may not do with your data. Buried deep in the TOS document is the following dense verbiage that explains this:

> **6. INFORMATION RIGHTS AND PUBLICITY. Google and its wholly owned subsidiaries may retain and use, subject to the terms of its Privacy Policy (located at** `http://www.google.com/privacy.html`**, or such other URL as Google may provide from time to time), information collected in Your use of the Service. Google will not share information associated with You or your Site with any third parties unless Google (i) has Your consent; (ii) concludes that it is required by law or has a good faith belief that access, preservation or disclosure of such information is reasonably necessary to protect the rights, property or safety of Google, its users or the public; or (iii) provides such information in certain limited circumstances to third parties to carry out tasks on Google's behalf (e.g., billing or data storage) with strict restrictions that prevent the data from being used or shared except as directed by Google. When this is done, it is subject to agreements that oblige those parties to process such information only on Google's instructions and in compliance with this Agreement and appropriate confidentiality and security measures. Unless You notify Google otherwise in writing, You hereby grant to Google and its wholly owned subsidiaries a limited license to use Your trade names, trademarks, service marks, logos, domain names and other distinctive brand features ("Brand Features") in presentations, marketing materials, customer lists, and financial reports.**

Google's use of your data is governed by their privacy policy located at `http://www.google.com/privacy.html`.

Basically, this means that Google will share your information only when it's necessary to do so; however, the company does reserve the right to mention your site or brand name in marketing materials. To our knowledge, Google does this only with express permission from the site or brand owner. But, as with all legalese, you should take the time to read through all of the details, understand them fully, and only then decide if you're in agreement with the terms of service.

Now, enter your Contact Information as in Figure 4-5. It might be wise to actually read the web form. Mary tried to enter her first name in the box where it said Last Name, which would have been embarrassing for the rest of the screenshots.

The next window is the standard terms of service agreement (TOS), called Terms and Conditions. You should read the TOS. There's important information in the TOS about how your site analytics may be used. Click **Yes, I agree to the above Terms and Conditions**, but only if you do agree with them. You should know, however, that if you don't agree to the TOS, you cannot create a

Google Analytics account. When you've read through the TOS and agreed to it, click **Create New Account.**

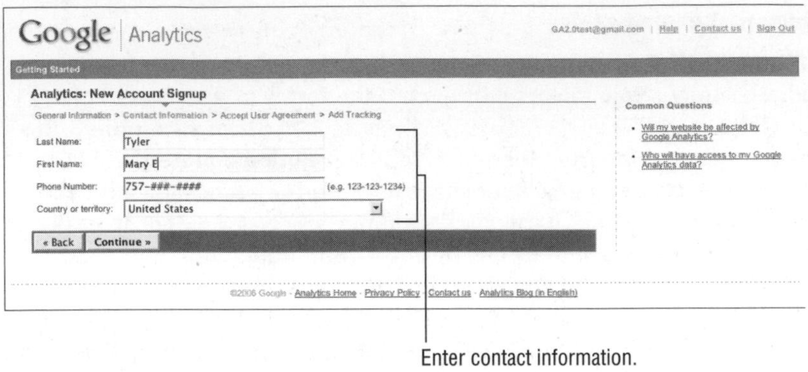

Enter contact information.

Figure 4-5: Enter your Contact Information here.

Activating Tracking

Analytics uses a snippet of JavaScript code to track the traffic on your web site as shown in Figure 4-6. You have to place that code on your site before the Analytics tracking is activated. It's not hard to do. All you have to do is copy the code that Google provides when you set up your account and paste it into your web site code before the `</body>` tag at the end of the page.

Save and republish the page, and Google Analytics will automatically detect the correct placement of the code. This may take a couple days. Or it may happen quickly. We've seen it happen both ways.

The key piece of information in the tracking code is the line that begins `uacct=UA` followed by a seven-digit number. This number is unique to each web site profile, and it tells Analytics which profile owns the ping your site sends when a page gets loaded.

After you've pasted your code into every page you want to track, click **Continue**. You will be brought to your Analytics Settings Dashboard shown in Figure 4-7.

On your Analytics Settings dashboard (which you'll learn more about in Chapter 5), you should see a message that indicates the code has been detected and data are being gathered for the analytics. The detection of the code should be immediate, but it could take a couple of days for any analytics to appear. In the meantime, if you click the **Check Status** option, you'll be taken to the **Status Tracking** page, as shown in Figure 4-8.

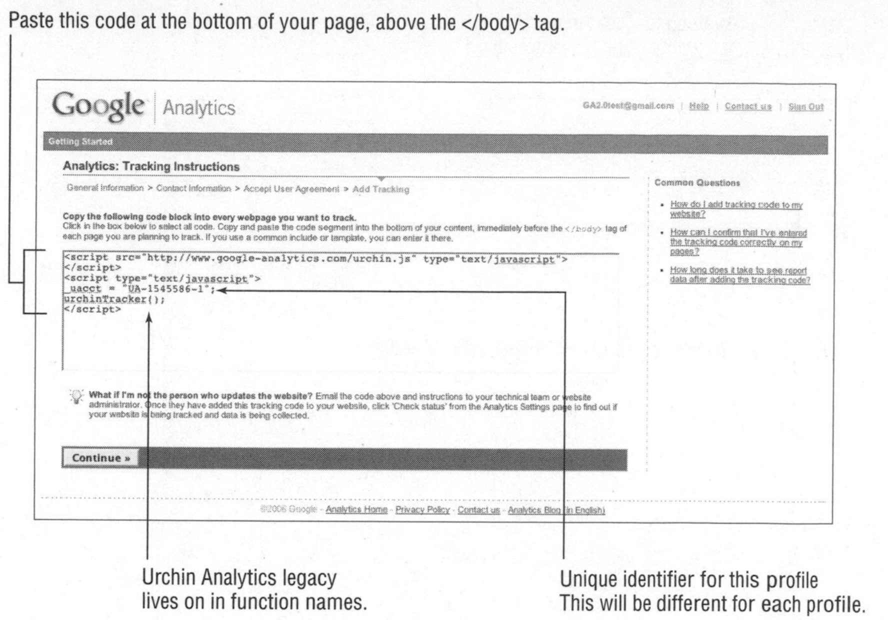

Paste this code at the bottom of your page, above the </body> tag.

Urchin Analytics legacy
lives on in function names.

Unique identifier for this profile
This will be different for each profile.

Figure 4-6: Copy tracking code and paste it in web pages before the </body> tag.

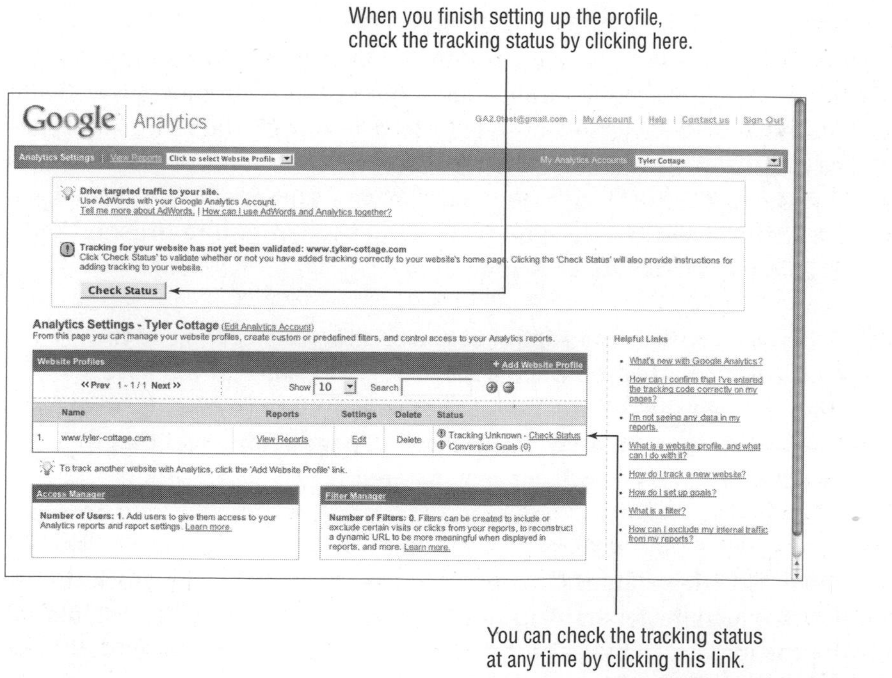

When you finish setting up the profile,
check the tracking status by clicking here.

You can check the tracking status
at any time by clicking this link.

Figure 4-7: Analytics has many dashboards. This one controls your profile settings.

"Waiting for Data" means Analytics
has detected the tracking code.

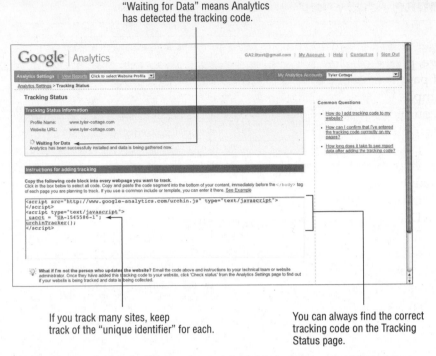

If you track many sites, keep
track of the "unique identifier" for each.

You can always find the correct
tracking code on the Tracking
Status page.

Figure 4-8: This time Analytics was quick and found the code right away.

Analytics will say whether it detects your tracking code or not and whether it is waiting for data or receiving data. Depending on how busy your web site is, it can take several days to several weeks to get enough data into Analytics to make the graphs mean anything. Regardless, Analytics always shows a listing of your code on the Tracking Status page in case you misplace it somehow (for instance, during a site redesign). Click **Done** when you're finished with the page to go back to Analytics Settings.

> **NOTE** To track more than one page of your web site, you need to add the tracking code to every page you want to monitor. For example, if you have 15 pages in your web site and you want to track all of those pages, you need to place the code snippet on every one of those 15 pages. Any pages that do not contain the tracking code will not be monitored.

At that point, all of the reports and graphics for your site metrics should appear in your Google Analytics account. Google Analytics is a historical analytics program, which means statistics are not tracked in real time. The statistical data that appear in your analytics reports will be one to two days behind. It's not a perfect solution, but despite the delay, the depth of information provided is both accurate and useful.

Navigating Analytics

By now, you've had a taste of navigating through the Google Analytics site. It's an intuitive, point-and-click navigation method that lets you start at the most general of pages and takes you deeper into more specific pages as you go on.

For example, when you sign in, you're taken to the Analytics Settings Dashboard. If you click one of the **View Reports** links on that page, you're taken to the reports for the corresponding web site. The first page for each account (or web site) that you're monitoring is the Dashboard page. This page, shown in Figure 4-9, is an overview of the reports that are available to you through Google Analytics for that specific account or web site. It allows you to see quickly the most important measurements for your site.

From the Dashboard page, you can navigate to every other report in Google Analytics 2.0. The navigation bar on the left side of the screen is where you'll find links to all the reports. Each section of reports is divided into a group that includes all of the reports related to that aspect of analytics. If you click the title of the report section, the navigation bar expands to show links to each of the reports in that section.

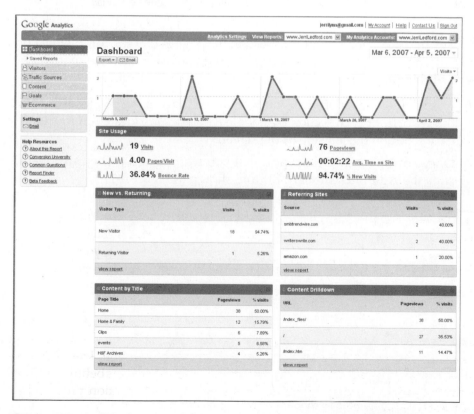

Figure 4-9: You'll find your most frequently used reports in the Dashboard.

Next to some reports within a section, you may notice there is a small arrow that points right. This arrow, shown in Figure 4-10, indicates there are additional reports under that category. For example, within the Visitor report section, there is a category for Visitor Trending. When you click the Visitor Trending link, the navigation bar expands even further to show the reports that are available on that next level down. The important thing to remember, when navigating through Google Analytics 2.0, is that the more clicks you make, the deeper into the collected information you're drilling.

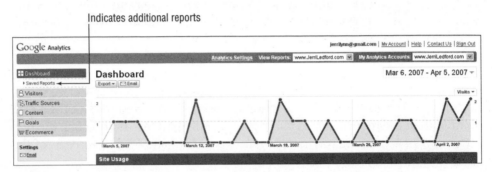

Figure 4-10: Each level of navigation leads you deeper into collected data.

One of the nice things about the Dashboard page is that it's completely customizable. You can quickly add the reports that you use most often to this front page by following these steps:

1. Navigate to the report that you want to include on the dashboard. All of the reports for each section of Google Analytics are located in the navigation bar on the left side of the screen.

2. Once you've reached the report that you want to add to the Dashboard, click the **Add to Dashboard** button, shown in Figure 4-11.

Figure 4-11: Customize the Dashboard by adding reports used most often.

3. The report is added to your dashboard and a message (shown in Figure 4-12) is displayed on the current screen. The next time you view your dashboard, you should see that report at the bottom of your screen.

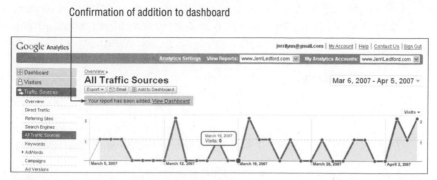

Figure 4-12: A confirmation message lets you know the report has been added.

You may find it irritating that this new dashboard system does not enable you to remove one report. The Site Usage report that appears at the top of the page is there to stay. You cannot remove it, and you can't move it to a different location on the page, which you *can do* with the other reports that you place there.

To move a report from one place to another on your Dashboard, all you have to do is place your pointer over the gray bar at the top of the report. Your pointer will change to a four-pointed arrow. Click-and-hold that bar while you drag the report to the desired location. Using this method, you can arrange all of your reports (except that Site Usage report) in any order that works best for you. Kudos to Google for making this element of Google Analytics 2.0 much more user-friendly than in the previous version of the program.

There are also some changes to the way in which you get help in Google Analytics 2.0. In the previous version of the program, getting help was most difficult. The online help system was set up in a very circular, hard-to-navigate way. With this new system, however, all you have to do is navigate to the report on which you need help, then click the **About This Report** link on the left side of the page. A tooltip appears, explaining the purpose for the report, and the basic "need-to-know" information.

For more in-depth information, click the **Conversion University** link just below the **About This Report** link. Again, a tooltip opens, giving you a preview of the additional information that's available in Conversion University — Google's training system. If you want to know more than what's provided in the tooltip, click the **Read More** link at the bottom of the tooltip box, and you'll be taken to the relevant article at Conversion University.

Finally, as you navigate through Google Analytics 2.0, you may notice two buttons near the top of each report page. These buttons — **Export** and **Email** — indicate new functionality that users of Google Analytics have been waiting for. Use the **Export** button to export any report or Dashboard to a file. You have your choice of file types: PDF and XML are file types that are available for all reports. But CSV and TSV file formats are also available for some reports. If you want to export a report to one of these file types, all you have to do is navigate to the report, click **Export,** and then select a file type from the links that appears. After you click the link, a dialog box appears prompting you to open or save the report. Use the dialog box to specify where you want to save the file and what the file name should be and then click **OK.** The report will be saved.

When you click the **Email** button, you're taken to a page like the one shown in Figure 4-13. From this page, you can send a report to an e-mail address as an attached file.

Figure 4-13: Reports can be e-mailed to others in one of four formats.

To send a report in e-mail, all you need to do is add the e-mail address the report should be sent to, create a subject and description for the message, and then select a file format. On the right side of the page is a preview of the message that will be sent. When you've finished entering the information, click the **Send** button and the message will be sent to the specified recipients.

The e-mail option also allows you to schedule a regular mailing of a report. If you click the **Email** button from within a report you'll be taken to the **Setup Email** page. From this page, click the **Schedule** tab. The page will reload and you'll notice that there is now a Date Range/Schedule drop-down menu, and the **Send** button has changed to **Schedule.**

Set up your e-mail just as you would if you were sending a single e-mail, except set the schedule for the report you would like to have sent. You have some options there also for the frequency of the data you'd like sent. For example, if you choose Weekly, then the report that's sent will include all of the data from the one-week period since the last report was sent.

Once you've set all of the options, click the **Schedule** button and the message is scheduled to be sent, on the schedule you have chosen, to each of the recipients you specified. Once the message is sent, you'll be returned to the report view, but a gold bar at the top of the report will display a confirmation that your report sending schedule was set. In that bar, there is also a link to **Manage Scheduled Reports.** Click this link to view scheduled reports, stop sending them, or modify them.

If there is more than one report you would like sent on the same schedule, then you can add a report to an existing schedule. Navigate to the report that you would like to include in the scheduled send, then click the **Email** button at the top of the page. When the page reloads and the e-mail form is showing, click the **Add to Existing** tab. This takes you to a page that displays the reports that you have scheduled to send at specific times. Select the schedule to which you would like to add the report and then click the **Add Report** button. The report is added to the existing schedule and you're returned to the report page.

The ability to send your reports by e-mail or to export them to files makes Google Analytics 2.0 an even more useful tool than it has been in the past. It's no longer necessary to take screenshots or captures to share this information with other people inside or outside your organization. Now all you need is an e-mail address. With a few mouse clicks, you'll have your reports delivered to whoever may need to see them, or you can even schedule regular mailings so that you don't have to think about such things. This feature adds much more usability to the Google Analytics application.

CHAPTER 5

The Settings Dashboard

It's one thing to collect data. Any web statistics program will do that. But to go beyond gathering data to producing usable information — that's something completely different. While most analytics programs produce almost any kind of data your heart could desire, they don't make it easy to use. And if you can't figure out what the data mean, you can't use that data to your benefit.

To produce meaningful data, even with the easiest of analytics programs, you have to set up the program correctly. Set-up should be easy. The first dashboards, after all, were on horse-drawn buggies. Far from those horse-and-buggy days, most professional analytics programs require experienced professionals to configure them. Google Analytics is strictly DIY, beginning with the simplest dashboards first. The more complex settings are no more than a few clicks deep.

Analytics Settings

When you log in to Google Analytics, the first page is the Analytics Settings dashboard shown in Figure 5-1. This dashboard is your gateway to creating and managing your profiles, controlling access to those profiles, and setting filters.

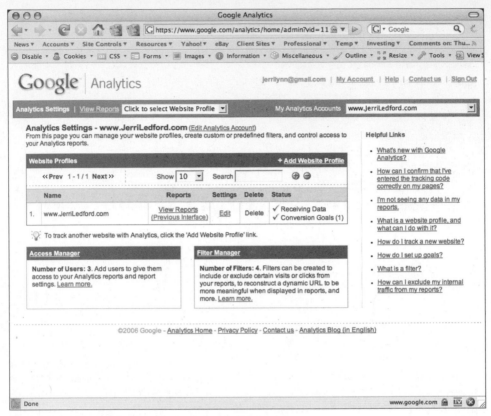

Figure 5-1: The main Google Analytics dashboard

The main (top) menu bar of the Analytics Settings dashboard has two basic choices: Analytics Settings and View Reports. If you have more than one profile, you can select which one you'd like to view from the drop-down menu, as shown in Figure 5-2. Otherwise, the default profile (whichever one you added first) will load when you click **View Reports**. Jerri has only one web site profile in her account, her freelancer's site, www.JerriLedford.com.

If you've been given access to profiles in another account, you will have a second drop-down menu on the far right. As Figure 5-3 shows, this is the menu that contains the different accounts connected via your Google Analytics account. For example, the www.JerriLedford.com profile is the default in Jerri's account, whereas the SkateFic profile is in Mary's account. Using the Access Manager, Mary gave Jerri administrative privileges to the SkateFic profile. Jerri can see all the metrics and make changes to settings in the SkateFic profile.

CAUTION   One thing you should be aware of when adding someone else to your Google Analytics account is that once you grant that person access to your account, they have access to any other web sites that you're tracking. For example, Mary tracks eight web sites within her Google Analytics account.

Because Jerri has access to her account, she can also see all of the metrics for each one of those web sites. Use caution when adding other users to your account. However, you can add access to specific profiles, so make sure that when you add someone, you add them where you want them, and restrict them from what you don't want them to see.

Website Profiles menu

Figure 5-2: The Website Profiles menu contains up to five different profiles.

My account menu

Figure 5-3: You can give other people access to your Google Analytics profiles.

Website Profiles

How many web sites do you own? Do you have just one or do you collect them the way Monopoly players hoard hotels? Maybe you've got a web site and a separate blog or a personal site and an e-commerce one? If you have multiple sites to track, you know it can be a hassle if you have to track all those sites separately. It takes time to keep up with each site, and it's always hard to come up with extra time.

Google Analytics makes it easy for you to track the analytics and metrics for multiple sites or even subdomains by creating profiles that you can manage from one location. Below the Analytics Settings ribbon is a Website Profiles table. This table contains all the links you need to administer your various profiles, to add a profile, or to change or delete a profile. There's also a status category that gives you a quick look at the tracking status of each profile you've created. If for some reason your tracking code isn't working properly, you'll be able to see that very quickly in the Status column of this table.

Adding a Profile

When you sign into Google Analytics for the first time, you'll be directed to a web site where you set up your first profile (you may remember doing this back in Chapter 4). Once you get that first profile set up, you can add additional profiles through the Website Profiles dialog box.

Here's how to add a new profile to those you're tracking:

1. In the Website Profiles table on the Analytics Settings dashboard, click **Add Website Profile**.

2. As Figure 5-4 shows, the information page for the new web site profile appears. Select from the options to add a new domain to track or to add an existing domain to track. The new domain is for a site that you are not currently tracking. The existing domain would be a portion, or page, of a site you're already tracking that you would like to track separately. (The way time-zone information is presented may differ slightly among users.)

3. After you select the Profile Type, select whether your site is an HTTP site or an HTTPS site (HTTPS is usually used for secured pages, like checkouts or registration pages). Then enter the URL of the web site that you want to track in the Add a Profile for a New Domain text box.

4. If you're adding a page to an existing profile, then click **Add a profile for** an existing domain, select the Domain Name you want to add the profile to, and give the profile a name.

Figure 5-4: Adding a new profile takes only a few seconds.

5. Click **Finish.**

6. You'll be taken to the Tracking Status screen, as shown in Figure 5-5. The code that makes it possible for Google to track your site is located below the Instructions for Adding Tracking. Copy that code and paste it to the bottom of your Web page before the `</body>` tag, and the site will be added to your profiles for tracking.

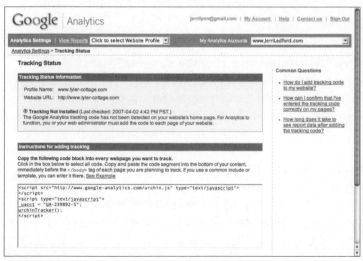

Figure 5-5: The Tracking Status screen shows status information and tracking code.

Checking Status

Once you've added the code to your web site, it will appear in the Status category on your Analytics Settings dashboard as pending. You should see the status of the tracking on your site whether it is Pending or Receiving Data. Pending means that Analytics is still gathering information.

It could take a couple of days for Analytics to gather enough information to begin producing reports. When enough tracking information has been gathered, the message Receiving Data will be displayed in the Status category.

NOTE Even though Google Analytics may gather enough information within a couple of days to start showing you populated reports, many of the analytics measurements that you'll use won't be truly useful until data has been collected for two months or more. Because Google Analytics offers historical tracking, the true value of this data is how it varies over time. Try to be patient and not make too many decisions about how effective your marketing or SEO efforts are until there is really enough data to show you truly useful information.

Editing a Profile

Once you've created your Analytics profiles, you can edit or change the profile information by clicking the **Edit** command that's on the same row as the profile name in the Website Profiles table. The profile name is usually the URL of the web site you're tracking, though it might be something like "Web Store" if you're tracking the part of your web site where e-commerce takes place.

The profile settings page is shown in Figure 5-6.

This page enables you to change four types of profile settings:

- **Main Website Profile Information:** Change the profile name or the URL of the site you're tracking, or set a default page — the index page of the site you're tracking. Add query parameters, set your time zone and currency settings, or choose which reports you would like to have access to.

NOTE Query parameters are variables that could possibly cause your web page to be counted more than one time. This duplication can skew your analytics, so it's important to add any query parameters that might make a page appear more than one time in your analytics. This includes session identifiers (such as `sid` **and** `session id`).

Figure 5-6: You can edit profile settings for several categories from this page.

- **Conversion Goals and Funnel:** A conversion goal is a target page you want users to reach. For example, if you want to drive traffic to sign up for your corporate newsletter, your conversion goal would be the "thank-you" page for the sign-up process. The number of people who actually reach the "thank-you" page is then counted toward the conversion goal. Funnels are pages that you expect your visitors to pass through to reach your conversion goal. You can specify up to 10 pages as funnel pages. Those pages are then monitored to show traffic patterns and how users navigate through your site to your conversion goal — and where people drop out of the process that leads them to a goal. You'll learn more about creating and tracking goals and funnels in Chapter 7.

- **Filters Applied to Profile:** Filters help you achieve more accurate measurements of the traffic on your site. For example, you can choose to filter visitors who enter your site from a specific domain as a way to ensure more accurate reports. The most common use of this feature would be to filter out traffic from your IP address. Say that your browser loads your web site's home page when you open a new window. You don't want to skew data about real visitors by counting hundreds — if not thousands — of your own visits and page loads. A filter can tell Google Analytics to ignore anything that comes from your IP address, resulting in more accurate metrics. Filters can be quite complicated, especially when you begin to create advanced filters with Regular Expressions, so you'll find more information on this topic in Chapter 6.

■ **Users with Access to Profile:** In many organizations, more than one person will want or need to have access to the information that Analytics collects and the reports that it returns. There are two levels of access: View Reports and Account Administrator. View Reports allows the user to look at any reports in that profile. Administrator privileges allow the user to make changes to View Reports and make changes to settings. This is where you add users for individual profiles, instead of adding them to the whole account.

All these settings can be changed at any time. If you try something and it doesn't work, you can change it again until it does work. Each web site you're tracking has its own profile settings, so you can manage each profile in a way that works best for that profile.

Deleting a Profile

Change happens, and it's a good bet that your needs will change over time. You may change the name of your web site, add profiles you want to track, or delete profiles. To delete a profile, navigate to the Analytics Settings page; then find the name of the profile that you want to delete. Click the **Delete** link that's in the same row as the name of the profile. As Figure 5-7 shows, you'll be prompted to confirm that you want to delete the profile. Click **OK** and the profile will be deleted.

Make sure you really want to delete the profile from Analytics before you click **OK**. Once you confirm, there's no way to get the profile back. If you change your mind, you'll have to recreate the profile from the beginning and you'll lose all your historical data.

> **NOTE** Deleting a profile from your account will work only if you are tracking more than one profile. If you have only one profile to track, you cannot delete it. You can, however, create another profile and then delete the first one.

Confirm deletion.

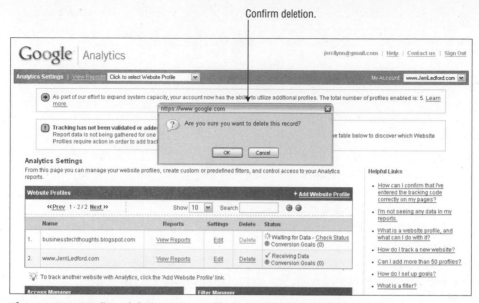

Figure 5-7: Confirm deletion of a profile before the process is complete.

Access Management

One very helpful feature of Google Analytics is the ability to give other people — your IT manager or administrator, other executives, or your partner — the ability to see and manipulate your Analytics account.

If you've ever worked with someone else and had them inadvertently change something that you didn't want changed, you may be nervous about which privileges you grant to other users. Maybe you want them to control everything. Maybe you only want to allow them to look at the reports. The Access Manager lets you control who can see what and who can do what with your whole account. You can control who has access to individual profiles from the settings page for each profile.

The Access Manager is located near the bottom of the Analytics Settings page. Click the Access Manager link and you'll be taken to the Access Manager dashboard, shown in Figure 5-8. From this dashboard you can add users and manage those users' privileges.

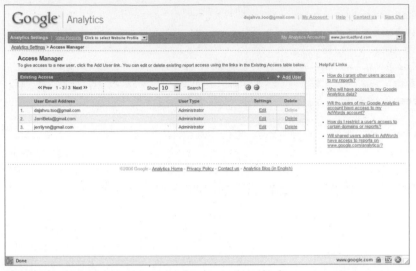

Figure 5-8: The Access Manager lets you control who can access your account.

Adding a User

Recently there have been several studies about how executives want to be involved in the collection and reporting of business intelligence, such as the information gathered by Google Analytics. According to these reports, executives want to be right in the middle of the action. They want access to the reports and to receive information about what data are being gathered, how often, and from where.

Google Analytics is built for multiple users. If you have an executive screaming over your shoulder every day that he wants information about the ROI (return on investment) of your web site, Analytics makes it easy to overload him with all the information he could ever desire. All you need to do is add your executive as a user on one or more profiles.

To add a user to your profile, go to **Analytics Settings ⇨ Access Manager**. In the Access Manager window is an Existing Access box that shows who your current users are and what levels of user they are. Click **+ Add User** in the upper-right corner of the box to give another person privileges.

You'll be taken to the Create New User for Access page, where you should enter the user's e-mail address and name, and set the access type, as shown in Figure 5-9. If you are allowing the user viewing privileges only, you can choose to permit access to individual profiles. If you select Account Administrator, the user, by default, will have access to all profiles and the profile lists will disappear. When you've entered the relevant information, click **Finish** and the user account will be created.

NOTE When creating a new user profile, the user you are adding must have a Google account, and that's the e-mail address you should use to register the user to have account access. If you use an e-mail address that isn't attached to an active Google account, the user won't be able to access the site. However, that person can use that address to set up a Google account that will then be able to access Analytics.

If you're not sure you want the executive (or anyone else) to have complete control over your Analytics account, you can always add them to a report mailing list, like the one that you learned to create in Chapter 4. This is an easy way to give your executives the information they demand without having them poking around in areas where they could create havoc.

Figure 5-9: To add a new user, enter some simple information and click Finish.

Setting User Permissions

When selecting the Access type, you can set permissions so that your users have Administrator Access or authorization to View Reports Only, as shown in Figure 5-10.

Administrator Access to a profile gives the user the ability to do anything you (the owner) could do. That user can make changes to settings, add other users, and even delete the profile. That user can even hand out administrator privileges like beads at Mardi Gras. An inexperienced admin can neatly sabotage a web-analytics strategy. View Reports Only allows the user to view reports but not to make any changes to the profile.

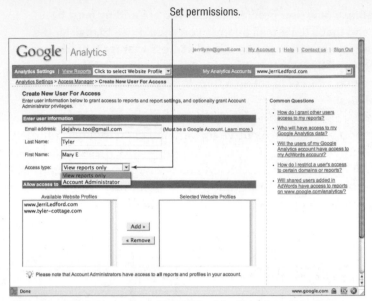

Figure 5-10: Set user permissions in this drop-down menu.

You can select and also restrict which web site profiles the user can access. If you have multiple profiles for multiple sites, you can give users access to some and keep them out of others. For example, if you work in a bigger company, you could set up several profiles for your company's web site. You might have a profile for your site's web store for the e-commerce division and another profile of the content pages for the editorial division.

Deleting a User

People leave. They find better jobs, get downsized, move to Tahiti, or transfer to different departments. In the business world, it's inevitable. Even in small family businesses, sometimes mom and pop choose to go separate ways. You need to have the ability to delete a user from your Analytics account. Google knows this and makes deleting users easy, even for non-propeller heads.

To delete a user, go to Analytics Settings ⇨ Access Manager and find the user you want to delete. Select the **Delete** option in the same row as the user's name. You're once again prompted to confirm that you want to delete the user, as shown in Figure 5-11. Click OK and the user is immediately removed and no longer has access to that — or any other — profile.

Just be sure that you really want to delete the user, because once it's done, you can't undo it. You'll have to recreate the user's access.

Confirm deletion.

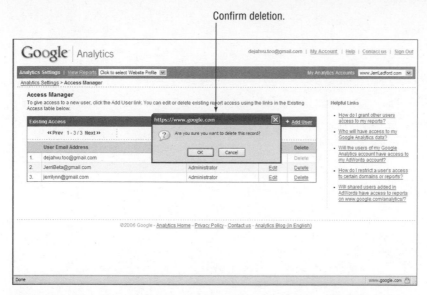

Figure 5-11: You're prompted to confirm that you want to delete users from your program.

Google Analytics makes everything point-and-click easy. It might take you a few minutes the first time you access the program to get it set up and become familiar with navigating through the controls, but once you're comfortable, adding and changing profiles and users is just a matter of clicking a few links.

Filtering Your Data

Most people look at a bolt of fabric and see nothing more than cloth. A seamstress looks at it and sees a shirt. The data collected by Google Analytics are just about the same — it's only meaningless data until you view it from the right perspective. That's when it begins to look like something useful.

In Google Analytics, a filter provides the right perspective. Filters help to separate data into two categories: the data that are used to create reports and those that have no value to you. Google Analytics provides filtering capabilities that help you see through the myriad facts, numbers, and values it collects.

What's a Filter?

Suppose Google Analytics simply collected information about your web site statistics and then dumped it in your lap without any kind of organization. It would take you longer to make sense of the statistics than it takes for a toddler to clean his room.

To help you understand what the facts that Google Analytics collects mean, data go through filters. These filters can exclude information collected about certain domains or IP addresses (an Internet site's numerical address), or they can simplify complex sets of numbers or facts, making them easier to understand.

Because understanding data can be a real chore, Google has created a standard set of filters that give you the ability to separate your collected metrics by plugging in key pieces of information or patterns expressed in a language called Regular Expressions, also known as RegEx. More about that later (although you'll see some RegEx wildcards in the following examples). The following standard filters are located in the Filter Type drop-down menu on the Create New Filter page:

- **Exclude all clicks from a domain:** This filter lets you exclude visits to your site from a specific Internet site. This is especially helpful if your company web site gets a high number of visits from people on the corporate intranet looking for dirt to dish on their coworkers.

- **Exclude all clicks from an IP address:** Remember that girl who had a crush on you and now follows you everywhere, making untoward suggestions for weekend activities? She visits your web site 150 times a day from her always-on cable modem connection 68.68.68.68. You could filter out that IP. But say she also uses her dial-up connection, which has the IP address 68.68.68.67. This filter will also exclude information about visits that match a particular kind of pattern. Filtering on `68\.68\.68\.6[78]` will match either 68.68.68.68 or 69.69.69.67 and will keep her obsession from screwing up your web site metrics. Now, if you could only use a filter to keep her out of your favorite restaurant.

> **NOTE** Some unsavory characters have discovered ways to mess around with your stats and analytics. One way they skew the numbers is by copying your web site's source code (which they use to create their own site) and leaving your Google Analytics code embedded within it. Another is to copy your source code to the header on their web site. In either case, the result is screwy measurements for your site. To straighten out your measurements, you need to use a filter that excludes the rogue's IP address from the data that Google Analytics collects.

- **Include only traffic from a specific subdirectory:** Your hot, new product finally has a page on your web site, and now you want to know how much traffic that one part of the site gets. Disappointing or not, this filter will show you how your baby is doing at the expense of all the other data on your site. "Include only" will include only the specific information that you tell it to.

In addition to these, you can create custom filters that separate out the information that you don't want or that isolate the information you do want. Custom filters allow you to:

- **Exclude a pattern:** This filter will exclude data from visits that match a certain pattern. Say you want to collect information only on your catalogue's regular products, not the sale ones. All sale products have a special e-commerce Item Code that begins with "SALE." You could filter that field to exclude any hits from those e-commerce items by filtering with SALE.* as the pattern.

▪ **Include a pattern:** Just as you can exclude, you can choose to include information that matches a certain pattern. Say you want to measure only the visitors who have really big screen resolution because you're going to launch a new game that requires it. You could include traffic where the Visitor Screen Resolution matches \d\d\d\d X \d\d\d\d, which would match resolution only with two four-digit numbers.

TIP The custom Exclude and Include filters are much more flexible than the predefined filters that Google has included. You can use pattern-matching with any of the data fields that Google monitors, more than just the domain, subdomain, or IP address. Use these custom filters to drill deeper into the vast oil field of data that's available to you.

▪ **Search and replace:** Much like the search-and-replace function in your word processor, this filter lets you search for specific types of information related to user visits and replace it with other information.

▪ **Lookup table:** Certain specific information isn't in a format that you can understand, even if you have it in front of you. So the lookup table collects that information and translates it into a format you can understand. For example, you can use a lookup table filter to show readable names for unrecognizable or confusing URL patterns. There's more to come on lookup tables, so don't fret if you don't get it just yet.

▪ **Advanced:** Do you wish you could exclude one pattern at the same time you're including another? You can. Simply use an Advanced filter that looks at multiple pieces of information at one time. Advanced filters are trickier than avoiding anthills in Mississippi, though, and Google documentation is circular, but that's why you bought this book, right?

▪ **Uppercase/lowercase:** Got something against capital or lowercase letters? Use this filter to change them. Why? Maybe your web developer is lazy and sometimes used title style for tokens and sometimes all caps. Google Analytics doesn't know that there's no difference between "Sale" and "SALE." With the uppercase filter, you could change "Sale" to "SALE," or with the lowercase filter, you could change "Sale" and "SALE" to "sale," which would make for much more accurate metrics.

A Short Lesson in Regular Expressions

Creating many of the Google Analytics filters requires some knowledge of Regular Expressions. Don't get too excited. Regular Expressions aren't phrases like "well, bless her heart" — the Southern disclaimer for every comment uttered under any circumstance. Life couldn't be that easy.

A Regular Expression is a string of text that uses characters, numbers, and wildcards to match patterns in a string of characters. RegEx has been accused of being obtuse, and that is not wholly unjustified. While basic RegEx is pretty easy, patterns can be complex, and RegEx follows right along.

The characters and numbers used in a Regular Expression are the same ones you use in English every day: letters A–Z (and a–z), numbers 1–9, and certain symbols from your keyboard. The wildcards are specific symbols or combinations of symbols. Here are the wildcards used in Regular Expressions:

. A period by itself will match any single character: letter, number, punctuation, or space but not an end-of-line character such as a carriage return. To match a literal period, use \. which uses the back slash to "escape the wildcard" and make it literal.

* An asterisk added to a character or wildcard will match zero or more of the previous items. So x* will match a string with nothing in it, x, xx, xxx, or any number of x's in a row together. More generally, .* matches nothing (empty string) or any series of characters (including numbers and punctuation but not including end-of-line characters). But take great care with the * modifier; it's greedy, meaning that it seeks the largest match possible — not always the one you mean. Say you have a paragraph with several sentences ending in periods. You would think that .*\. would match the first sentence, but it doesn't. It matches the whole paragraph!

+ A plus sign added to a character or wildcard will match one or more of the previous items. Use this modifier when you definitely know you don't want to match an empty string or when you want to require that a particular character be present. So x+ would match x, xx, xxx, and so on but would not match a blank string or a string of characters with no x's in it.

? Match zero or one of the previous items. So x? will match x and xx but not xxx. Adding ? to * produces something interesting. Remember we talked about .* being "greedy" — that it produces the largest match possible, which is not always what you want? Well, .*? de-greed-ifies .* faster than jail time drains the avarice off a CEO. Still want to match the first sentence of that paragraph of sentences? Well .*?\. will do it.

You can also use ? with the + modifier to the same effect. The pattern .+? will match at least one character in a non-greedy way.

{ } Use curly braces to repeat an exact number of times. So [0-9]{4} would match any group of exactly four digits. You can also have several values inside curly braces. So {2,5} would be "match any two or five characters."

( ) Put parentheses around a part of a pattern when you want to store that tidbit of information for use later. To reference that stored bit of text later, you use escaped numbers: \1 for the first saved bit, \2 for the second, \3 for the third, and so on.

[ ] Put square brackets around a list of characters you want to match. So when we wanted to match both 67 and 68 in your crazy crush's IP address, we used the pattern 6[78], which matched both. Don't make the mistake of putting a word in square brackets and think you'll match the word. You won't. It's strictly character by character. Use alternation with the | to match words.

- Create a range in a list. So if you want to match any digit, you can use [0-9] rather than [0123456789].

| The vertical bar or "pipe" character is used for alternation. Think of it as the word "or." Say you wanted to match "this" or "that"; you'd use a pipe this|that.

^ The carat has two possible matches depending on where it is. If it's inside square brackets, it means "not." So [^0-9] means "anything that is not a digit." But when you find ^ outside of square brackets, it means "at the beginning of the line." So ^Help will match the word Help if it appears at the beginning of a line.

$ Just as the carat is the beginning of the line, the $ is the end of the line/field. So help me$ will match only if it appears at the end of a field (or if it's followed by an end-of-line marker like a carriage return or line feed).

\ Escape any wildcard. When you escape a wildcard, it becomes a literal. When you escape certain literals, they become wildcards (for example, \d is "any digit" and comparable to using [0-9] but quicker to type). Only certain literals can become wildcards when escaped. What happens if you escape something that doesn't have a special meaning? Nothing. You're safe. You can even escape an escape, like \\, which you'll need if you want to match a literal back slash. RegEx behaves like Amelia Bedelia, a beloved character from a series of children's books who takes every direction completely literally unless you tell her not to.

Here are some additional tips that you'll need for working with wildcards in Regular Expressions:

- The characters ^ and $ represent the beginning or end of an expression. They're called *anchors* and can speed up the processing of your request when used properly.

- Use the | to group patterns together. For example, if you need to return graphics with the extensions .jpg, .gif, .bmp, and .png, you don't need to escape the period in front of each extension. Instead, you can use the expression \.(jpg|gif|bmp|png) to group the pattern (and preserve the exact text of what you've matched).

- The expression .* matches everything, so don't forget how greedy it is! Use .*? when you don't want to match everything and it's dog and cat and bird and fish and — well, you get the idea. Also remember that .* and .*? will match the empty string (i.e., nothing, "") as well as strings containing characters. If you definitely want to make sure that you're not unintentionally matching empty strings, make sure to use .+ or .+? instead.

- Keep it simple. The more complex you make your Regular Expressions, the longer it will take them to process. With a very complex Regular Expression, you also introduce more opportunity for error. As my editors are fond of telling me, add only what you have to and leave everything else out.

You could spend months — even years — learning Regular Expressions and still not learn everything there is to know. What you need to know right now is that you will need some simple Regular Expressions, like the ones in the preceding examples, to create an advanced filter. Of course, more advanced expressions will result in more advanced filtering capabilities, so if you'd like to know more than what's here, check out the sidebar later in this chapter for some additional resources on Regular Expressions.

A Slightly Longer Lesson on Regular Expressions

As with most programs you run on your computer, Regular Expressions was developed rather than just springing like Athena from the mind of the creator. It's one thing to understand what the symbols mean and quite another to be able to read or write one. As one reviewer of the first edition properly pointed out, we didn't have enough examples. So in the coming section, we're going to try to develop the RegEx for certain situations you might commonly meet as a webmaster.

Matching an IP Address

In the last section, we talked about wildcards that match various subsets of characters. The most flexible, powerful, and dangerous character is the period aka "dot." The period will match any character except the end of line marker (\n in RegEx-speak). It will match letters of either case, digits, punctuation, spaces, tabs — you name it. It will even match periods. So how do you match a literal period?

To make the wildcard period into a literal period in a Regular Expression, you escape it by putting a back slash in front of it like this:

```
\.
```

So say that you want to match the specific IP address: 192.168.0.1? What if you wrote the RegEx like this:

```
192.168.0.1
```

It would match `192x16830,1` as well as `192.168.0.1`. Instead, you write:

```
192\.168\.0\.1
```

Now the RegEx parser knows that you mean literal periods not "match any character." What if you wanted to match a range of addresses? Say that you'd like to match `192.168.0.1` through `192.168.0.5`. It's still fairly easy:

```
192\.168\.0\.[1-5]
```

Don't forget that escaping works for a variety of wildcards. For example, the ampersand is a wildcard. You should always escape it with a \&. Some wildcards are created by escaping letters: \n means "end of line" and \t means "tab." To refer to a previous match that you have "saved" by putting it in parentheses, escape a number. The first match is \1, the second match is \2, and so on. Sometimes, you even need to escape the escape \\ when you want to match a literal black slash.

What happens when you escape a character that has no special meaning when escaped? Nothing. If you escape a character that is not a wildcard when escaped, nothing happens.

Matching a Directory Name

The first thing you need to do when putting together a Regular Expression is think about what the pattern is. How does it begin and end? Are there markers that appear every so often? In programming-speak, these are called "delimiters." If you've ever opened a CSV file (created by Excel) in a text editor, then you've seen that it's all Comma Separated Values. The comma is the delimiter.

So what kind of delimiter does the directory structure of your web site have? Let's look at an actual URL:

```
http://www.skatefic.com/serials/ote/index.php
```

See how the forward slashes separate the protocol http: from the domain name `www.skatefic.com`? Then there are forward slashes between each directory name. In Chapter 3, we used RegEx to match the serials directory to filter information in AWStats. First, the name of the directory we want to match:

```
serials
```

Next, the delimiters — the forward slashes come before and after the directory name:

```
/serials/
```

SkateFic has an old, basically abandoned domain name, `DejahsPrivateIce .com`, which still points to the site, much as `egroups.com` still leads to `groups.yahoo.com`. So we can't just put the whole `http://www.skatefic.com/` in the pattern, because sometimes it's `http://www.skatefic.com/serials/` and sometimes it's `http://www.DejahsPrivateIce.com/serials/`. We don't know exactly what comes before the directory we want. We also have a variety of serials, and each of those serials has a lot of different documents. So we need to express this understanding that there's "some stuff" before and "some stuff" after the directory name serials.

Yes, "some stuff" is a technical term. In RegEx, `.+` means "some stuff." We're going to use `.+` instead of `.*` because `.*` might match the word serials by itself, and we want to make sure it has "some stuff" before and after. So, placing `.+` before and after our current expression, we get:

```
.+/serials/.+
```

Wait a minute. Why are the slashes important? Couldn't we do just as well without them?

Nope. If we wrote the RegEx like this:

```
.+serials.+
```

then it would match things like:

```
http://www.skatefic.com/skating-serials-rule.html
```

It fits the pattern, after all, being "some stuff" before and after the word serials. Without the delimiting forward slashes, you can end up matching things you don't intend to match. Now, do we need to make those `.+` matches not greedy? It probably wouldn't hurt. Up to now, Mary's been fairly careful about what she names things. The word "serials" is only used for that directory name. So there's no way for the RegEx to mess up if it's greedy. But what if she sells the site and the new owner does not follow her careful naming convention?

Better safe than sorry.

```
.+?/serials/.+?
```

Matching a Variable Name/Value Pair

Some URLs, like product catalogue pages, end like this one with a question mark (`?`) and a series of variables:

```
http://www.example.com/catalogue/index.php?ItemID=4963
```

A variable is something that can change. In this case, it can be one ID or another and identifies the catalogue item you want to display. But say you don't want to display that meaningless number in the Google Analytics results. Say you want to display something meaningful to the average human . . . like your boss.

First, just as an exercise, let's develop a generalized expression for a name/value pair. The name part of the pair can be letters and numbers, but must always start with a letter. The value, for this example, will always be a four-digit number. Names and values in URLs are always separated by an equal (=) sign. Let's also say that we know there is never more than one variable in the example site's URLs. For this example, let's also try to use escape sequences when we can — it makes for a more human-readable RegEx.

Okay, we need the first character to be a letter. You can denote that letter as [a–z]. Because we want one or more letters at the beginning, we need a plus sign (+) as well, like so:

```
[a-z]+
```

Now, the rest of the name can be letters or numbers. We could write it like [a-z0-9] or we could use the escape shorthand and use \w, which means "any word character." Now, since we want to allow, but not require that a number be included, we need an asterisk (*) rather than a plus sign (+). Make sure not to put a space between the characters inside the square brackets. We don't want any spaces in our Name tokens! Now we have:

```
[a-z]+\w*
```

That's our Name token. We know that the Name token is always followed by an equal sign (=). So that's next:

```
[a-z]+\w*=
```

Now, we know that the Value is always going to be a four-digit number. We can write that a couple different ways. You could, if you wanted, repeat `[0123456789]` four times, but that would be long, long, long, long. You can also write `[0-9][0-9][0-9][0-9]`, which is still long. If you like escape sequences, you can write four digits as `\d\d\d\d` (note that here we don't need the square brackets). Or, if you are a propeller-head, you can write `\d{4}`, which reads as "digit, exactly four times." And let's say that we want to capture that four-digit number for use later. We need to put our expression in parentheses `( )` for that. For clarity's sake, let's use the `\d\d\d\d` notation:

```
[a-z]+\w*=(\d\d\d\d)
```

Wow! We actually developed something that might be useful.
Not.
There's not much point in being able to match any Name/Value pair. For filtering, you want to be able to match particular ones. So, let's replace that generalized Name pattern, with the literal one used in our example URL:

```
ItemID=(\d\d\d\d)
```

But let's also add a bit more complexity. Let's say that the item number is not always going to be four digits. It could be one to four digits. How would you write that? There are all kinds of complex ways, but you don't need to rack your brain for them because there's one simple way:

```
ItemID=(\d+)
```

Huh!?
The reason we can write it that way is that we know this RegEx will only match digits. A `\d` won't match the `&` that delimits variable pairs on the hind end. And we know that the filter will either reach the end of the URL or there will be an ampersand and the match will complete. And, if some day, you have more than 9,999 items in your catalogue, your filter isn't going to break when it sees `ItemID=10000` (five digits).

LEARN MORE ABOUT REGULAR EXPRESSIONS

If you're interested in learning more about Regular Expressions, these resources will give you something to chew on:
Beginning:

■ *Beginning Regular Expressions,* by Andrew Watt. ISBN: 0764574892.

Intermediate:

■ *Regular Expressions: The Complete Tutorial*, by Jan Goyvaerts. ISBN: 1411677609.

Advanced:

■ *Mastering Regular Expressions,* by Jeffery Friedl, ISBN: 0596002890.

Articles on the Internet:

■ Regular Expressions Wikipedia Entry

```
http://en.wikipedia.org/wiki/Regular_Expressions
```

■ Common Applications of Regular Expressions, by Richard Lowe at 4GuysFromRolla.com

```
http://www.4guysfromrolla.com/webtech/120400-1.shtml
```

■ Understanding Basic Regular Expressions Patterns, by Tom Archer at Developer.com

```
http://www.developer.com/net/cplus/article.php/3485636
```

More resources can be found by Googling "how to"+Regular+Expressions."

But what if we want to be able to use letters and numbers in our values? You may well want to do that if you need to capture a long, complicated session ID. It's not too difficult. Remember that we decided that \w* meant "letters and numbers" (word characters, really, but let's not be nit-picky). Except in this case, we don't have to have a letter first. So we need a + instead of a *:

```
ItemID=\w+
```

Again, we don't have to worry about the ampersand or the end of line. But what if your site has two different catalogues? Or if a combination of variables has a meaning? Like this:

```
http://www.example.com/index.php?CatID=1A&ItemID=4309
```

Say that Catalogue 1A is Ice Resurfacers and ItemID 4309 is the Zamboni Deluxe 9000. If you wanted to capture these two variables separately, you could use these two separate Regular Expressions, which we have already developed:

```
CatID=(\w*)
ItemID=(\d+)
```

What if you want to capture them together? We just concatenate them — a fancy propeller-head term that means "moosh together."

```
CatID=([\w]*)\&ItemID=(\d+)
```

Notice that the ampersand (&) in this pattern is escaped. In RegEx, the & is a wildcard meaning the whole match, so if you intend to use it as a literal (an actual ampersand) you need to escape it.

In Analytics, we wouldn't do a compound pattern like this. In the Advanced Filters section, we'll show you what we would do. But first, let's take care of the administrivia of how to create and assign filters.

Managing Filters

Setting up filters begins with the Filter Manager, which is located near the bottom of the Analytics Settings dashboard. Click the **Filter Manager** link — not the **Learn More** link, which will take you into the help system — and you'll be taken to the dashboard shown in Figure 6-1.

Creating New Filters

To set up a new filter, click the **Add Filter** link in the upper-right corner of the Existing Filters box. This opens the Create New Filter page, as in Figure 6-2.

Enter the filter name, filter type, and domain name, if necessary. Then select a web site profile to apply the filter to and click Finish.

> **NOTE** If you have multiple domain profiles on your Google Analytics account, you can apply the same filter to all of the domains (or any number of the domains) at one time. For each domain you want the filter applied to, highlight the domain name in the Available Website Profiles menu and click Add. The domain will be moved to the Selected Website Profiles menu. Complete the filter setup, and the filter will be applied to all selected domains.

You'll be returned to the Filter Manager Dashboard, and as Figure 6-3 shows, your new filter will appear in the Existing Filters box.

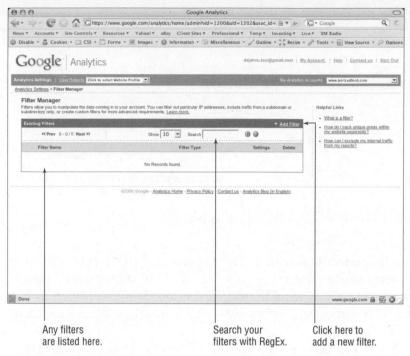

Any filters
are listed here.

Search your
filters with RegEx.

Click here to
add a new filter.

Figure 6-1: Manage your filters on the Filter Manager Dashboard.

Name your filter.

Select the type of filter you want.

Content of this box
depends on filter
type you chose.

Select profile to
apply your filter to.

Figure 6-2: Create a new filter by entering the requested information.

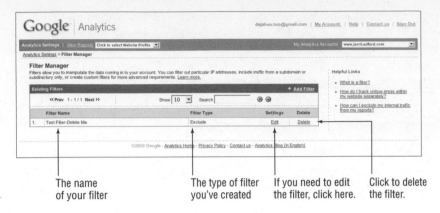

The name   The type of filter   If you need to edit   Click to delete
of your filter   you've created   the filter, click here.   the filter.

Figure 6-3: New filters appear in the Existing Filters box.

For example, if you want to create a filter to exclude the internal traffic from your network because your home page is set to the front page of your web site, from the Filter Manager you would select **Add Filter**. Now, as shown in Figure 6-4, enter a filter name; for the purpose of this example, we'll use the name Exclude Internal Example.

Next, go to **Filter Type** and select **Exclude All Traffic from an IP Address**. When you select this option, the IP Address field will automatically show a default IP address. This is an example address and should be changed. Replace the address with your own IP address using the exact same format as the example that is filled in for you. Don't forget, this is RegEx; make sure to escape the periods in your IP address.

Finally, select the web site profile to which you want to apply the filter and click **Add** and then **Finish**.

Now you have set up your first filter to exclude any internal traffic to the web site that you're measuring.

> **NOTE** You can find your IP address by going to www.WhatIsMyIP.com.
> But remember that if you're on a dial-up, your IP can change every time you
> dial in. In that case, you will probably want to contact your ISP and ask them
> what range of IP addresses your dial-up number uses. Then create a Regular
> Expression that will match that range. You'll lose some visitors who might
> happen to use the same dial-up as you do, but there's nothing that can be

**done about that. If you're on DSL or a cable modem, it will probably change
every two to six months. So if you filter your own traffic out, you should make
a point to check your IP address at least quarterly.**

There's one more thing you need to understand about filters, and that's the
order in which they are applied. Many people have trouble with Google Analytics' filters because they don't realize that all of the filters that you apply to a
web site profile are applied in the order in which they are set.

If you happen to have an exclude filter set as the very first filter, only what
remains after the filter action will be affected by the next filter in the list.
Unfortunately, these sorts of effects are most often found by trial and error, as
in "Why the heck isn't such-and-such data showing up? Duh . . . it's
excluded." This is where you conk yourself on the head and reorder the filters.
Changing the order of the filters is easy enough. From your Analytics Setting
page, click **Edit** in the same row as the web site profile for which you want to
change the ordering of the filters.

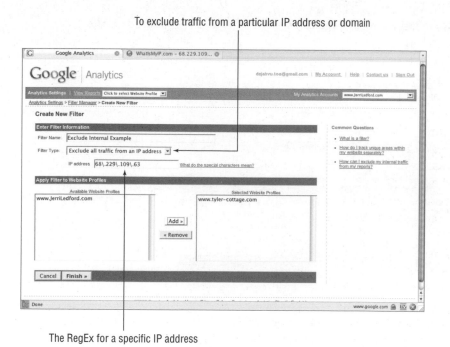

Figure 6-4: Exclude traffic from your own IP like this.

On the Profile Settings page, navigate down to the Filters Applied to Profile box and click the **Assign Filter Order** link, as shown in Figure 6-5.

You are taken to a page like the one in Figure 6-6. Highlight the filter that you want to move and then click the **Move up** or **Move down** buttons to rearrange your filters into the order that you want them to be accessed.

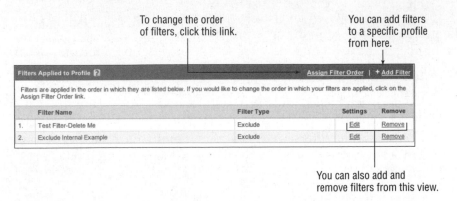

Figure 6-5: In the site profile, you can see the order filters get applied to data.

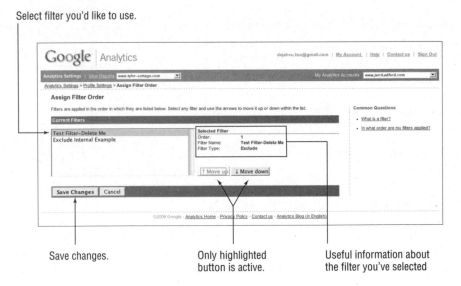

Figure 6-6: Rearrange the order in which filters are accessed.

FILTER VALUES IN PREDEFINED FILTERS

If you're using the filters that Google Analytics already has predefined, there are a few fields that you might want to know a little more about. Here's a quick list of the fields you might encounter and how you can use them:

■ **Domain:** This allows you to determine the complete domain or a portion of a domain that you want to filter. So if you want to keep your brother-in-law's traffic out of your stats (because you share a domain) you could set up your filter to exclude his subdomain (sub.domain.com) by using the expression `sub\.`

■ **IP Address:** You can filter an IP address or a range of IP addresses using Regular Expressions to tell Google what to look for.

To filter a single IP address, like your own, enter the IP address like this: `192\.125\.1\.1`

To filter a range of addresses, as you would if you worked in an office with multiple computers each with its own IP, such as `192.125.1.1 to 192.125.1.25`, you would use the expression: `192\.125\.1\.[1-9]| 1[0-9]|2[0-5].`

To filter two or more addresses, which you might need to do if you have two separate local area networks, use a | symbol between the addresses. This technique is called "alternation" and the vertical bar is read as "or." If you want to match `192.168.0.1` or `10.0.0.1`, the expression is `192\.125\.1\.1|10\.0\.0\.1` and is read `192.125.1.1 OR 10.0.0.1`.

■ **Subdirectory:** Again, you can use Regular Expressions to include (or exclude) the subdirectory of a site. So, if you wanted to include a specific subdirectory (and exclude everything else), the expression that you would use is: `subdirectory/` where you replace the word subdirectory with the name of the subdirectory you want to include.

Translating RegEx in English can be confusing, even for experienced users. This is not to say that it's too hard for us mortals. Rather, if you find RegEx tough going, don't feel dumb, because you're in good company. RegEx is a cryptic language — and maybe it's new to you. That makes it seem even harder than it really is. The more you use Regular Expressions, the more they will make sense. Until you're comfortable with RegEx, you may need to refer to the opening portions of this chapter to help you figure out how to write the Regular Expressions you'll use in your filters.

Custom Filters

When you're creating a new filter, one option you have is to create a custom filter. When you select the **Custom filter** option, as shown in Figure 6-7, the menu for custom filters expands to show you additional options for that filter.

Figure 6-7: Additional options on the custom-filter menu

These custom filters can be used to dig deeper into the statistics that Google Analytics collects. Use them to filter for specific activities such as including only a subset of traffic or excluding a type of visitor. You can also perform search-and-replace functions and rely on a table function to clarify the data that is returned. Let's look closer at each of those types of filters.

Include and Exclude Filters

Include and exclude filters are just what they appear to be — filters that include or exclude specific data. But the custom include and exclude filters go beyond simply filtering web site domains and IP addresses. With these filters you can choose to include or exclude specific fields or capabilities. If you don't want to know about any of the users hitting your site who have Java capabilities installed, you can choose to exclude them. Or maybe you want to include only the users who have Java capabilities. In that case, all of the visits from users who don't have Java capabilities will be discarded, and you'll see information only from those who do.

Here's what you need to remember:

- **Include filters** include only the data that match the inclusion pattern and discard everything else.
- **Exclude filters** exclude only the data that match the exclusion pattern and include everything else.

The reason it matters? Multiple include and exclude filters can result in no traffic at all. Say you want data only from users who use IE7 with Java turned off. So you include only the data from people with Java turned on. Then you exclude all of the people running all browsers other than IE7. What if there are no users among your visitors running IE with Java turned off? Right. No data.

Think of it this way. When you decide to buy a car, you go to the lot and first choose a model that you like. That choice (which you could call an include filter because you want to include only cars that are that specific model) cuts your choices down by at least half and probably more.

Then you decide that you want this specific model only in blue. You've added another include filter that reduces your number of choices again.

Your last decision is that you don't want a standard transmission. Now you've added an exclude filter and the result is that there might not be any cars on the lot you can choose from. Include and exclude patterns work the same way to narrow your results.

Search-and-Replace Filters

Ever look at something and have no clue why you're looking at it? Chances are, if you were looking at it from a different perspective, you'd understand it immediately. Let's say you're selling jet skis, snowboards, and surfboards through your web site. Each category of items appears on a single dynamic page. Which page you get is determined by the category ID tag on the end of the URL: 1000 for surfboards, 2000 for jet skis, and 3000 for snowboards. When your look at the metrics, you'll need to remember what those numbers mean because Analytics will show your results by the category number. If you have more than three categories — whoa, baby! Unless you have a photographic memory, learning all of the category ID numbers could take forever.

On the other hand, if you can convert those numbers to readable, easy-to-understand text on your reports, your hair might not go gray for another month or so.

That's what a search-and-replace filter does. This nifty tool lets you turn mundane, hard-to-recognize results into something that's immediately understandable by replacing a matched expression with a different string or group of numbers or text. You can use the search-and-replace filter to change those mundane category IDs to something that has meaning. Like this:

Go to **Analytics Settings** ⇨ **Filter Manager** ⇨ **Add Filter** and then enter a filter name. For this example, we're using Search & Replace Example. From the drop-down menu, select **Custom Filter** and then click the radio button beside **Search and Replace**.

A new information section that has to this point remained hidden (Google doesn't want to scare you off with confusing stuff before it's necessary) appears. In the Filter Field, select **Request URI.**

Now for Search String, type **/docs/document.cgi?id=1000**. (This is just for the example, not for your actual site. For your site, you would replace this information with the actual part of the URL that you want to find.) Then, for Replace String, you type the information you want to replace it with. Let's use "Surfboards."

Now you can select whether you want to make this filter case-sensitive. In most cases, you do not want case-sensitive searches. For now, leave it alone.

At this point, your filter should look like the one pictured in Figure 6-8. All that's left is to select the web site you want the filter to apply to and click **Finish.**

Figure 6-8: An example search-and-replace filter

Now you're seeing the meaningful label, "surfboards" instead of ID=1000, which really means something only to your web server. You won't have to wonder if your customers are looking at surfboards. The answer will be right in front of you in an easy-to-read format.

Lookup Table Filters

But what if you have more than three generic items in your catalog? What if you have 100 models of surfboards and 55 different jet skis and hundreds of snowboards? You're not going to want to enter a different filter for each model, but you might want to be able to break down your metrics by model as well as by general category.

As with search-and-replace filters, lookup table filters substitute something understandable for the incomprehensible numbers tagged on the ends of your URLs. But there are some differences. Let's look at the surfboards again. Say your product IDs are set up like this: http://www.supersurfing.com/catalog .php?id=1691 (where the number represents the specific product ID of a particular model of surfboard).

The lookup table filter takes the product ID and compares it against a big list of possible values and their corresponding substitutes. When it finds the one that matches, the filter does the replace with the value that corresponds to the value that you "looked up." This is like search and replace with a range of possible "finds" and "replaces." And this requires Google's help.

> **NOTE** At the time of this writing, Lookup Table functions are disabled in Google Analytics. You can use existing lookup tables, but they are not installing new ones. We've included information on lookup tables in this chapter so that when they go live again, you can use them.

To begin using a lookup table, the first thing you need to do is create a spreadsheet saved as a *tab delimited plain text file* with the format discussed in the following format:

In cell A1, type **# Field**. In cell B1, type **request stem**. Now, in column 1, list all the possibilities for your product ID. In column B, list the corresponding replacement value for each product ID. For example, our surf shop's spreadsheet looks like Figure 6-9.

Once your spreadsheet is complete, save it as a tab-delimited, plain-text file with the extension .lt for lookup table. If you're using Excel, you'll probably receive a program prompt that tells you that you can only save the active sheet rather than the whole workbook. This is exactly what you want to happen, so click **OK**.

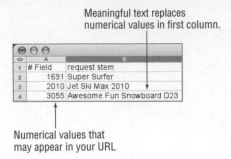

Meaningful text replaces
numerical values in first column.

Numerical values that
may appear in your URL

Figure 6-9: The basis of a lookup table filter

Now you have to send the sheet to the folks over at Google for processing. Attach the file to an e-mail to `analytics-support@google.com`. And because a human will be reading your message, make sure you specify which account and web site profile you want the table applied to. Then wait. It could take a few days for the team at Google to get you fixed up, so be patient. When they do get you ready to roll, you need to create an advanced filter to put that file to use. That information is in the next section.

Advanced Filters

Advanced filters are where things get hinky because creating one isn't as easy as picking two options from a list and then clicking okay. You actually have to work a little to put an advanced filter into place. The payoff is that you can create filters that meet your specific needs, including customized tracking for advertising campaigns and tracking specific measurements.

Creating Advanced Filters

Now that you understand just enough about the other types of filters to be dangerous, it's time to learn how to create advanced filters. Buckle in. It's going to be an interesting ride.

Step back just a bit and remember where we were with the lookup table filters. We're going to continue that example by using the surfboard information to create an advanced filter.

You start creating an advanced filter just as you would start any other type of filter. Go to **Analytics Settings** ➪ **Filter Manager** ➪ **Add Filter**. The Create New Filter page appears. Enter a name for your filter (for the example, I'm using Advanced Filter Example as a filter name); then, from the **Filter Type** drop-down menu, select **Custom filter,** as shown in Figure 6-10.

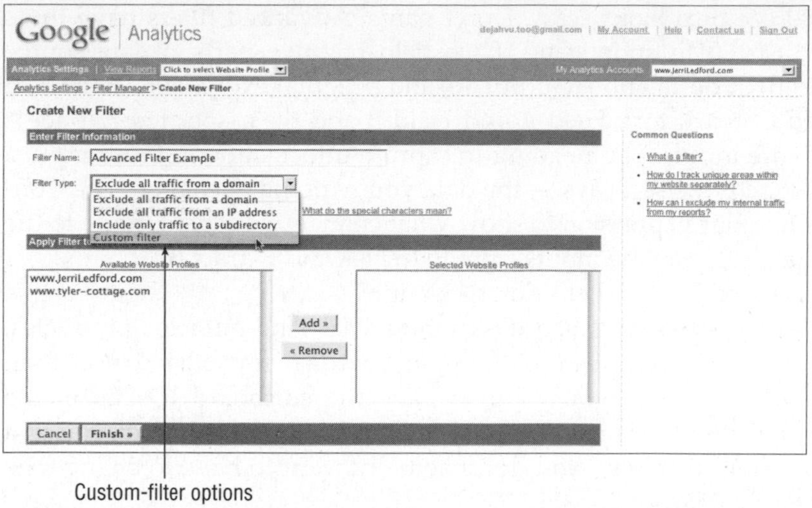

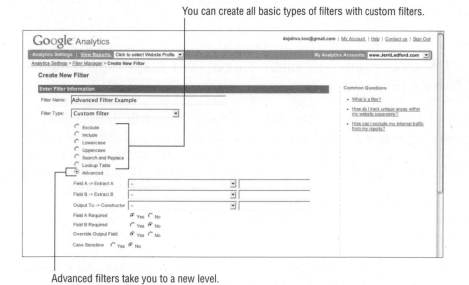

Custom-filter options

Figure 6-10: The custom filter is located in the Filter Type drop-down menu.

The custom filter menu expands to show several options. Select the radio button next to the **Advanced** option, as shown in Figure 6-11, and the advanced filter fields appear on the page.

You can create all basic types of filters with custom filters.

Advanced filters take you to a new level.

Figure 6-11: Advanced filters use a combination of input data and RegEx to produce the output.

What you'll see next looks scary. Don't panic. Advanced filters have three fields that you need to understand. Each field has two parts: a data source (Field A, Field B) or destination (Output To) and a regular expression (Extract A, Extract B, and Constructor). Field A and Field B and the associated Extract A and Extract B are inputs. You're going to capture information in those inputs. Output To is exactly what it says — the data you're going to change. The Constructor uses Regular Expression to show what changes you want made to the Output To data, based on the inputs from Extract A and Extract B.

Sorted that out yet? Good. Let's do an example.

Say that all your surfboards had IDs in the 1,000s. And miracle of miracles, you've sold and/or discontinued so many surfboards that you have more than 1,000 surfboard IDs. Now, you want to have the surfboard IDs be in the 10,000s, with the first thousand reserved for the legacy boards. But you just want to count them that way; you don't actually want to have to change the numbers in your catalogue.

> **NOTE** This may not be the most realistic of examples, but it's a good one for showing how advanced filters work. In the next section, we give some real-life examples. Never fear.

In order to capture the fields, you need to enter two pieces of information. The first is the source of the data you want to capture. You select this from the drop-down menu shown in Figure 6-12. Field A, Field B, and Output To all use the same menu.

> **NOTE** To see what all the filter fields represent, search Google Analytics Help for "filter field represent."

For Field A, select Request URI. This is the part of the URL of the incoming page after the hostname — the `www.your-domain-here.com`. For this example, that is `catalog.php?id=1691`. We'll also assume that we know all the IDs are going to be four-digit numbers. Now, you need to enter a Regular Expression in the Extract A text box to the right of the Request URI menu line. The one we developed earlier in the chapter for a four-digit number was:

```
id=(\d\d\d\d)
```

But that captures all the digits in one clump, and it captures all possible four-digit IDs. You want only IDs that begin with the digit 1 and we want to capture only the last three digits. So you modify that RegEx to:

```
id=1(\d\d\d)
```

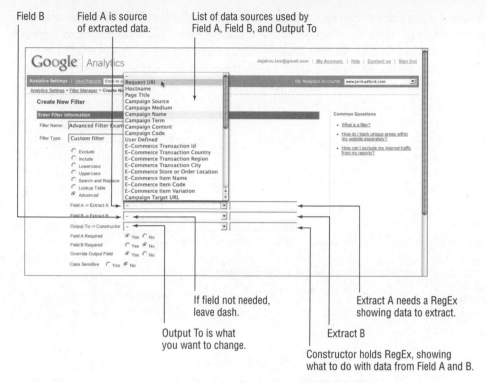

Figure 6-12: You can cull your fields from many possible sources.

Enter that in the Extract A field. Remember that the parentheses in the Regular Expression mean we're capturing the part of the source data that matches the pattern we've described. That's the connection between Extract A and the RegEx in the parentheses. Whatever part of the RegEx you put in parentheses will be what Extract A captures.

We are not going to use Field B for this example, so leave the data source as "-".

Now, for the output. First, you have to choose what data you're modifying. Choose **Request URI** from the Output To menu. Next, let's develop the RegEx, which will describe the changes we want made. What are we changing? Right, the ID. So the first part of the RegEx is:

```
id=
```

We want to go from a four-digit number beginning with 1 to a five-digit number beginning with 10 (from 1,000s to 10,000s). So you want to specify the first two digits as a literal 10:

```
id=10
```

Here's the meat of the change. We've captured the three digits after the 1 in the original ID. We need to refer to them in the Constructor. How? Easy. There's only one set of parentheses in the pattern for Field A, so the reference is $A1. (Most propeller-heads read $ as "string" as in "string A one."). So now we need the digits we saved from Extract A:

```
id=10$A1
```

You come out with the filter shown in Figure 6-13.

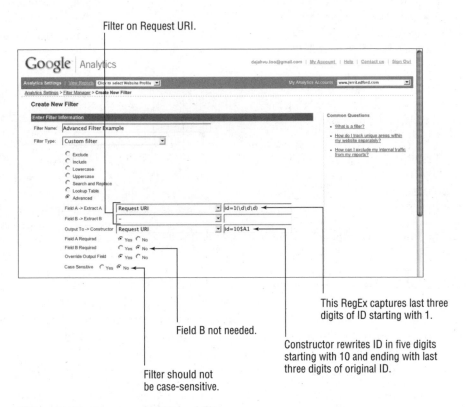

Figure 6-13: Your nearly finished filter

How should this work in practice? Let's say our ID is 1691. That pattern in Extract A matches `691` and saves it in `$A1`. Then the Constructor builds `id=10691`.

Let's do another. Say the ID is 2353. What happens?

You're right! Nothing happens. Why not? Because `id=1(\d\d\d)` won't match 2354 at all.

Now that we have some confidence that our RegEx is right and we've set the filter up correctly, we can move on to the other options. If you're only using one field, of course you want to require that the data you're trying to access and match in that field be present. No data and the filter won't apply to that pageview. So in this example, we want to click **Yes** for Field A Required and **No** for Field B Required. In this example, the ID output field already exists; we want to override what is already there with our new value, so we click **Yes** for Override Output Field. We want the filter to match ID, id, Id and iD, so we click **No** for Case Sensitive. At the bottom of the page, you can select which profiles will use the filter and then click Finish.

Now, let's extend this example a little bit. We have our same four-digit numbers, but let's say that in addition to the product ID (`itemID`) we also have a category ID (`catID`), like this: `catalog.php?itemID=1691A&catID=2900`. Note that the `itemID` is now four digits and a capital letter and the `catID` is just four digits. Now, you want to append the first two digits of the `catID` to the end of the `itemID` with a dash between them, and you want to take the letter on the end of the `itemID` and put it on the front. If there's no category ID in the URI, don't worry about it.

We need to make a couple of changes to the filter. First, choose Request URI for all three sources. Next, the RegEx for the `itemID` needs to change. It's `itemID` instead of just `ID`. And we want to capture the digits and the letter separately, so we need two sets of parentheses. With the modifications, it looks like the following:

```
itemID=(\d\d\d\d)([A-Z])
```

We'll also need to use Field B and Extract B in this example to capture the category information. We need to capture the first two digits; they'll need parentheses around them in the RegEx. The pattern for Extract B looks like this:

```
catID=(\d\d)\d\d
```

With those two things in place, we can work on the output. We want to modify the `itemID`: and add the letter to the front, and the partial category ID to the back if it exists. Now, note that we have two captures from Extract A. The four-digit number is `$A1` and the letter is `$A2`.

> **NOTE** When you capture multiple parts of a Regular Expression (by using several sets of parentheses) the notation is $ followed by A for Field A or B for Field B and then a number: 1 for the first set of parentheses, 2 for the second set, 3 for the third, and so on. The first match in Extract A is $A1. The second match in Extract A is $A2. The first match in Extract B is $B1. The second match in Extract B is $B2. And so on.

We'll have `itemID=` plus the second match from Extract A (the capital letter), plus the first match from Extract A (the four-digit number), plus a dash, plus the first match from Extract B (the first two digits of the `catID`). That looks like this:

```
itemID=$A2$A1-$B1
```

Just a little bit more and we'll be done. Field A is required, but Field B is not. So click **Yes** for Field A Required and **No** for Field B Required, **Yes** for Override output Field, and **No** for Case Sensitive. The filter will come out looking very much like Figure 6-14.

Let's look at some boundary conditions. These are situations in which the filter might fail — problem areas. For example, what will happen if there is no `catID`? It's not required, so the filter won't run screaming from the room. Here's an example:

```
catalog.php?itemID=1234B
```

There's no `catID`. So there also won't be any `$B1`. The Constructor will build `itemID=B1234-` and go no further. In the real world, a situation like this may or may not be a bad thing. It might be that you will want to require that there be a Field B, or you might just cope with the fact that some `itemIDs` might end up with a dash and no partial `catID`.

Another boundary condition: What if there is no `itemID`? Well, Field A is required. The filter is going to be bypassed since it will not apply. This is only a problem in situations where you miss counting visits because of it.

Now that we've mastered the basics of Advanced Filters — is that ever a contradiction in terms! — we'll do some more work with Advanced Filters in

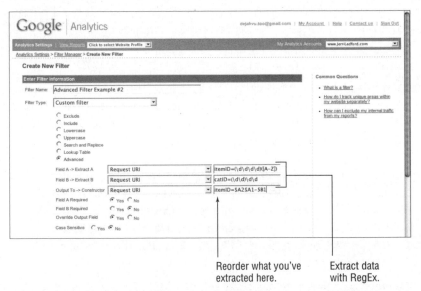

Reorder what you've extracted here.

Extract data with RegEx.

Figure 6-14: An advanced filter for an advanced user (congratulations!)

a later Advanced Topics section. At that time, we show you some real-life uses for Advanced Filters based on real filters used by real businesses

Editing and Deleting Filters

Filters don't run off to Tahiti to hang out under palm trees and slurp umbrella drinks. But you may find now and then that they need a vacation — maybe a permanent one. So you need to know how to change or delete them. (And Tahiti could still be a problem if the boss spent a week there and came home with some grand ideas that require different analytics.)

Before the tropical high wears off, change your filters and then ask for a big raise. We can't help you with the raise, but we can tell you that you change or delete filters by clicking the **Edit** or **Delete** links in the Existing Filters box.

Editing will take you to the same page you saw when you set up the filter, and then you can change anything about the filter that you want (or need) to change. Just make the changes and click the **Finish** button and the updated filter will be changed and will automatically take effect.

> **NOTE** If you need to keep a filter around, but you don't want it to be applied anymore, edit the Apply Filter to Website Profiles list so that it's not applied to any profiles. Then you can save the filter, but not have it mucking with your data anywhere.

When you select the option to delete a filter, you are prompted to confirm that you truly do want to delete it, as shown in Figure 6-15. By now you should be familiar with this routine. The confirmation is there for your protection, so double-check everything and then click **OK** and the record is deleted.

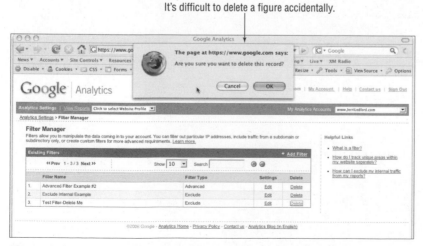

It's difficult to delete a figure accidentally.

Figure 6-15: Confirm that you want to delete the selected filter.

The Power of Filters

What you can do with filters is limited only by your ability to create them. If you're not familiar with Regular Expressions, it is well worth your time to learn more. As with any new language, RegEx can be confusing in the beginning, but as you become familiar with how the wildcards work, it will get easier to create Regular Expressions for your advanced filters. Before you know it, you'll be filtering with the best. Don't worry; those monkeys in the back room banging away at keyboards won't care that you're filtering them out as long as you keep them supplied with bananas.

Using Analytics Goals

What's the point of tracking web site metrics if you don't have some reason for tracking them? It's like jumping on the interstate in your super-efficient car with no particular destination in mind. You've got the vehicle to get somewhere, and the road to follow — and you're not doing this for the joy of travel. Without a destination, how will you know if you're headed in the right direction?

That's where goals come in. They're the "where you're going" of collecting user data. Why do you want to know how many users dropped off your e-commerce web site during the checkout process? Because knowing will help you decide if you've reached your goal of providing an easy, effective means for users to purchase your products through your online channel.

Google Analytics actually has a capability that allows you to decide where you want to go and then gather data to show you how fast, how far, and whether you're getting there at all. You can add goals to web site profiles so you can track your progress toward reaching those goals.

Before we get any further into the specifics of Google Analytics' goal capabilities, let's run through some of the management-speak you'll encounter in this chapter. The keywords are objectives, goals, and specifics.

- **Objectives:** An objective is your big picture or what you want the big picture to look like when you're finished. An objective for a company that imports and sells Russian nesting dolls might be to sell more dolls and make piles of money. It's a long-term outlook.

- **Goals:** If objectives are long-term aims, goals are shorter-term aims. What has to happen for you to sell more nesting dolls? And specifically, what do you want to accomplish with Google Analytics? Your goal could be to increase sales by 20 percent and to do it using Google Analytics.

- **Specifics:** Now you're getting to the heart of what you want to accomplish, both in the short term and the long term. Specifics are the "how" — the action steps — of goal setting. A good set of specifics for the nesting-doll goal would be to use Google Analytics to find the most efficient way to funnel traffic to a sales confirmation page (the "thank you for placing your order" page that appears after an order has been approved), to reach a sales goal within six months, and to generate proof of your efforts and successes in the form of reports to get the boss off your back.

Now, back to an important question: Why should you have analytics if you don't have goals? The answer is that you still should, but that you'll get less out of analytics without goals.

Understanding Goal Setting

Pop quiz: What's a frequent response to the question, "Why do we need this or that technology, application, or program?"

Give up? Try: "Because it's the best." To which the typical reaction is to scratch your head and keep your mouth shut because you don't want to look like a complete idiot to the obvious genius trying to explain that "having the best" means the tech gods smile on you, revenues flow from the heavens, and the door on the corner office automatically opens.

Yeah, right.

Every technology, application, or program should have a purpose to fill: a goal to reach that leads to the big-picture objective. If you're putting a firewall in place, the purpose (or goal) of that firewall is to keep the wrong sort of people off your network. And if you want to track analytics, what you track will be determined by the business problem that you're trying to solve with your web site.

Of course, this whole theory assumes that you have taken the time to develop a web site for a purpose. Are you selling a product, collecting customer information for marketing purposes, or trying to recruit the next downline star for your network marketing group? You need a goal. Simply saying the business problem is the goal isn't enough. Yes, you want to sell more of your Russian nesting dolls. But that's your objective, and alone it isn't enough to drive business or increase sales. And trying to track that goal will have you pulling your hair out by the roots.

What you need is a goal or set of goals that specifically tracks the behavior that leads to the sale of the nesting dolls. So the goal we mentioned earlier — to increase sales by 20 percent and do it using Google Analytics — is more measurable than a goal of simply selling more nesting dolls.

That's an important point: To be effective, you need a goal you can measure or track. With that goal in mind, you can develop a set of metrics, or specifics, that shows how visitors navigate through the site to complete the sale. The information returned by these metrics will illustrate what works and what doesn't, making it easier for you to alter your marketing campaign or customer approach to achieve your goal.

For example, to the real-estate giant RE/MAX, driving traffic to the RE/MAX web site seemed like a good goal. A study conducted by the National Association of Realtors in 2004 found that nearly three-quarters of all home buyers begin their search for a new home online.

But simply driving traffic online isn't enough. It's like herding cattle in the direction they're already going. You sit in the saddle and let the horse follow the cows while you watch the scenery.

RE/MAX needed to do more than just drive traffic to its web site; it needed to turn online traffic into sales — that is, make "conversions." Kristi Graning, senior vice-president of IT and e-business for RE/MAX, said that instead of just pushing users to the web and tracking how many visitors the site had, the company created a goal to help people find a house and select an agent, which follows the general objective of increasing sales.

To reach the goal, RE/MAX used Google Analytics to learn more about why people were visiting the RE/MAX web site, where they were coming from when they visited the site, and how they behaved while on the site.

Those analytics were then turned into a strategy — the specifics — to make it easier for people to find houses and select agents. Then RE/MAX redesigned its web site to better suit visitors' property-search behaviors, to capture lead information that's passed to agents, and to track the lead-to-sale-conversion rate.

RE/MAX set a goal it could act on and then went to work using Google Analytics to create strategies to reach that goal.

Why Set Goals?

There's some consensus in the business world that those who set goals tend to get farther than those who do not. Look around your organization, circle of friends, or family group. How many of the people there have solid goals and can voice those goals in a clear, understandable way?

Now consider where those people are in comparison to Cousin Danny, who really doesn't seem to have a goal in life, or Colleague Jenny, who's very happy with her position in your company. Contrast that with your manager, Amy, who always knows where she's going and what she wants to do, or your dad who retired at 55 after a lifetime of careful saving. Do the people with goals accomplish more than the people without goals? You bet they do!

Setting analytics goals works the same way. If you have a clear, reachable goal in line with your overall objective, there's a better chance you'll take action to achieve that goal. It's the difference between passive and active. If you're passive, the world happens to you. If you're active, you make the world happen.

Setting goals is the precursor to action. You set a goal with an overall objective in mind. Then you can choose specifics that will make things happen to reach that goal.

Choosing Which Goals to Set

Here's where the waters start to muddy just a bit. How do you know what goals to set? No worries. It's easy. There's this glass jar with the word GOALS painted on the front. Someone in the office has it. Just reach in and pull one out.

Okay, maybe that won't work. But it still seems to be some people's approach. They grab at thin air and hope that something will magically appear for them to latch onto. Instead, try asking yourself this question: What business am I really in?

It's not fate, magic, or divine intervention that makes a goal great. It takes a solid understanding of your business — or your objective — and how your web presence fits into that larger picture. If your business is management training, how will your web site improve that business? Maybe you want to expand training beyond your local area by offering online classes to management wannabes still living in their parents' basements. You could also use your web site to gather sales leads by enticing potential management trainees (or even corporations that might need your services) to sign up for a monthly newsletter.

What you need to accomplish with your web site is what should drive your goals in Google Analytics. A good goal for your management training business might be to increase sales by providing training services that are more accessible to individuals and companies in the region (or U.S. or world).

That goal applies to the actions your management training company takes with your web site.

Ultimately, you determine your analytics goals by your specific situation and needs. A goal that puts you on a path toward fabulous results might put a similar company on a path toward certain doom. So examine your business. Determine what *your* needs are. And then create goals that help you fill those needs.

One company that truly understands the business it's in is the Warren Featherbone company. Back in the 1800s, Warren Featherbone made corset stays — those horrid, rigid pieces of hard material that ensured a woman couldn't slouch or bend over at the waist. Obviously, corset stays went out of style. So, in the 1920s, Warren Featherbone got into bias tape. It's a sewing notion that simplifies making secure hems on fabric that frays.

Over time, however, customers' needs changed again. No longer did customers have time to sew all the garments their families wore. There were even — gasp — women who couldn't sew!

Because the Warren Featherbone company knows what business it's in — the fabric and clothing business — it shifted gears yet again to meet the needs of the customer. Today, Warren Featherbone sells kids' clothing under the Alexis label.

Warren Featherbone completely understood its business, which led to a clear understanding of its objectives and the survival of the business — all because it's a company that can create and achieve effective goals.

Now, let's see if we can help you do the same thing.

Setting Up Goals

When you first set up a web site for tracking on Google Analytics, you're given the option to create goals for the site. Most people don't set those goals up at the very beginning because they're not sure what they're doing. That's okay. You can set the goals up anytime you're comfortable with the process.

It'll be easy. We'll lead you through the steps. All you have to provide is the goal.

To set up a goal after you've created your web site profile, go to Analytics Settings. Under the Website Profiles menu, find the profile to which you want to add the goal. Click the **Edit** link in the same line as the web site name, and you are taken to a page like the one in Figure 7-1.

The Conversion Goals and Funnel menu is the second box on the page. It lists the name of any goals you've created, the URL of those goals, and a status area that shows whether the goal is active or not. Click the **Edit** link in the line of the goal number that you want to change or set up.

NOTE Google allows only four goals for each web site profile that you set up. Should you need to track more than four goals for your web site, you should set up another web site profile for a section of your site. This allows you to have four goals for that section and four goals for any other sections of the web site that have their own profiles.

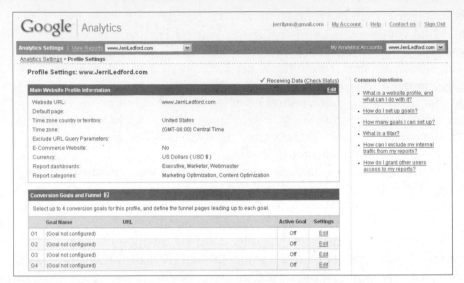

Figure 7-1: Create goals in the Conversion Goals and Funnel menu.

After you click the **Edit** link, you are taken to the Goal Settings page shown in Figure 7-2.

Here's the information you need to enter to create a new goal:

- **Goal URL:** The Goal URL is the web page within your site that you want your customers to reach. If you have an e-commerce site, the Goal URL might be the purchase confirmation page after the transaction has been submitted. It could also be a confirmation page on a site where the goal is for users to sign up for a newsletter.

- **Goal Name:** Choose the name you want your goal to have. In the preceding example, the name Purchase Complete would be a good choice.

- **Active Goal:** Select the **On** or **Off** radio button to activate or deactivate your goal.

- **Define Funnel:** For every Goal URL, there is a logical way that consumers reach that goal. In the case of the e-commerce site, a funnel might include the index page, the products page, the shopping-cart page, the checkout page, and then the Goal URL, which is the confirmation page.

  A funnel is used to measure how often users take the logical path to your Goal URL. If they deviate from that path frequently, you know that what you think is the logical path may not be logical for the consumer. This allows you to redefine the funnel and creates additional opportunities for you to reach your customers.

  Enter the URLs for the funnel in this section.

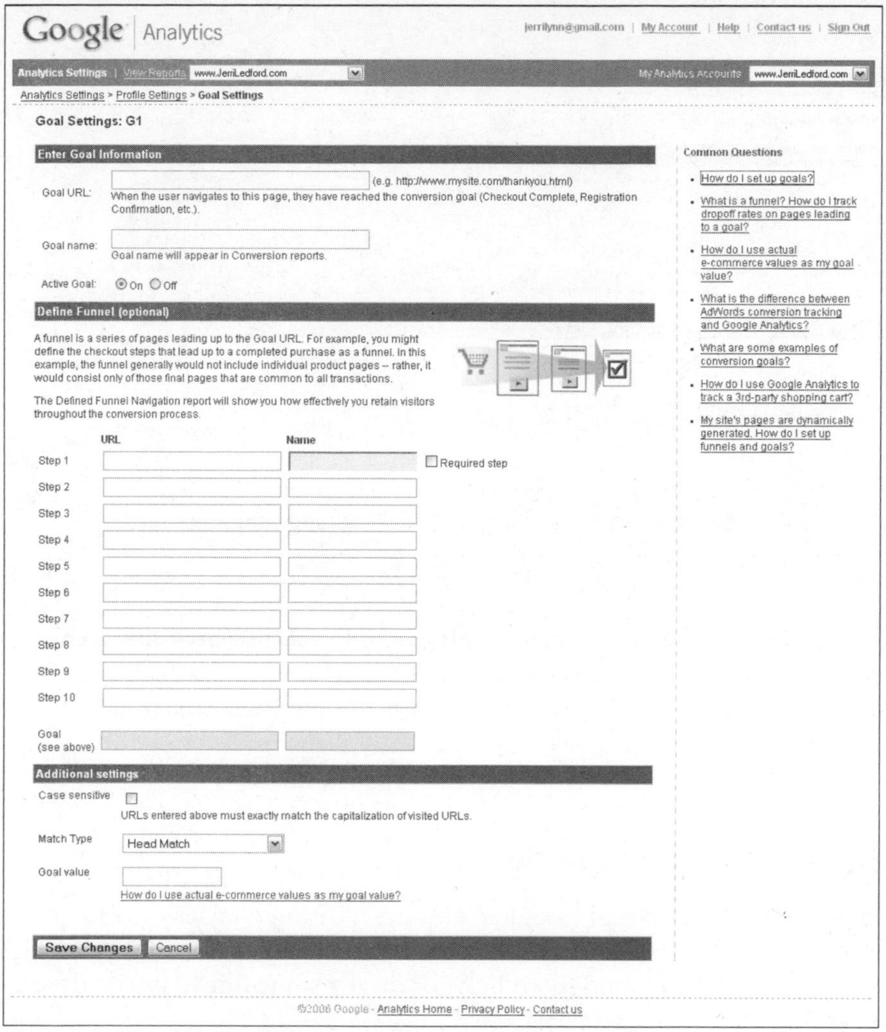

Figure 7-2: Create a goal to track on the Goal Settings page.

- **Additional Settings (**Match Type): There are three options for Match Type. Exact Match requires the URL to be exactly what you've entered as the funnel or goal URL. Use Head Match when you always have the same URL but when you have user or session identifiers after the URL that are unique from visitor to visitor. You can also specify a Regular Expression Match, which is useful when you're dealing with subdomains.

When you finish entering all the information requested, click the **Save Changes** button and your new goal will be created. Then you'll be able to see it in your goals list, as shown in Figure 7-3.

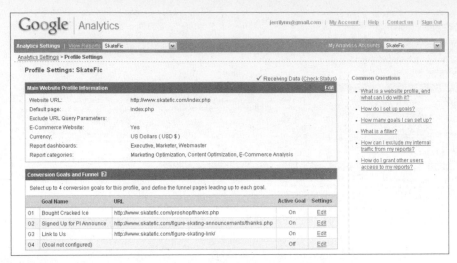

Figure 7-3: Once created, goals appear on your Profile Settings page.

TIP To quickly determine how many goals you have set for a particular web site profile, all you need to do is look in the status column on the Analytics Settings page. The number of goals for each web site profile is displayed there, but you can't see the actual goals.

Editing and Inactivating Goals

As with the other functions of Google Analytics, editing goals is easy to do. To edit your goals, enter the Goals Settings screen by going to Analytics Settings ➪ Profile Settings and then click **Edit** in the same line as the goal number that you want to edit or delete.

If you're editing the goal, your pre-populated Goal Settings screen will appear, as shown in Figure 7-4. All you have to do is edit the information that you want to change and click **Save Changes**.

The one failing here is that you can't actually delete a goal once you set it up. You can change it or turn it off, but you can't remove it entirely. It's not a problem unless you happen to be the minimalist type who can't stand clutter. In that case, having an unused goal just floating around in your web site profile might drive you a little crazy, but it won't hurt anything at all.

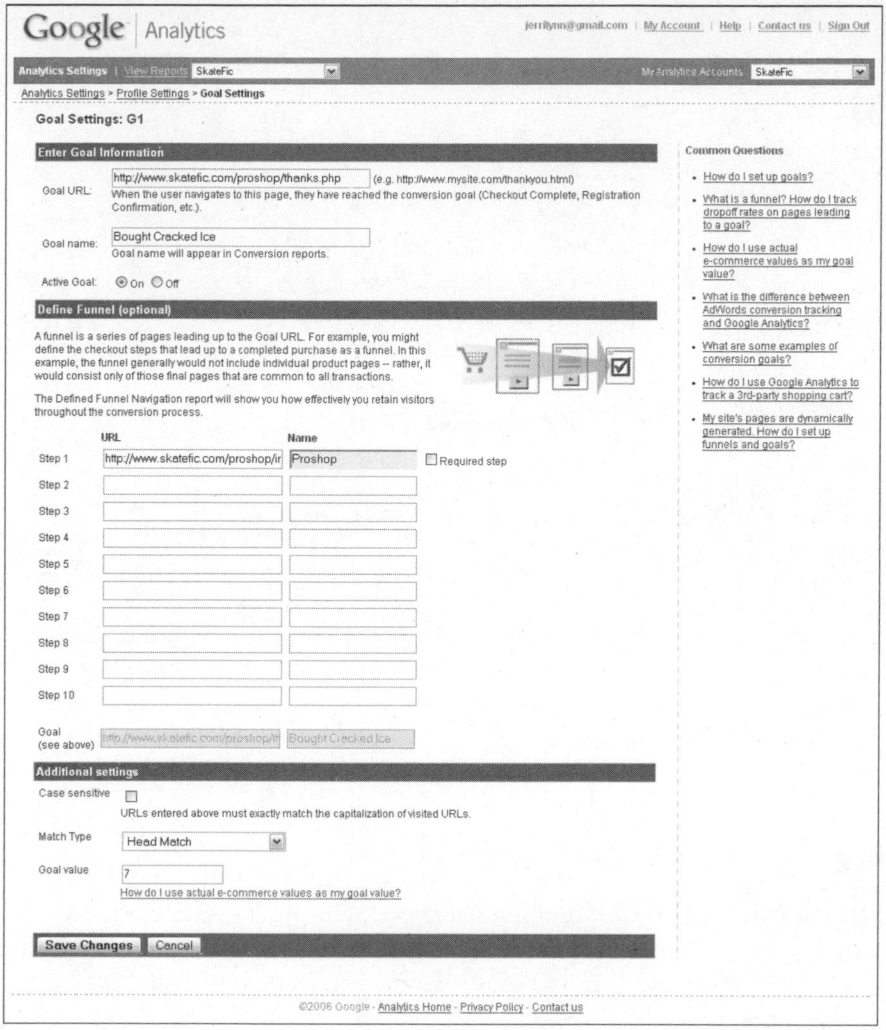

Figure 7-4: Make your changes on the Goal Settings screen.

CHAPTER 8

AdWords Integration

Whatever else Google Analytics is, it's a power tool for Google's AdWords program. Like the radial-arm saw that you use to create the perfect shelf for your entertainment hutch, Google Analytics is the tool for building the perfect AdWords campaign.

So which came first, the chicken or the egg? Analytics has been around for a long time, but until AdWords, there was less of a reason for the little guys to have Analytics. If you're spending money on AdWords, you absolutely want to have Analytics.

Why Google Analytics with AdWords?

If you're not already using AdWords, you might be wondering why you would want to put the two together. Even without Google Analytics, AdWords has decent reporting capabilities. But when you add Google Analytics, what you get is a picture of your campaign performance worth a thousand (Ad)Words.

Using Analytics' tools, you can measure the ROI (return on investment) of your ad campaign by tracking not just your AdWords campaigns but also any banner ads, referral links, e-mail newsletters, or offline advertising campaigns that drive visitors to your web site and entice them to buy.

Once you link the two accounts, Analytics will automatically track any active campaigns in your AdWords account. You get a single view with all the information you need. It saves you a ton of flipping back and forth between windows, trying to figure out what's working and what's not — not to mention all the work that you save in trying to tag ads so that Analytics tracks them. If you're already tagging, never fear; you can use your own tags, too.

Linking Analytics and AdWords

Not much is different between a lone Google Analytics account and one linked to AdWords.

Linking AdWords and Analytics Accounts

If you didn't link your Analytics account to an AdWords account when you signed up for Analytics, you can still do it. First, you need an AdWords account. If you don't have such an account, sign up for one right now. We'll wait.

It's best to sign up for your AdWords account under the same Google account as your Analytics account. If you did not sign up under the same Google account (or e-mail address), go into your Analytics account and add your AdWords account as a user with administrative privileges. If you need to flip back to remember how to do this, the instructions for adding accounts are in Chapter 4. Now, log in to your AdWords account and add your Analytics account as a user with administrative privileges.

Once you've done that, click the Analytics tab across the top of your AdWords Dashboard. In the splash page that follows, click I already have a Google Analytics account in the lower left, and you'll see something that looks a whole lot like Figure 8-1.

If you have access to multiple Analytics accounts, there will be more than one listed in the drop-down menu. In our case, our test account has access to only one Analytics account.

> **NOTE** You can link an Analytics account to someone else's AdWords account. When we did the first edition of this book, Jerri linked her Analytics account to Mary's AdWords account. Mary is also linked to her own Analytics account from her AdWords account. It is a many-to-many relation, not a one-to-one relation.

At any rate, choose the Analytics account you want to link from the drop-down menu. The default is to have auto-tagging on and to apply cost data from AdWords to your Analytics calculations. You can turn auto-tagging off depending on whether you tag your own data (we get into that in the next section). We don't recommend that you turn off the application of cost data. Applying the cost data is the whole point of linking Analytics and AdWords.

Now click **Link Account** and you're done. You can now access Analytics from your AdWords login just by going to the Analytics tab.

Once you've connected the two accounts, you can create profiles, add users, set up filters, set goals and funnels, and much more. Much more? Read on, intrepid explorer. The wonders of AdWords integration await.

Figure 8-1: Link Analytics and AdWords from your AdWords Dashboard.

Tag, Your Link Is It!

How does Google AdWords know that a certain visit is the result of clicking an ad? Very simple. Whether it's a banner image on a web page, a text link in an e-mail, or any other advertising vehicle, the link is tagged with a variable that says, "Ooo! Ooo! Me! Me!" There are two ways of doing this. You can let AdWords auto-link the incoming links — auto-link is on by default. To turn it off, go to **My Account ⇨ Account Preferences**.

Auto-linking takes the work out of tagging your links by using a special parameter, called `gclid`, which adds an extension to your URL containing the information Google needs to track the details about how users behave when they click the link. The URL is then referred to as an *arbitrary URL*.

An auto-tagged link will look something like this:

```
http://www.yourwebsite.com/?gclid=hit475
```

That's the good news. The bad news is that some sites won't display arbitrary URLs properly. So, instead of seeing the page displayed, users will see a server error. To be on the safe side, you should test your site's reaction to the tags before you call it done.

For more control, tag links on your own. Each tag has a name and a value in the format `name=value`. If you want more than one tag, you separate name/value pairs with an ampersand, like this: `tag1=value1&tag2=value2`. You've seen this in other chapters — a URL followed by a question mark (?) and then one or more name/value pairs. We just didn't have a name for it. Those name/value pairs can be called "tags," "variables," or "parameters." They modify the URL much as an adjective modifies a noun. Which page? The big page. Or as a tag `page.html?type=big`.

Google Analytics uses specific tags for tracking. Say SkateFic advertises on SkateWeb `<www.frogsonice.com/skateweb/>`. Mary would set the link underlying the banner ad to:

```
<http://www.skatefic.com/?utm_source=skateweb&utm_medium=banner&utm_
campaign=rebate>.
```

See the part of the URL after the question mark? Those are tags. AdWords requires three particular tags. They are:

- **Campaign:** If you're running more than one advertising effort, the campaign variable uniquely identifies each one. The default variable name is `utm_campaign`. In the preceding SkateFic example, `rebate` is the value of the campaign variable. It's your choice what you call your campaigns. You could call this one "Kevin" if you wanted.

- **Source:** This is where the advertising actually appears. The default name of this tag is `utm_source`. In the preceding SkateFic example, `skateweb` is the value of the source variable because that is the web site where this link will appear. If you were using an ad aggregator, you might use the name of the aggregator because you won't necessarily know the specific site name where your ad is appearing.

■ **Medium:** This is the type of advertising you're placing. The default name is utm_medium. In the preceding SkateFic example, "banner" is the value of the medium variable because it's a banner ad we're tracking.

If you want to use your own variable names, maybe because you already have your campaigns tagged from your previous efforts, you can, but that's an advanced topic. And if tagging by hand seems too taxing, you can use Google's tagging tool. We cover both points in Chapter 9. If you're still not sure about all of the various aspects of AdWords, there's a thorough training section in the AdWords Learning Center.

LEARN MORE ABOUT GOOGLE ADWORDS

Google's AdWords program is a great tool for advertising. But it can get a little complicated. We don't want to distract you from Google Analytics too much, but if you're interested in learning more about AdWords, there are several really good books on the subject. Here's a sample of books that you might find useful:

Beginner:

■ *Winning Results with Google AdWords,* by Andrew Goodman. McGraw-Hill, ISBN: 0072257024.

■ *Google Advertising Gorilla Tactics: Google Advertising A-Z Plus 150 Killer AdWords Tips & Tricks,* by Bottletree Books, LLC. ISBN: 1933747013

Advanced:

■ *Google Advertising: Cashing in with AdSense, AdWords, and the Google APIs,* by Harold Davis. O'Reilly Media, Inc. ISBN: 0596101082

And if you just happen to want to know more about key-word marketing in general, there's also a great book called *Pay Per Click Search Engine Marketing For Dummies,* by Peter Kent. Wiley, ISBN: 0471754943

Why Track AdWords Campaigns with Analytics?

The reason people stampeded Google Analytics like bulls charging a red cape was its capability to track AdWords campaigns. There are hundreds of thousands of AdWords subscribers. And all of them want to know more about how their AdWords campaigns are performing.

AdWords does provide a tracking and reporting mechanism. But Figure 8-2 shows what an AdWords tracking page might look like — not very descriptive is it?

And then there's the reporting. Figure 8-3 shows what a simple report might look like.

Google AdWords

jerrilynn@gmail.com | Help | Contact us | Sign Out
Customer ID:

Campaign Management | Reports | Analytics | My Account
Advanced Search
Campaign Summary | Tools | Conversion Tracking
Search

Campaign Summary > Free Skatfic > Free Skatefic

2 keyword(s) are currently inactive for search.
These keywords are marked in the status column below. Improve their quality through optimization, delete them, or raise the keywords' maximum CPCs to the minimum bids indicated. (Raising the bids will activate the keywords.) [?]

Ad Group: Free Skatefic Active | Pause Ad Group | Delete Ad Group
1 of 1 Ad Groups
Default bid: USD $0.05 Max CPC [edit]

Apr 20, 2006
Tools: Filter Keywords | Add Keywords | Edit Keywords | Keyword Tool Updated!
1 - 2 of 2 keywords.

Free Skating Fiction
Serial fiction, humor and poetry.
Read ours or get yours published.
www.skatefic.com

+ Create New Ad: Text Ad | Image Ad | Local Business Ad
20 Clicks | 0.08% CTR | $0.05 CPC
Served - 100.0% [more info]
Edit - Delete

yesterday
Apr 20 2006 - Apr 20 2006 Go
Include deleted items that were active in this date range

Edit Keyword Settings | Delete

Keyword	Status [?]	Current Bid Max CPC	Hide Settings Sort by: Bid | URL	Clicks	Impr.	CTR	Avg. CPC	Cost	Avg. Pos	Conv. Rate
Search Total	Enabled	Default $0.05 [edit]		0	0	-	-	$0.00	-	0.00%
Content Total [?]	Enabled			20	24,864	0.08%	$0.05	$0.89	3.3	0.00%
figure skating	Inactive for search Increase quality or bid $0.10 to activate	$0.05	Settings $0.05 Max CPC [edit]	0	0	-	-	-	-	0.00%
ice skating	Inactive for search Increase quality or bid $5.00 to activate	$0.05	Settings $0.05 Max CPC [edit]	0	0	-	-	-	-	0.00%

Reporting is not real-time. Clicks and impressions received in the last 3 hours may not be included here. There is a 24 hour delay in conversion tracking reporting. Lower CTRs for content ads do not adversely affect your campaign. [?] Inactive for search keywords have a Quality Score and Max CPC too low to trigger ads on searches for Google or the search network, but they remain active for content impressions. These keywords may occasionally accrue search clicks as we re-assess their quality. [?]
Time zone for all dates and times in data tables, reports, and billing: (GMT-08:00) Pacific Time. Learn more.

©2006 Google - AdWords Home - Editorial Guidelines - Privacy Policy - Contact Us

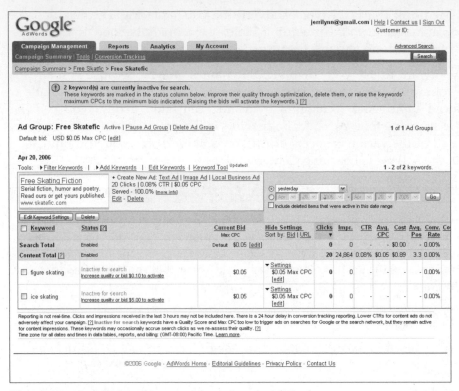

Figure 8-2: A typical tracking page from Google AdWords

Google AdWords Ad Text Report | All Time -- (GMT-08:00) Pacific Time
CAMPAIGNS: All | ADWORDS TYPE: All

Showing rows 1 - 6 of 6.

Campaign	Ad Group	Headline	Description Line 1	Description Line 2	Display URL	Destination URL	Impressions	Clicks	CTR	Avg CPC	Cost	Avg Position
FS Cracked Ice	Cracked Ice	Skating Scandals Exposed	Insider Sonia Bianchetti tells all.	Intrigue, graft, back room deals.	www.skatefic.com	http://www.skatefic.com/proshop/	9,047	33	0.4%	$0.21	$6.81	4.3
FS Cracked Ice	Cracked Ice	Cracked Ice: an exposé	Intrigue, graft, back room deals.	What They don't want you to know.	www.skatefic.com	http://www.skatefic.com/proshop/	7,657	13	0.2%	$0.19	$2.48	4.2
FS Cracked Ice	Cracked Ice	Figure Skating Scandals	A figure skating insider tells all.	Intrigue, graft, back room deals.	www.skatefic.com	http://www.skatefic.com/proshop/	47,010	215	0.5%	$0.13	$28.61	2.4
FS Cracked Ice	Cracked Ice	Cracked Ice: an exposé	Intrigue, graft, back room deals,	figure skating's dirty secrets.	www.skatefic.com	http://www.skatefic.com/proshop/	1	0	0.0%	$0.00	$0.00	9.0
FS Cracked Ice	Cracked Ice	Cracked Ice: an exposé	Intrigue, graft, back room deals,	ice skating's dirty little secrets.	www.skatefic.com	http://www.skatefic.com/proshop/	14,980	42	0.3%	$0.14	$6.01	2.6
Free Skatfic	Free Skatefic	Free Skating Fiction	Serial fiction, humor and poetry.	Read ours or get yours published.	www.skatefic.com	http://www.skatefic.com	8	0	0.0%	$0.00	$0.00	8.1
Totals and Overall Averages:							78,703	303	0.4%	$0.14	$43.91	2.8

©2006 Google - AdWords Home - Editorial Guidelines - Privacy Policy - Contact Us

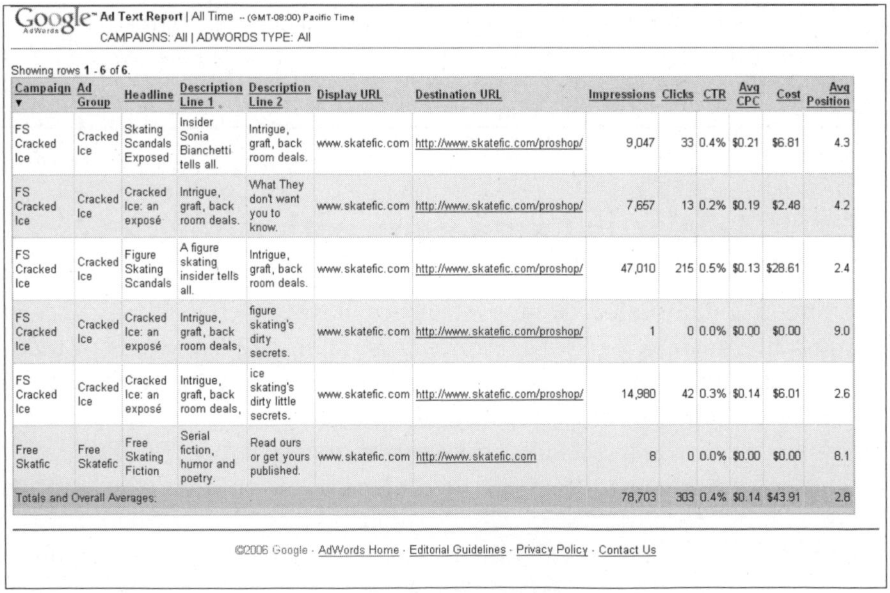

Figure 8-3: AdWords' reports contain only essential information.

Rather than a dry listing, Analytics graphs the effectiveness of your AdWords campaigns, as shown in Figure 8-4. See the difference? In this Analytics report, you can quickly see how AdWords (google[cpc]) drives traffic relative to other source/medium combinations.

Connecting AdWords to Analytics gives you access to all of the reporting power in Google Analytics — all of it.

Figure 8-4: Google Analytics gives you a clearer picture of your AdWords results.

CHAPTER 9

Advanced Topics

There are two aims to this book. The first is to take the beginner through basic proficiency. The second is to ease the now competent beginner into expertise. To that end, this chapter will cover the beginnings of expertise — the hurdles that most new users of Google Analytics have to surmount before they feel completely comfortable with their understanding of analytics and how to use analytics to improve web site performance.

Monetizing Goals

It's one thing to set up your "thank you" page as a goal, and quite another thing to know what reaching it is worth. For an e-commerce site, the value of a goal is fairly easy — it's the value of the transaction. For a content site, it's not so apparent what the value of a particular page of content is, or how much a new subscriber to the mailing list is worth.

OVERWHELMED? OR IS THIS IS ALL TOO SIMPLISTIC?

At this point, some readers are going to be completely overwhelmed by the sheer volume of skills they're expected to master. That's okay. Some of this stuff *is* rocket science. Don't feel dumb if you're not getting it. Meanwhile, other readers may be saying "This stuff is too simple, I really need XYZ, why aren't those stupid authors giving it to me?! My company needs professional level analytics help, not this dumb book."

Both kinds of readers need professional intervention, which you get from companies such as ROI Revolution www.ROIRevolution.com. ROI Revolution offers high-end services to companies that need more than a how-to book can provide, and they also help out "Mom and Pop" web sites, which are up RegEx Creek without a paddle.

ROI Revolution's Timothy Stewart was kind enough to help us with some of the more technical bits on Google Analytics 2.0. Tim also suggested subjects to cover in our advanced topics chapter so we could make sure to hit the most common "expert" questions. ROI Revolution is a good company. Look them up if you need more help.

Content Site Goals

The content site issues aren't as intractable as they first seem, but getting a goal value does require some voodoo and wand-waving. Your content has to lead to some monetary gain. It may not be immediately apparent what the gain is.

For a site where the primary purpose is marketing, there's a sale down the line. That sale is worth something and you probably have some information on how many of your leads turn into sales. For a publication, where the content *is* the product, the monetary gain involved is usually revenue from advertising. You have information on returning visitors and on page views per visitor, and you probably know what your average (or even specific) ad revenue from a page is.

Goal Value of a Sales Lead

The easy case is when your content collects leads that end in an offline sale. Let's say, for example, that you sell consulting services. Your average sale is $2,300. And you know that you get one sale for every 23 leads. You've set up a goal that is similar to the one in Figure 9-1.

There's no funnel to define, so you can leave that blank. Depending on the structure of your individual site's URL you'll want to choose the right kind of match. The calculation for the goal value is fairly simple:

```
Average Sale/No. of leads = $2,300/23 = $100
```

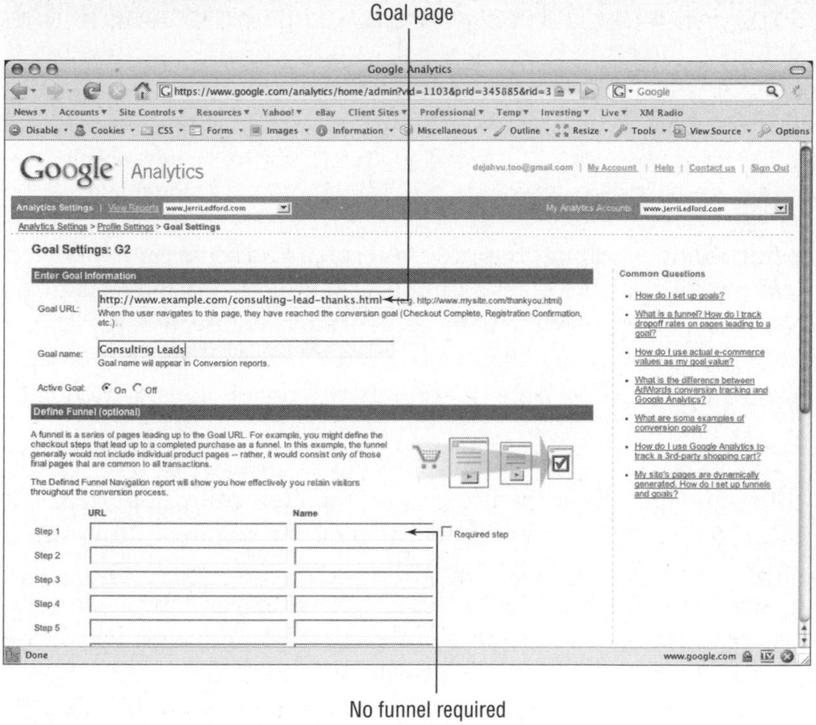

Goal page

Figure 9-1: A simple lead acquisition goal

So each time you get a lead, it's worth $100. That's your goal value, as shown in Figure 9-2.

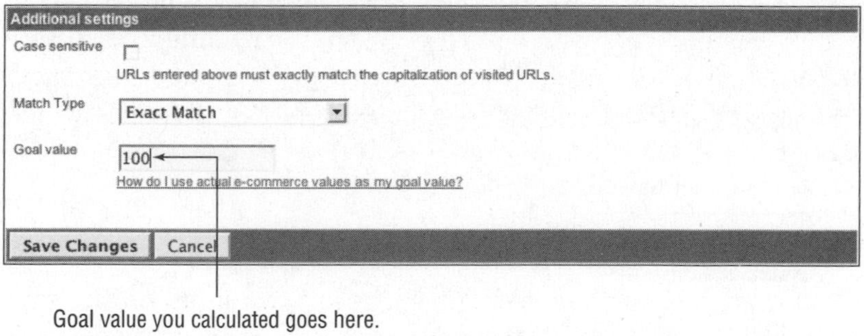

Goal value you calculated goes here.

Figure 9-2: The goal value for each lead goes in the Additional Settings.

NOTE You can do a similar calculation even if your numbers are not as neat as the ones in the preceding example. For instance, if you're getting three sales for every 10 leads, that's one sale for every 3.33 leads. Just divide your $2,300 by 3.33 and you'll see that each lead is worth about $690.

Now, when you acquire a lead because the visitor made it to the goal page, the financial data will flow into your reports. If you have AdWords integrated or you track other advertising campaigns, those costs will go into reports and you will begin to see ROI (return on investment) calculated.

Goal Value of a New Subscriber

What if you're not selling anything? Suppose you run an advertising-supported content site. This model applies to sites as small as SkateFic.com and as large as Salon and the *New York Times*. As with many content sites, yours probably has an announcement or headline e-mail that you send out when there is new content. A reader who signs up to receive content announcements obviously intends to return. This can be quantified.

Now, you need some data. Click View Reports for the appropriate Google Analytics Profile, and go to the Visitors: New vs. Returning report. Click Returning Visitor to the left of the graph. Now, click the Segment drop-down menu and choose Source, as shown in Figure 9-3.

Now, if you scroll down a bit, you'll see a list of whatever sources you are tracking. We're going to assume for the moment that you have set up all the URL's in your content announcements with tracking for the Source (more about how to do that later in the chapter). For the sake of this example, say that the content announcement URLs are tagged as `DejahsPrivateIce.com`. Then announcements would account for 178 visits (12.7 percent), as shown in Figure 9-4.

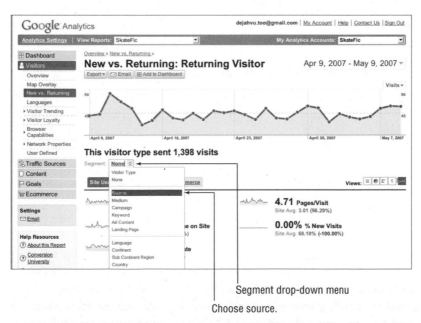

Figure 9-3: If you're tracking sources, you can see where people are coming from.

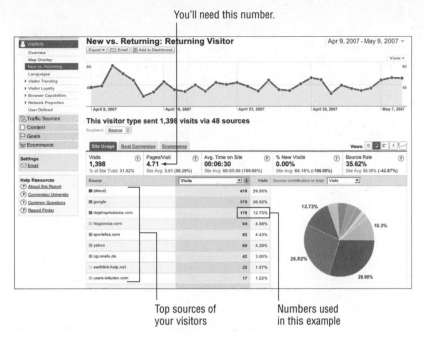

Figure 9-4: The source of returning traffic holds the key to returning visitor value.

Take note of one more number from this report — the number of pages per visit. In this case, that's 4.71 pages per visit.

NOTE These two numbers should be representative of the traffic your content announcement brings in every month. You'll have to look at several months or at a longer period of time to get an idea what the correct numbers are.

Remember, this is an estimate; it's not going to be exact. The important thing is to get as close as you can so as not to overcount or undercount by too much. For example, when we change the date range to a full year instead of just a month, we get 2,010 visits (12.66 percent) and 4.61 pages per visit. Those numbers are very close to the monthly percentage (12.73 percent) and 4.71 pages per visit. This means we have a pretty good estimate. If possible, use a yearly figure — unless you had a wildly non-typical year. But if you don't have a year of data to go on, use a monthly estimate and update it quarterly until you do have a year of data.

We're going to use the monthly numbers, even though they are slightly less representative because they are close enough. We have 178 visits at 4.71 pages per visit; that's 838 pages.

Now on to the next key piece of information. This has to come from your advertising aggregator (like AdSense). If you use AdSense, log in and you'll see a report much like the one for `SkateFic.com` in Figure 9-5.

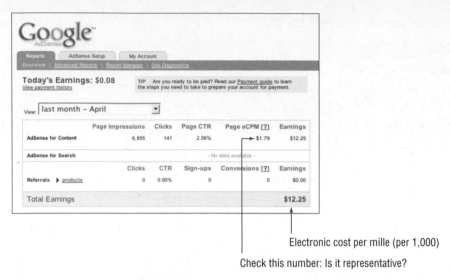

Electronic cost per mille (per 1,000)

Check this number: Is it representative?

Figure 9-5: What's your CPM?

Locate the eCPM (that's electronic cost per mille, or thousand) for a representative time period. It may be last month, or this month, or today, depending on how much you make on advertising. You may choose "since last payment" as your time period. This is your call. If you over-estimate, your Goals Value will be inflated. If you underestimate, you'll undervalue your content-announcement subscribers. We chose "last month" as our time period, since the total payment of $12.25 for that month was fairly representative of what the site brings in — don't laugh, it pays half the hosting.

The eCPM for that time period is $1.79, which means that we made $1.79 for each 1,000 ad impressions. Let's assume that each of your pages holds a standard Google AdSense vertical banner showing four ads. That's four impressions per page, and 250 pages will make 1,000 impressions. You have to show 250 pages to make $1.79, so each page in our example is worth $1.79/250 or $0.00716.

Putting that altogether, we have 838 page views worth $0.00716 each, or $6 altogether. Okay, so it's not a huge amount, but it's for a single month for a low- traffic site.

Now, we need one last piece of information: the number of "absolute unique visitors" — actual people who visited your site in a stated period, regardless of how many times they visited. (You can find more about these visitors in Chapter 13.) Go to Visitors: Visitor Trending: Absolute Unique Visitors and read off the number of absolute unique visitors for a typical month, one without any unusual circumstances to skew the numbers. In this example, April 9 to May 9, 2007, is such a period. In that month, there were 3,238 absolute unique visitors to SkateFic.com. (We haven't given you the screenshot for this, but if we had, you would see 3,238 in big type at the top.)

Now go to Visitors: Visitor Loyalty: Loyalty, using the same time period. Read off the number of visitors who visited only once as shown in Figure 9-6. Although there were a fair number of return visits, a lot of first-timers didn't come back, so this is a picture of at least moderate disloyalty. However, it's the ones who did come back that we're interested in.

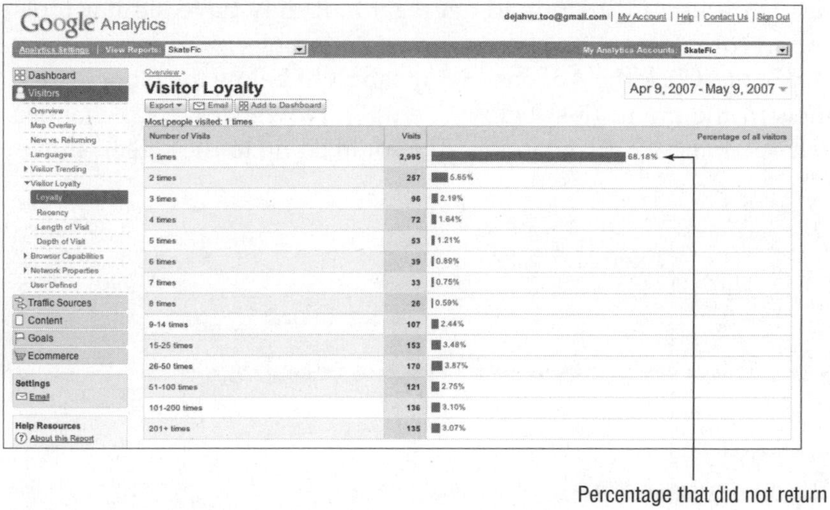

Figure 9-6: Results show a moderate degree of "disloyalty."

The number of one-time visitors in Figure 9-6 is 2,995, which means that some of those 3,238 absolute unique visitors from the other chart (remember, we're counting actual individuals here) did not drop out after just one visit during the period. In fact, 243 of them apparently were interested enough in the site to come back one or more times. These folks have value and are responsible for that $6 in AdSense revenue. Divide 243 into $6 and you find that each of these 243 returning visitors is worth just less than two and a half cents a month.

How much is a visitor worth over a lifetime? It's hard to say. You have to make some sort of assumption or use some heavy-duty software to send out tailored e-mails to every subscriber. If you assume in the example above that a visitor will keep returning for three months, then each new subscriber is worth about seven and a half cents. If you think this person will be back for a year, then 30 cents might be closer to right. If you assume people will visit and revisit over the course of years, then you might make even more. This estimate is your call, based on whatever final total you think is likely.

Now, whatever that number is for you, put it in the Goal Value box shown earlier in Figure 9-2.

Goal Value of a Content Page

What if the pages you want to get people to visit are just content pages? To work with these, you have to know what a content page is worth. This may require some extra tracking or custom reporting. We'll do this example with AdSense, but if you use a different ad aggregator, it may have similar tools. Ask tech support for information about your aggregator.

Log in to AdSense. Click the AdSense Setup tab right below the Google logo. Click Channels in the menu (just below "Setup"). Now, click URL channels and then click + Add new URL channels and you'll come to the screen shown in Figure 9-7.

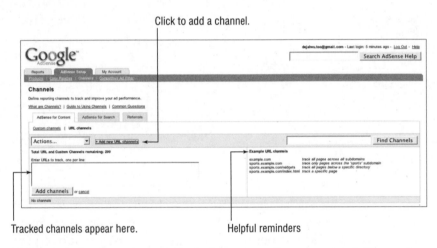

Figure 9-7: Track revenue on single (or groups of) pages using AdSense channels.

Now enter the URL you want to track. You can track a specific page, all the pages in a directory, all the pages in a subdomain, or all the pages in a domain. AdSense provides a neat little shorthand beside the entry box in case you forget how to enter the URL to track what you want to track. Click Add channels.

One thing that Google doesn't say in the reminders is how to track dynamic pages. If you want to track dynamic pages — ones with name/value tags that control the output of the page — you should just use the bare URL before the question mark (?). For example, on SkateFic.com, Chapter 1 of the serial On the Edge is produced by the URL:

```
http://skatefic.com/serials/ote/chapters/index.php?Chapter=1
```

To track that chapter alone, you would enter the whole URL. But every chapter in the serial gets produced by the same script. The only thing that changes is the number after `Chapter=`. If you want to track the revenue from all the chapters, you would enter the URL up to `index.php` excluding the `?` and everything after it. After adding the channel, you can turn it on or off or remove it altogether from the result screen shown in Figure 9-8.

Now, to see the data on your new channel, click Reports. Then click Advanced Reports. Then click the Channel data radio button. The channel controls will appear and you can select the channel (or channels) you want to see, and click the **Group by** Channel radio button at the bottom, as shown in Figure 9-9.

Unfortunately, AdSense will not process historical data. So you'll have to wait a short time — anywhere from a couple hours to a couple weeks, depending on how busy your site is — to generate the data you need. You may want to wait a month or more, to generate "typical" data. If you don't want to wait that long, then keep checking back so that you can fine-tune your page value as time goes on.

So have you waited a bit?

Then click Display Report. You'll see something similar to what you see in Figure 9-10.

If you click on the URL for the channel of interest, you can break performance down by day for that particular channel as shown in Figure 9-11.

This is actually the same view you would get if you clicked **Group by** Both radio button instead of **Group by** Channel before you displayed the report.

At any rate, the tidbit of interest is the total earnings. We're assuming this total is representative of how much revenue the page usually generates. But this may not be a good assumption.

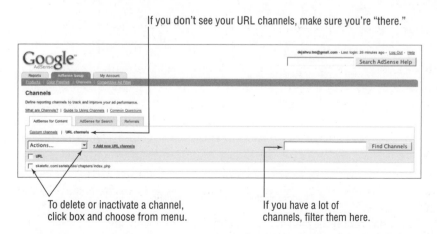

Figure 9-8: From this screen, you can turn your new channel on and off or delete it.

Click to display report.   Click channel data.

Select channels you want to see.

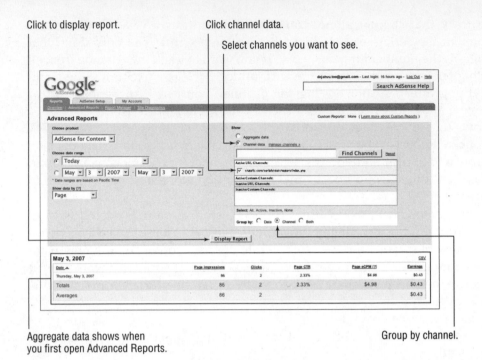

Aggregate data shows when   Group by channel.
you first open Advanced Reports.

Figure 9-9: Use the channel controls to select which channels to show in the report.

Click the channel URL to dig deeper.

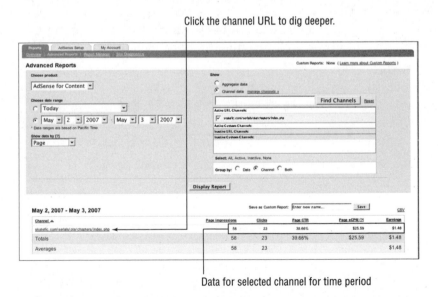

Data for selected channel for time period

Figure 9-10: A two-day report for the *On the Edge* channel of advertising

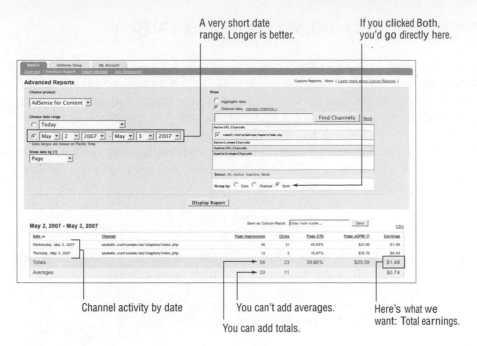

Figure 9-11: The *On the Edge* channel by day

The total is based on a very small sample size (only two days in this case). You want the total you use to be based on at least 30 days. That will give you some level of confidence that it's statistically accurate.

These two days are also not exactly normal days. In fact, SkateFic had just sent out an e-mail reminding its subscribers to support SkateFic by clicking on the ads in this section. This bumped the revenues from these pages for these few days. If your traffic is distinctly cyclical, you may want to be careful not to use your highest days' values, but rather to include the whole cycle in your total.

As an example, SkateFic gets very busy around the Winter Olympics. Ad revenue also soars during that month. It would be highly inaccurate if we were to use that month to calculate the value of a particular channel because during the other four years of the cycle that channel doesn't produce remotely the same level of revenue. So rather than using that month, we might use the whole year including that month — which would slightly overestimate value — or we might use a whole year not including that month, which would slightly underestimate that value of that channel.

Lecture over. Now, take the Total Earnings and divide it by the Total Page Impressions — not the Total Clicks. In this case, it's $1.48 divided by 58 or $0.026. This would be the Goal Value of any page in that channel (i.e., any chapter in the serial *On the Edge*).

Google Analytics on Secure Pages (https)

A secure page has to use all secure resources. An unsecured resource could be a data-leak and compromise the secure nature of the page. Thus, using `http://www.google-analytics.com/urchin.js` to touch Google Analytics causes an error because it's not a secure resource. The protocol is `http://` rather than `https://`. If you have a shopping cart or you use a secure server for collecting customer information, you may well be tearing your hair out when the script that calls Google Analytics causes this error. There's an easy solution and a difficult solution.

The Easy Way

The easy way? Just use the secure source URL for all your pages. You'll have to modify the first portion of the tracker code, which looks like this:

```
<script src="http://www.google-⏎
analytics.com/urchin.js"type="text/javascript">⏎
</script>
```

It needs to look like this:

```
<script src="https://ssl.google-analytics.com/urchin.js"type="text/
javascript">⏎
</script>
```

The second portion of your tracker code looks like this:

```
<script type="text/javascript"> ⏎
_uacct = "UA-xxxxxx-1"; ⏎
urchinTracker();⏎
</script>
```

It will remain unchanged — except that your code will have your `_uacct` code filled in, of course.

The Hard Way

But that's the easy way! A real propeller-head doesn't do things the easy way, and in fact there are some reasons why you might not want to use the previous solution. For one thing, it would be considerate not to overuse Google's secure servers — and also considerate of the sites that are actually secure and would be slowed if the servers were hit unnecessarily. This would also discourage Google from purposely breaking the previous technique because said servers got abused. There is something to be said for doing something the right way, not just the convenient way.

The basic idea here is that you want to check if you're on a secure page or not, and then include the correct piece of code. This code replaces the first part of the script that you touched above in The Easy Way.

First, we'll do it in PHP:

```
if($_SERVER['HTTPS'])↵
{$GA_URL = "https://ssl.google-analytics.com/urchin.js"; } ↵
else {$GA_url = "http://www.google-analytics.com/urchin.js"; } ↵
print ("<script src='$GA_url' type='text/javascript'>\n</script>");
```

The "if" checks the global $_SERVER variable to see if it's using the https protocol (i.e., this is a secure page). If the page is secure, it sets the $GA_url variable to the URL for the secure version of urchin.js. If the page is not a secure page, the "else" clause sets the $GA_url to the non-secure URL. The print statement prints out the upper script tags. Your lower set of script tags (the one containing the $_uacct tag) remains unchanged.

Now, we'll give it a go in Javascript:

```
<script type="text/javascript"> ↵
document.write ('<script src="');↵
if (window.location.protocol == 'https:') ↵
{document.write('https://ssl.google-analytics.com/urchin.js'); } ↵
else {document.write('http://www.google-analytics.com/urchin.js'); }↵
document.write (' type="text/javascript"></sc'+'ript>'); ↵
</script>
```

The Javascript version is a tiny bit different. Rather than checking first and cobbling together the full script tag at the end, we first print the opening part of the script tag. Then we check the window's location property to see what protocol the page is using. If it's https — a secure page — we write the secure URL (remember, we've already written the opening part of the script). If it's not an https page, we write the non-secure URL. Then we write the last part of the script with a final document.write. Note that at the end of the document .write statement, the word script is broken up into two pieces as sc'+'ript so that the browser doesn't exit the script prematurely when it comes to a </script>!

The code for use of this technique ASP (CGI/Perl, Ruby, et al.) is left as an exercise for the reader. If you don't like typing the code, you can find it on our blog at www.google-analytics-book.com in the Code Samples directory.

Manual Tagging and Tracking with URLBuilder

Do you have a newsletter for your site? Perhaps you make announcements when you have new content. Do you send out e-mail sale flyers now and again? Or maybe you have two AdWords ads with the same title and different ad copy. Yes, AdWords will auto-tag those ads, but they'll be listed under the same title! You can't compare their performance unless you can separate one ad from the other. You have to tag newsletter, banner, and other online and offline campaigns yourself. But don't despair; Google Analytics has a web-based tool that will tag your URLs for you until you get the hang of it (in our case that's forever, because we're forever looking up syntax).

"Tagging tool! Google has a tagging tool?" you ask. If you called the URL Builder one of the best-kept secrets of Google Analytics, you wouldn't be far wrong. It's buried in the help documentation and doesn't even seem to have a permanent URL of its own. There are actually multiple instances of the tagging tool in Google's Help files; which one you get depends on where you start from. Luckily, all of the URL Builders work the same way and give the same results.

To find one of the tagging tools, click Help at the top of any Google Analytics page and in the search box look for "tagging tool." Clicking on the URL Builder link in the search results will bring up that tagging tool as shown in Figure 9-12.

Our first example is tagging a newsletter link. The first tidbit of information you need is the URL of the page you want people to visit when they click the link in your newsletter. In this example, it's `http://www.skatefic.com/news/index.php`.

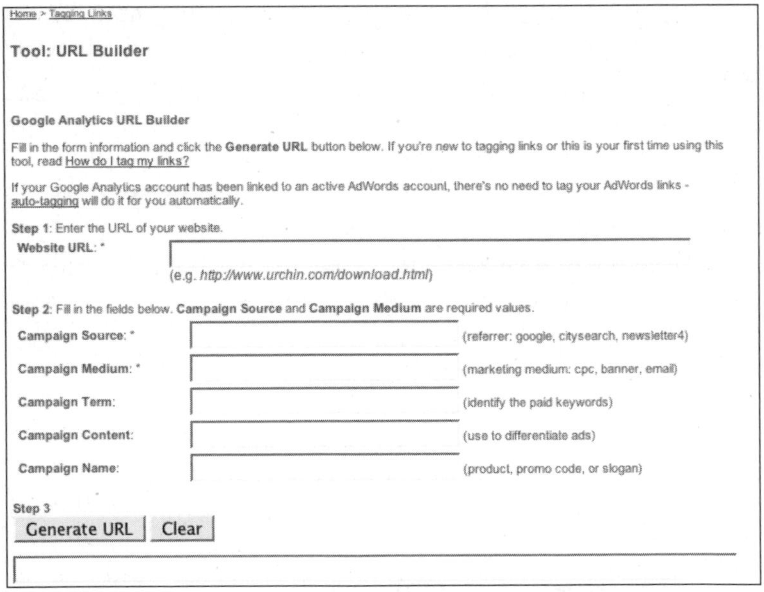

Figure 9-12: Google Analytics' best kept secret — the tagging tool

First, we'll start with the **Campaign Source**. We're dealing with a newsletter, so the obvious Source here might be newsletter. However, you should decide at the outset if you want to track all issues of your newsletter as the same source or differentiate your newsletter's Campaign Sources from issue to issue, or perhaps across a series of issues. If you wanted to track a particular issue, you might choose a Campaign Source such as news20070512, for the newsletter that went out on May 12, 2007. Or, if you're running a series of content announcements for a particular property, you might choose a Campaign Source to aggregate results across the whole series. In our example, we want to track visits from content announcements about the serial On the Edge, so we're going to use ote_news as our Campaign Source.

This is an e-mailed newsletter, so the natural choice for **Campaign Medium** is email. If you were tracking a print newsletter that you hand out in your retail location, you might enter *print_retail* for Campaign Medium. If you were tracking a direct mail piece, then *direct_mail* or *snail_mail* might be appropriate, depending on your sense of humor.

NOTE When you need to concatenate two words into one in a URL, you can either run the words together or use an underscore. Don't use spaces!

The **Campaign Term** tag is used when you have a search term associated with your advertisement. Pay-per-click advertising is a prime example. There are other pay-per-click advertising vehicles besides AdWords (which we'll handle later). You can use this to tag them. If you advertise for a single keyword, enter it. If you use a keyword phrase, put plus signs (+) between the words of the phrase. So, for example, if the keyword phrase was "figure skating fiction," you would enter "figure+skating+fiction" for **Campaign Term**. However, in this example, we're talking about a newsletter, which is not associated with a keyword or keyword phrase. There is no **Campaign Term**, so leave it blank.

Depending on what kind of campaign you're running, there are lots of possible values for the **Campaign Content** tag. You can use the content tag to differentiate between **types** of content, like a link that appears under your company's logo from a text link. Or you could be marking different locations because you want to know if links that appear at the top of your newsletter are more effective than links that appear at the bottom. You could also use the tag if you have ads with different content pointing to the same URL. Say that SkateFic has different sections in the newsletter — one for fiction and one for poetry. If we were tracking response from the link in the first section, we might put "skating+fiction" for the **Campaign Content** of the URL for that section and "skating+poetry" for the link in the other section. In this case, this is a simple text link in a one-section newsletter, so we're going to mark it **textlink** and move on.

Campaign Name is a tag you may or may not need. This might be your spring sale (tag: spring_sale) or you might be doing a special promotion with a coupon code (tag: COUPON124). Or you might be tracking several sources or media under the same overarching campaign. In our case, this is our "content+announce" campaign whereby we remind readers that they really like our content and should come read more of it.

Now, click Generate URL and there's a nifty, tagged URL we can use in the newsletter, as shown (partially) in Figure 9-13.

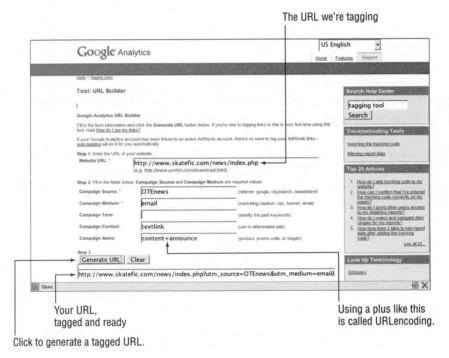

Figure 9-13: Voilà! One URL tagged to order.

Let's do one more quick example. Say you have two AdWords ads with the same title and different ad copy. AdWords will auto-tag those ads, but with the unfortunate result that the response to the two ads will be aggregated. You want it separate. All you have to do is manually tag those two ads with different content tags and then know where to look for the resulting data.

WHERE'S THE TAGGING?

The tagged URL is excessively long:

```
http://www.skatefic.com/news/index.php?utm_source=ote_news&utm_medium=
email&utm_content=textlink&utm_campaign=content%2Bannounce
```

It's not exactly the kind of textlink you want to put in a newsletter, although you could if you did it in HTML. But what about direct-mail postcards? You can't expect people to type that monster and not make mistakes. Or they'll get frustrated, or just not try at all. What do you do?

Do what the experts do: redirect. You can do a redirect either from a dynamic page generation language like PHP or have your web server do it. Ask your web host if your site has these capabilities before attempting the following techniques.

With a redirect, you send a visitor to a dummy page with a simple URL, which then sends the visitor to the real page with the long, complex, tagged URL. Let's try it in PHP, shall we?

Figure out a simple URL you want to use for your dummy page. Let's use `http://www.skatefic.com/otenews/`**. Create a folder called** `otenews` **and in it create an** `index.php`**. Open the** `index.php` **file and put the following code snippet in it, alone, with nothing else:**

```
<?php header('Location: your URL here');?>
```

Replace the *your URL here* with your URL, of course. Ours looks like:

```
<?php ↵
header('Location:http://www.skatefic.com/news/index.php?↵
utm_source=ote_news&utm_medium=email&utm_content=textlink&↵
utm_campaign=content%2Bannounce');?>
```

Now save the file. Go to your dummy URL in your browser. You should redirect to the page with the long URL. No excess typing or visitor despair necessary.

The Apache web server can also redirect URLs on the fly. This is called a "301 redirect." If you're on a Windows-based MS IIS web server, you can still do 301 redirects, but you'll have to look up the mechanics yourself.

To do a 301 redirect on an Apache web server, you put lines of code in the "invisible" `.htaccess` **file (pronounced dot-H-T-access). You can have multiple** `.htaccess` **files on your web site. This file may also control things like permissions to password-protected directories on your web site. The one we want is on the top level of your web site (where your home page resides). If you don't have a** `.htaccess` **file, you can create a blank file.**

Continued

WHERE'S THE TAGGING? *(CONTINUED)*

**Because we don't need the index.php file, delete it (or don't create it). You
can redirect from the directory** `http://www.skatefic.com/otenews/`**. A
redirect is one line:**

```
Redirect permanent /dummy-directory Tagged-URL
```

Note that you should use exactly one space **between each term in the
redirect. You should not include the domain name for the dummy directory,
only the path after the** `www.your-domain-name.com`**, and you need a leading
slash, but not a trailing one. Ours looks like this:**

```
Redirect permanent /otenews http://www.skatefic.com/news/↵
index.php?utm_source=ote_news&utm_medium=email&↵
utm_content=textlink&utm_campaign=content%2Bannounce
```

That's all there is to it.

It's very important, when manually tagging ads, that you make absolutely
sure you use the same `utm_campaign`, `utm medium`, `utm_source`, and `utm_term`
tags as the rest of your campaign. They must match exactly. Exactly. Exactly.
Exactly. If they don't, you'll find yourself unable to compare what you wanted
to compare, and you may mess up a bunch of other stuff as well.

But where do you find these crucial pieces of information? You can ferret
them out. First, the `utm_campaign` tag. This one is easy. Your AdWords Campaign Summary lists your campaigns, as shown in Figure 9-14.

All you have to remember to do is put plus (+) signs where the spaces are.
So if the campaign is called Free Skatefic, then it's `utm_campaign=Free+`
`Skatefic`.

You get `utm_term` from AdWords as well. Click the link for the campaign
you're tracking. Then click the ad group name to get down to the ad level.

NOTE Unfortunately, you cannot track ads at the group level, as there is no
tag for groups.

Click the Keywords tab and you'll get a list of keywords that are in use for
this campaign. You may have many keyword phrases, but you can only test
one at a time. We've chosen to track the Free Skatefic campaign, which uses
only one keyword, as shown in Figure 9-15.

Here, our keyword phrase is *figure skating*. When we replace the space with
a plus sign, our `utm_term` would be "figure+skating."

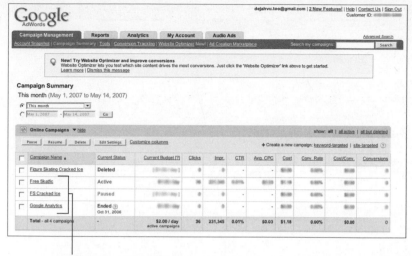

Nifty but un-URLencoded campaign names

Figure 9-14: AdWords kindly lists your campaigns.

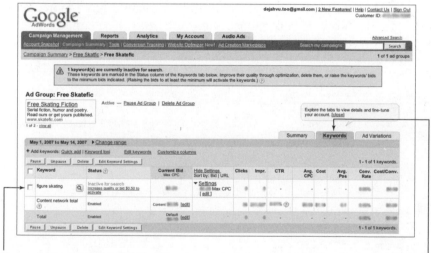

You can track only one keyword at a time.   Make sure you're on the Keywords tab.

Figure 9-15: There's only one keyword here.

The `utm_source` and `utm_medium` are fairly easy because for AdWords they are always the same, but just in case you forget, here's where to find them. In Google Analytics, navigate to Traffic Sources ⇨ Adwords ⇨ AdWords Campaigns. It will show your active campaigns. Select Source from the Segment drop-down as shown in Figure 9-16.

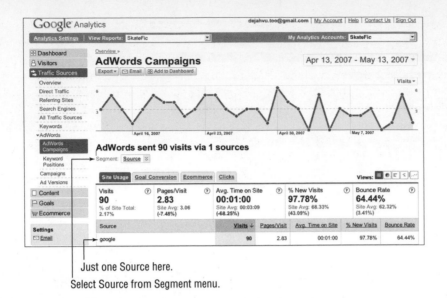

Just one Source here.
Select Source from Segment menu.

Figure 9-16: Just one here: google

There is just one source here, google, although you could have more. Your utm_source=google. Now, if you choose Medium from the Segment menu, you'll see a list of media. But the one we want, cpc (cost per click), is the only one shown in Figure 9-17.

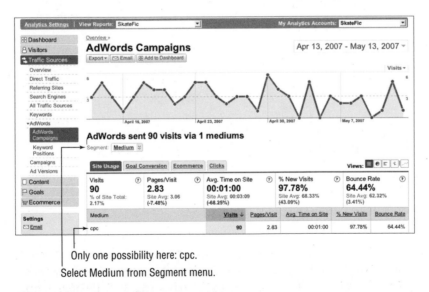

Only one possibility here: cpc.
Select Medium from Segment menu.

Figure 9-17: The medium you want: cpc

So now we have everything except the `utm_content` tag. This is up to you to choose. Remember that we are trying to characterize the ad copy of two ads with the same title. Let's say that one ad expounds on all the skating poems on SkateFic.com and the other ad concentrates on the serial fiction. Using the URL Builder, we'll tag the poetry ad with free+fantastic+poetry and the serials ad with addictive+serial+fiction as shown in Figure 9-18.

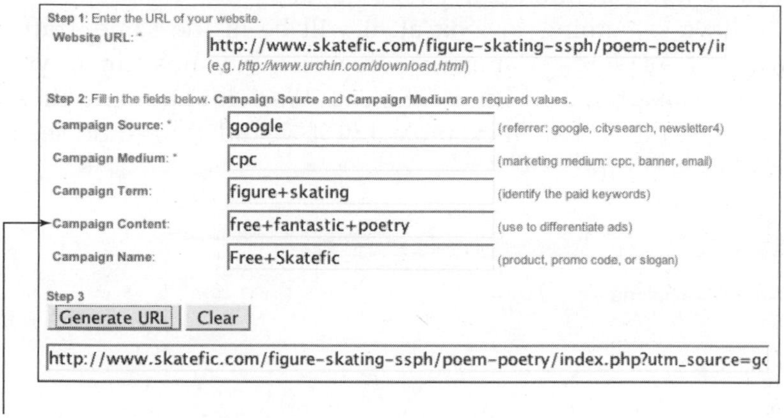

Change the campaign content to tag your ad copy.

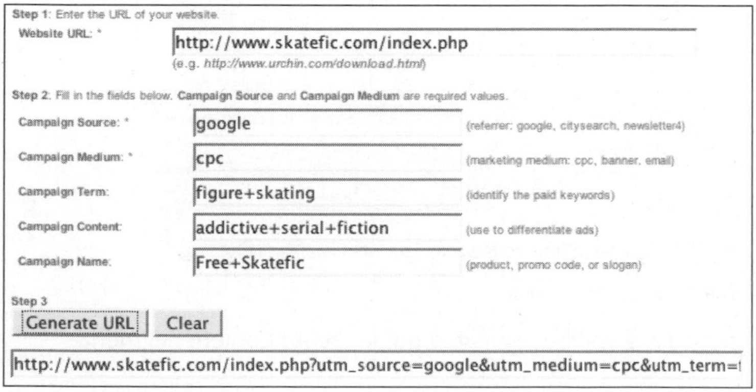

Figure 9-18: Tagging the URLs in URLBuilder

The URLs we get are:

```
http://www.skatefic.com/figure-skating-ssph/poem-poetry/↩
index.php? utm_source=google&utm_medium=cpc&utm_term=figure%2Bskating&↩
utm_content=free%2Bfantastic%2Bpoetry&utm_campaign=Free%2BSkateFic
```

```
http://www.skatefic.com/index.php?utm_source=google&utm_medium=cpc&↵
utm_term=figure%2Bskating&utm_content=addictive%2Bserial%2Bfiction&↵
utm_campaign=Free%2BSkateFic
```

When you're done generating the tagged URLs, you must actually put them into use for anything to happen. Edit each of your ads, and instead of the URL you were using, use the tagged URL that you generated in the previous step. Once you save the ads, you should begin gathering data.

When you do have something to look at, it will be in the same Traffic Sources ⇨ Adwords ⇨ AdWords Campaigns reports. But this time, you should choose Ad Content from the Segment menu. We don't have any clicks from these ads because this is just an example, but if we did, you could see it in beside the ad titles in Figure 9-19.

If we had actually created and tracked the ads, data would appear here.

Choose Ad Content from Segment menu.

Figure 9-19: Your tagged ads will be separated out in the Ad Content Segment.

Improve Your SEO/CPC Reporting with Filters

One thing drives Mary wild when she looks at her Analytics reports. The results of her search engine optimization (SEO) efforts and the money she spends on AdWords sometimes muddy the waters so much that she can't see what each is doing alone. There's a way to deal with this. Simply create one profile that sees only organic search engine traffic from the biggies and another that only sees cost per click (cpc) traffic. To do this, you of course need to filter the data coming in.

Organic Traffic Only

First, create a new profile for your web site and go to Analytics Setting ⇨ Profile Settings ⇨ Add Filter to Profile. Name your new filter Organic SE Traffic Only. Choose Custom filter for the Filter Type and click the Include radio button. Now, for Filter Field choose Campaign Source and for Filter Pattern, simply type **google|yahoo|msn|aol**, as shown in Figure 9-20.

This will include all your organic traffic from all search engine traffic, but no direct traffic, and no referrals from old domain names. Now that we have all the search engine traffic in, we want to get rid of the cpc traffic.

Create a new filter. Name it CPC Traffic Out. Set your **Filter Type** to Custom filter and click the **Exclude** radio button. Choose **Campaign Medium** from the **Filter Field** drop-down and enter **cpc** as your Filter Pattern, as shown in Figure 9-21. This filter will filter out Google AdWords traffic.

> **NOTE** If you do cpc advertising with Yahoo!, MSN, or AOL, they may have different ways of denoting their cpc campaigns, which you will also have to filter out. You may do this in a separate filter or by using a vertical bar in your pattern as we did above with the search engine names.

If you want only CPC traffic, your Include filter would have **Campaign Medium** as its Filter Field, and the Filter Pattern would again be **cpc** alternated with whatever campaign markers your other cpc advertising providers use. Remember that you can't run these two filters in the same profile! You'll filter out all your traffic.

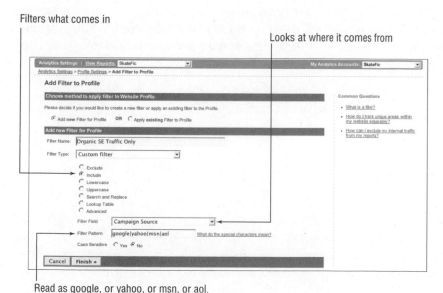

Figure 9-20: Filter in search engine traffic.

Now we filter out what we don't want.

Based on the medium . . . .

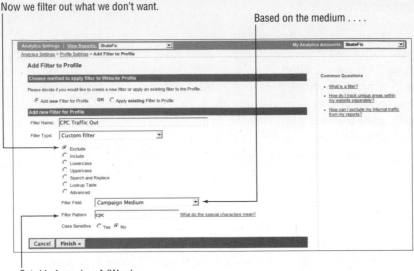

Get rid of cpc, i.e., AdWords.

Figure 9-21: Filter out cpc traffic.

Advanced Topics for Average Users

Google Analytics is so easy to use that even the advanced topics aren't rocket science — at least not the ones in this chapter. We hope that in exploring these advanced techniques in Goals, Tagging and Tracking, and Filtering you see you don't have to be a propeller-head to use — or to need — the advanced capabilities of Google Analytics. Even if you're just a baby copter-hat, you can begin to implement some of the things you've seen here and use them to improve your web site — and maybe your bottom line.

Three
The Dashboards

One of the most noticeable changes to Google Analytics is the appearance and functionality of the dashboard. Dashboards are now user-configurable, so you have the most relevant information available at your fingertips all the time.

In this part of the book, we show you just how to do that, too. Learn to add and remove reports from your dashboard. We even provide suggestions for dashboard layouts that you might find useful if you fall into a specific category of Analytics users.

If that's not enough, there is also a detailed explanation of how to use the new Date Range feature. You'll like it way more than the previous version of this capability. It's much more user-friendly, and it looks great, too!

The New Dashboard

There have been a lot of changes to Google Analytics, and one of the first things you'll notice is that the main dashboard (where you automatically go when you choose a web site profile) has changed a lot. These changes are all for the better, so don't panic. Google really listened when users made suggestions. And for that very reason you'll notice a whole new paradigm in the way the dashboard works.

A New Paradigm

When you first sign into Google Analytics, it's hard to know anything has changed. The Analytics Settings page still looks just the way it has always looked, but when you look at your reports, you'll see there are changes galore in this new version of Analytics. These changes are based on specific requests from users about how Google Analytics could be made more useful.

To that end, one of the best changes to Google Analytics 2.0 is in the main dashboards page. When you first sign into this page, you'll see that it is very different from the old main dashboard. Instead of having four reports, each taking up a quarter of the page, you now have five reports, as shown in Figure 10-1. The nice thing about these reports, however, is that all but one of them can be removed, and different reports can be added. Or if you prefer, you can keep all of the original reports and still add new ones. It's the ultimate in making sure that you have fast access to exactly the information you need.

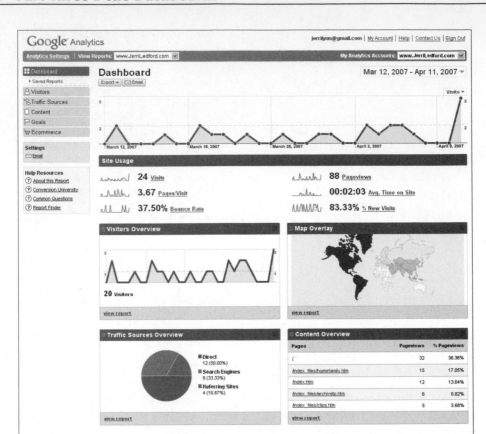

Figure 10-1: Customize the dashboard to meet your specific needs.

There is one report on this page that cannot be removed. The top report, Site Usage, is the default report for your dashboard. It's anchored at the top and cannot be replaced or moved. Also, the controls for date ranges are at the top. Date Ranges are covered in detail in Chapter 11.

Standard Traffic Reports

The default reports on your dashboard when you view your web site profile are the Standard Traffic Reports. These reports include the following:

- **Site Usage:** This report, shown in Figure 10-2, is the one you cannot remove from your dashboard. You also can't move it around on the dashboard. It's a useful report because it gives you a quick overview of your traffic statistics, but if it's not the most import report in your daily workflow, you might find it frustrating that you can't move or remove it. In one notable change from the previous version, Analytics no longer graphs the last (meaningless) point, the one that always dropped to zero because traffic data for that point in time had not been processed yet.

■ **Visitor Overview:** This report lets you see at a glance how many visitors came to your site during the selected time period (shown in Figure 10-3). If you hover over a point in the graph, the exact numbers associated with the nearest inflection point (where the graph changes direction) are shown.

■ **Map Overlay:** The Map Overlay lets you quickly see what continents your visitors are coming from. As shown in Figure 10-4, the continents are shaded, with white being the fewest visitors and bright green being the most. Of all the reports in Analytics, the reports underlying the Map Overlay have probably changed the most — and have become vastly more useful and powerful.

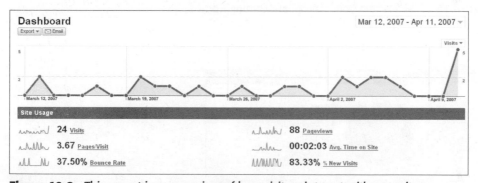

Figure 10-2: This report is an overview of how visitors interact with your site.

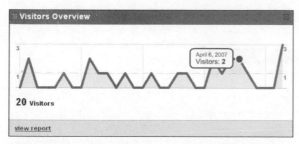

Figure 10-3: Learn how many visitors come to your site in this report.

- **Traffic Sources Overview:** If you want to know what your traffic sources are, the report shown in Figure 10-5 is where you'll find an overview of that information. The pie graph illustrates the sources from which traffic was directed to your site.

- **Content Overview:** If you want to know which pages on your web site were the most visited, this report is where to find an overview of that information. The report (see Figure 10-6) lists each of your pages along with the number and percentage of page views.

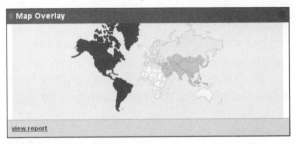

Figure 10-4: See where your visitors are coming from with the Map Overlay.

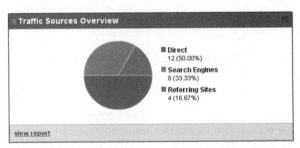

Figure 10-5: This report shows from where traffic came to your site.

Content Overview		
Pages	Pageviews	% Pageviews
/	32	36.36%
/index_files/homefamily.htm	15	17.05%
/index.htm	12	13.64%
/index_files/archivetp.htm	6	6.82%
/index_files/clips.htm	5	5.68%
view report		

Figure 10-6: Content Overview tells which page on your site is most popular.

All of these standard reports — and any other reports you choose to add to your dashboard — are interactive. You can mouse over portions of the reports to see more details, or you can click selections within a report to dig deeper into the information that is contained there. For example, if you click one of the URLs shown in the Content Overview report, you're taken to a Content Detail page for that specific URL. This page contains additional, more detailed information about that specific URL.

You can also remove all but one of these reports and replace them with your own selections. This makes the dashboard far more usable and more relevant to your specific needs. If you're part of a larger organization, you can also set up unique dashboards for different roles within your company. We'll talk more about that, and suggest dashboards for different roles, later in the chapter.

Adding Reports

Adding reports to your dashboard takes just a few clicks. First, you have to locate the report that you want to add. Using the navigation menu on the left side of the page, navigate to the report that you want to add to the dashboard. It can be any report that's not already located on the dashboard, and it can be as detailed a report as you would like. For example, if you go to the report **Content by Title** and then click one of the content titles to learn more about the number of visits to that specific page, you can then add that page to your dashboard. If your main focus is tracking your content, that might be a useful report to have on your dashboard.

Once you locate the report that you would like to add to your dashboard, all you have to do is click the **Add to Dashboard** button, shown in Figure 10-7. If the add was successful, an orange-ish bar that reads **Your report has been added. View Dashboard** appears below the **Add to Dashboard** button. The **View Dashboard** part of that message is a link back to your main dashboard.

When you navigate back to your dashboard, you should find the report you added at the bottom of the page. There are two things to remember here. The first is that the report shown on your dashboard is just a snippet of the information that's available in that report. To see the full report, click the **View Report** link in the bottom-left corner of the report preview. In some reports you can also click on information within the report preview to be taken to a deeper view of that information.

The other thing you want to remember is that with the exception of the Site Usage report that appears at the top of the dashboard, you can rearrange your reports in whatever manner suits you. To rearrange reports, place your cursor over the title bar of the report. As Figure 10-8 indicates, your pointer changes to a multi-directional pointer.

Click to add report to your dashboard.

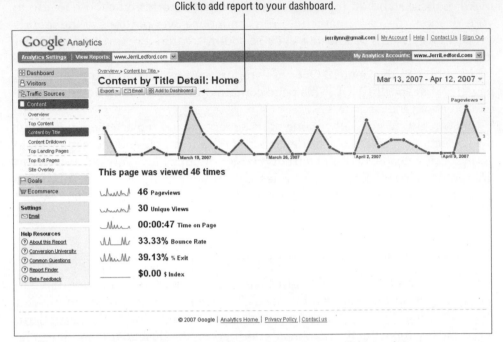

Figure 10-7: Adding reports to your dashboard is as easy as clicking a button.

Multi-directional cursor indicates report can be moved.

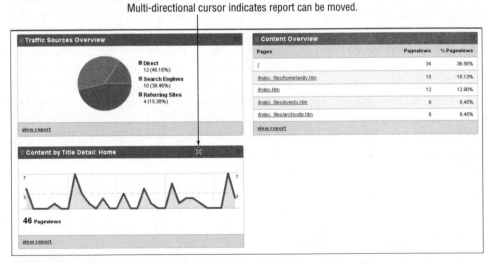

Figure 10-8: When the pointer changes, you can grab and move the report.

Next, click and hold that title bar. Drag the report, as shown in Figure 10-9, to the new location on the dashboard where you would like for it to reside. You can move that report again at any time, to any location on the dashboard except for the top space where the Site Usage report lives.

Original report location   Report being dragged to new location

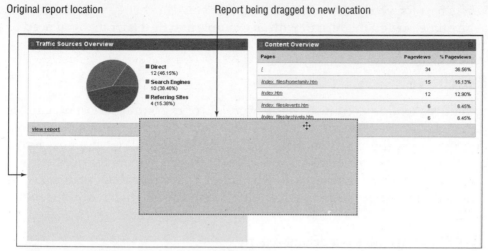

Figure 10-9: Drag your report to its new location.

Deleting Reports

If you're adding reports to your dashboard, then it's probably safe to assume that you'll also want to remove reports from that dashboard. Removing the reports is even easier than adding them. Each report has a small black X in the upper-right corner of the preview. To remove a report from your dashboard, click this X. A dialog box appears that reads **Are you sure you want to remove this module from the Dashboard.** Click **OK**. The report is removed from your dashboard, and if there were any reports beneath it, those are moved up to fill in the empty space.

If at some point you decide you want the deleted report back on your dashboard, then you have to go through the adding process again. Fortunately, that's a simple process, so it won't be horrible if you accidentally delete a report.

Suggested Dashboards for Specific Roles

Analytics can be a lot of different things to different people. Depending on your role in your organization, you may need different reports than someone else who is also using Google Analytics. Fortunately, with the new dashboard capabilities, you can have different dashboards for whatever role you play in your organization.

Below, you'll find examples of several different types of dashboards. These are just suggestions for how your dashboard might look if you fall into one of these categories. Your actual dashboard could vary considerably, depending upon your specific needs. Feel free to use these examples or not, whichever works best for you. And remember, too, that you can change your dashboard at any time, so you might start with an example and find later that you need to add or remove modules from it.

Executive

Executives tend to need just a basic overview of everything. Most executives don't want (or need) to know the specifics about what pages get most visitors and how long those visitors stay on the site. In general, what an executive needs to know is how many visitors came to the site, where they came from, how many of them were new, and what area of the world they reside in.

To meet those needs, then an Executive Dashboard might have these reports on it:

- Site Usage (this is a default report)
- New vs. Returning
- Map Overlay
- All Traffic Sources
- Visitors Overview

That example dashboard might look like the dashboard shown in Figure 10-10.

Of course, it's also possible that your Executive Dashboard won't look anything like this. What appears on that dashboard and how it's arranged are entirely dependent upon your specific needs.

Marketing

A marketing manager's job is vastly different from that of an executive. Marketing managers are looking for how well their marketing campaigns perform. It's all about the return on investment for them. So, when marketing managers create dashboards, it wouldn't be unusual for them to include reports that allow them to see how their pay-per-click advertising is performing, how keywords are performing, and how many goal conversions happen each day. Some of the reports that a marketing manager might include on a dashboard are:

- Site Usage (default)
- Keywords
- AdWords Campaigns
- Campaigns
- Ad versions
- Goals Overview
- Total Conversions

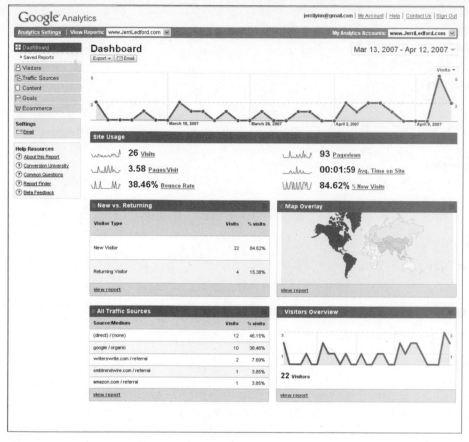

Figure 10-10: An example Executive Dashboard

Your marketing dashboard might resemble the one shown in Figure 10-11.

Webmaster

As a webmaster, you're constantly worried about the differing factors that affect how your web site is displayed. Everything from the browser your visitors use to find your site to the color capabilities of their screens can affect how your site works for them. And every webmaster knows that usability is a key factor to keep in mind when designing a site. So, as a webmaster, you might want to see reports that tell you what content was most viewed on your site, what types of browsers and operating systems most users have, even how visitors move through your site. All these things can be included on your dashboard. Unfortunately, because Google Analytics is cookie-based not log-based, there are no reports to show 401 errors (pages that don't exist or attacks on the site) or 301 redirects.

Figure 10-11: A suggested Marketing Dashboard

As a webmaster, your dashboard might look like the dashboard shown in Figure 10-12. It could include the following reports:

- Site Usage (default)
- Keywords
- Browsers and OS
- Goals Overview
- All Traffic Sources
- Abandoned Funnels
- Visitor Loyalty

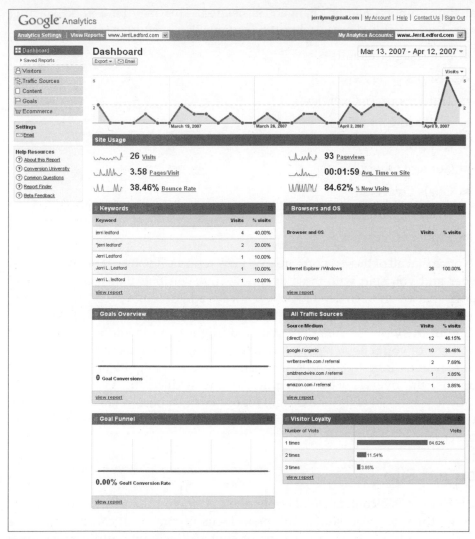

Figure 10-12: An example Webmaster Dashboard

Small Business

Small businesses are so widely varied it's hard to decide what an Analytics user might need on a dashboard. It's going to be very different from one business to another. However, there are some basic reports that are always a good place to start for small-business owners. You can see those reports in the example of a small-business dashboard in Figure 10-13. Remember, however, that those reports can be changed as needed. This may be a good starting point. This small-business dashboard contains these reports:

- Site Usage (default)
- Visitors Overview
- Traffic Sources Overview
- AdWord Campaigns
- Keywords
- Content Overview
- Goals Overview
- Average Order Value
- Product Overview

Notice that all of these reports are overview reports. If you are a small-business owner and you start with these overviews but you find that you really need reports that are more in depth, you can always add or remove reports according to what suits your specific needs.

If your business is primarily local, you might want to add a drilled-down map view of your city or regional area (more about that later in the chapter). If you're heavily invested in AdWords campaigns, you might want more details than just the overview. So, you might want to ditch the Visitor Overview (really just a repeat of the Site Usage) for one of the reports related to the return on investment. If you're concerned with "stickiness," you'll want a bounce-rate report.

Content Site

SkateFic.com is a content site. People don't go there primarily to "buy stuff"; they go there to "read stuff." The main focus is content. It can be articles, a newsletter, a blog, or whatever type of content (including audio and video) that you choose. But there are certain reports showing information that is key to the operation of a content site. If your main focus is that type of site, the dashboard shown in Figure 10-14 is a good place for you to start.

Here's what's included on that dashboard:

- Site Usage (default)
- Top Content
- New vs. Returning
- Bounce Rate
- Depth of Visit
- Map Overlay

Figure 10-13: An example Small-Business Dashboard

Figure 10-14: An example of a content-focused dashboard

In addition to the reports shown for this dashboard, if you sell a few things on your content site or if you use AdWords to draw new readership, you may also want to include some of the e-commerce or AdWords tracking reports. This is especially true if you offer content on your site for sale (e-books, special reports, teleseminars, and so on). However, even if you're selling nothing on your site, you can take advantage of some of the e-commerce capabilities by assigning value to your content. You'll learn more about how to do that in Parts 7 and 8.

E-commerce Site

One of the reasons Google Analytics is so wildly popular is that it has capabilities for everyone who has a web site. E-commerce sites have always presented a special problem for tracking and analytics programs because they are designed a little differently than "normal" web sites. However, Google has taken the time to add more bulk to its e-commerce offering. If your main focus is an e-commerce dashboard, then you might expect it to look something like the one shown in Figure 10-15. Here's what's included on that dashboard:

- Site Usage (default)
- E-commerce Overview
- Conversion Rate
- Average Order Value
- Products
- Transactions

In some instances, you may prefer to include more detailed reports than these. Or perhaps you want to add reports that show you the funnel navigation for a specific goal. All this is manageable with the new dashboard capabilities in Google Analytics. You can add or remove reports any time.

Figure 10-15: An example of an E-commerce Dashboard

Local Business Only

Local businesses often need to know what portion of their users comes from their local community. This is especially true if the local business is a brick-and-mortar business that uses the web site as a draw for local sales. If you have one of those local businesses, there's good news. You can set up a dashboard that includes only location-based information (or you can add the suggested reports to your regular Small-Business Dashboard). That dashboard might look like the one shown in Figure 10-16. Here are the main reports on geographics:

- Site Usage (default)
- Map Overlay

The flexibility of the new dashboard is a great addition to Google Analytics. All too often, users have wished they could have the information *they* need at their fingertips. Now they can. And there are only a few limits to that information. For example, you can add only 12 reports to your dashboard at any given time, but in most cases your most used information will be in six to eight reports. And of course, there's the annoyance of the Site Usage report that you simply can't do away with. We'll hope that Google fixes that in the near future.

Otherwise, the new dashboard provides a whole new capability in analytics and workflow. Everything you need is right there, and drilling deeper into the data is as simple as clicking a mouse.

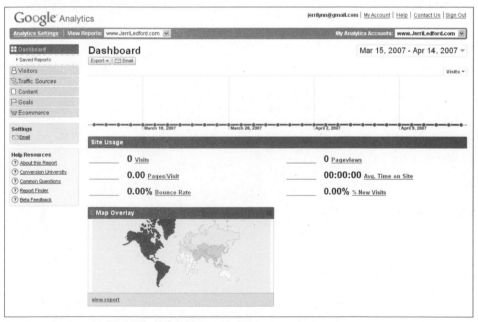

Figure 10-16: An example of a dashboard for local business only

CHAPTER 11

Setting Date Ranges

Date ranges are an important part of analytics, especially in historical analytics, which are what Google Analytics provides. Although it's not a huge lag time — 24 to 48 hours — the data that Google collects are not what's called *real time*. That means the data aren't up to the minute. So when you're looking at your analytics reports, you're looking at figures for activity that took place in the past.

In the previous version of Google Analytics, working with date ranges was a little cumbersome. Realizing how important date ranges are, and how often users change those date ranges around to obtain trending information, Google has completely revamped the date ranges capabilities for Google Analytics. The date ranges have moved, too. Right there on the top of the page (actually inside the Site Usage report) you'll see a date range inside a drop-down menu. That's where your new date range capabilities are located, as Figure 11-1 shows.

Date ranges drop-down menu

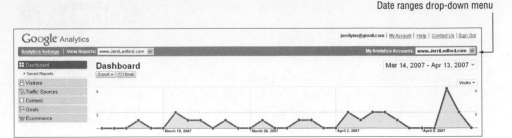

Figure 11-1: The new location for date range capabilities

Using the Calendar

The calendar looks very different now. Figure 11-2 shows that when you click the drop-down menu where the date range appears, the calendars expand for easy access.

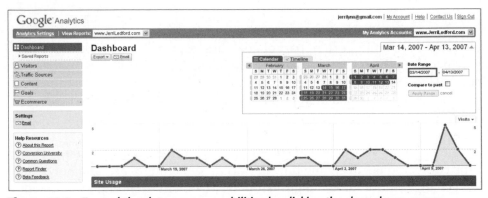

Figure 11-2: Expand the date range capabilities by clicking the drop-down menu.

The default date range is set to one month, so you should see blue highlighting over the last 30 to 31 days. To change your date range, click the first day you would like to include in the range and then click the last day you would like to include. This should change the blue highlighting to reflect the range between your beginning and ending dates.

> **NOTE** Default view for available dates is three months — two in the past and the current month. However, you can go back to earlier months by clicking the small arrow to the left of the month names. You can also advance to the future by clicking the arrow to the right of the month names. Advancing to future months does not provide predictive analytics.

Once you've selected the range that you would like to view, click the **Apply Range** button and the reports on your dashboard will change to reflect the new date range.

There are other ways to change your dates, too. For example, if you want to quickly switch between weekly displays, you can click the small tabs located to the left of each week and that week will be highlighted, as shown in Figure 11-3. Then to view the week's range data, click the **Apply Range** button.

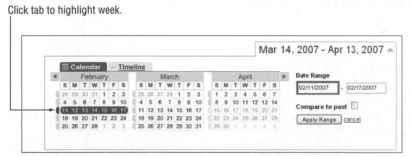

Figure 11-3: How to highlight a particular week

Another way to change the date ranges that you're viewing is to highlight the date inside the text box directly under the **Date Range** label. Type the new beginning date and then highlight the date inside the text box to the right and type the new ending date. The blue highlighting will change to reflect the date range that you typed. Click the **Apply Range** button, and the new date range will be applied to the reports on your Dashboard.

> **NOTE** When you change a date range, it applies to more than just the report previews on the dashboard. It is also applied to all the reports in Google Analytics.

Comparing Ranges

One other feature that you'll find on the **Date Range** module is the ability to **Compare to past**. This feature allows you to compare two date ranges.

To use this feature, first select the current date range that you want to compare to the past. Then click the small box next to **Compare to past**. This will open a second set of date-range boxes, as shown in Figure 11-4.

Notice that the new date range is highlighted in green, and is the same length as the previous date range. So, if you're monitoring a month of data, then your comparative range will also be a month in length.

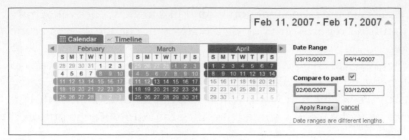

Figure 11-4: Compare two sets of date ranges.

You change the comparative date range the same way you changed the original date range. However, be aware that when you change the original date range, it will change the comparative range to match.

Once you have selected the current date range and the comparative date range, click the **Apply Range** button and both date ranges will be applied to your reports, as shown in Figure 11-5.

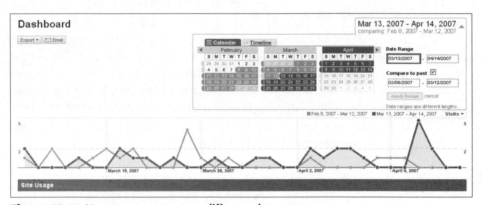

Figure 11-5: You can compare two different date ranges.

When you finish comparing your date ranges, you can go back to a single date range view by deselecting the **Compare to past** option.

Using the Timeline

When you open the Date Range dialog box, you will notice there is a second tab there labeled **Timeline**. This view of your date ranges shows you a small bar graph to help you better visualize your date ranges, as shown in Figure 11-6.

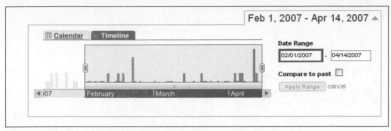

Figure 11-6: The Timeline feature gives you a different view of your date ranges.

The appearance of the date range view is the only change that you'll find on the Timeline tab. All the features of the date ranges and the comparative date ranges remain the same. To change the length of the timeline, grab one of the tabs at the right or left edge of the timeline and drag to the desired location. It's worthwhile to note that when comparing two timelines, you can overlap the time periods. This is easier to see in the timeline view than it is in the calendar view. One thing you should note, however, is that the Timeline feature does not change the graphics that are used in the various reports that are available to you.

There will be regular occasions when you need to change the date ranges that you're monitoring. Whether you're answering a question about the numbers from the last week or comparing this year with last, you'll find that date ranges are one feature you'll use all the time.

All Reports: Visitors

The layout of Google Analytics has changed quite a bit. Reports are now grouped together in a much more intuitive way, as you'll see when we begin to get into the first section of reports. This section includes all of the Visitor reports.

This part of the book includes everything from pinpointing just where in the world your visitors are to visitor trending and visitor segmentation. We explain each report, and all of the capabilities within the report. We've also tried to include some examples of how you might use each report.

Whatever visitor information you're looking for, this is the place to find it. And if Google Analytics doesn't offer a specific report to meet your needs (such as how many of your site visitors are male or female), then you can create a User Defined report to gather that information. And we show you how to do that, too.

Visitors Overview

The Visitors reports section is where you can find all the information you'll want to know about your visitors. This includes reports that show where your users are located, how they connect to the Internet, and how often they return to you.

The opening page for this report section is called Visitors Overview. This page, shown in Figure 12-1, gives you a quick overview of the most important data in the Visitors section.

Visitors

By default, the top chart shows the number of visitors who have been to your site in the given time period. The next figure shows how you can change that chart to represent several different views of your visitor data:

- Visitors (the default view)
- Visits
- Page Views
- Pages/Visit
- Avg. Time on Site
- Bounce Rate
- % New Visits

Figure 12-1: Visitors Overview highlights important numbers in the Visitors report section.

Access these options by clicking the **Visitors** drop-down menu in the right corner of the report, as shown in Figure 12-2. Select the option that you would like to view to close the menu and view the selected data. There is one thing about changing this data that you should know. The change is temporary. If you navigate away from the Visitors Overview, when you return the report will again reflect the number of visitors to your site.

Another nice feature in this section of the report is the ability to see how many visitors there were for a given day. Each dot on the chart represents a day. If you mouse over that report, the visitors from that day are shown, along with the date (also shown in Figure 12-2).

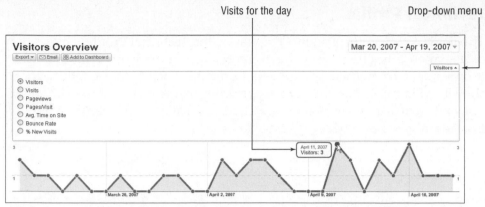

Figure 12-2: There is hidden functionality within the structure of a report.

Visitor Segmentation

The second section on the Visitors Overview is the overview of your visitor segmentation, as shown in Figure 12-3. On the left side of the overview is a recap of the visitors to your site. Numbers and chart previews are provided for each of the categories listed at the beginning of the last section. The right side of the report provides links to other visitor segmentation reports.

All the blue links in this section lead you deeper into segmentation data. Those reports are either covered later in this chapter (Map Overlay and Languages) or in Chapters 13 and 15, so they won't be covered here. Just be aware that clicking any of those blue links takes you to the full report for that facet of visitor segmentation.

29 people visited this site		
╮╱╮╲	**32** Visits	**Visitor Segmentation**
╮╱╮╲╱	**29** Absolute Unique Visitors	⑧ Visitors Profile: languages, network locations, user defined
╮╱╮╲	**116** Pageviews	▭ Browser Profile: browsers, operating systems, browser and operating
╮╱╮╲	**3.62** Average Pageviews	systems, screen colors, screen resolutions, java support, Flash
╮╱╮	**00:01:54** Time on Site	⊕ Map Overlay
╱╲╱	**34.38%** Bounce Rate	Geolocation visualization
╱╲╱	**87.50%** New Visits	

Figure 12-3: Visitor Segmentation provides a quick glance at segmentation data.

Technical Profile

The final section in the Visitors Overview is the Technical Profile. This section of the report briefly covers the technical aspect of your visitors — what browser and connection speed they are using. Each listing on this report, shown in Figure 12-4, is linked to deeper information. Clicking the link allows you to drill down into the data to see more detail about how many of your visitors use a specific browser or connection speed.

Technical Profile

Browser	Visits	% visits		Connection Speed	Visits	% visits
Internet Explorer	30	93.75%		Unknown	11	34.38%
Safari	1	3.12%		Cable	9	28.12%
Opera	1	3.12%		T1	5	15.62%
view full report				Dialup	3	9.38%
				DSL	3	9.38%
				view full report		

Figure 12-4: Technical Profile shows an overview of users' technical capabilities.

As with many of the other links on this page, these links lead you farther into reports that are covered in greater detail in another chapter. In this case, the technical information is covered in Chapters 15 and 16, so look for the complete explanation of these reports there.

Map Overlay

Wouldn't you be surprised if you looked at your site statistics and discovered that instead of the majority of visitors being from your country, they're from another country that you never thought to target? It happens. Many Japanese gaming sites find that U.S. visitors make up a large portion of their traffic, especially right before the release of a new gaming console or device. And they aren't the only sites.

So how are you supposed to know what country the majority of your visitors are from? The Map Overlay, shown in Figure 12-5, is just the tool to give you that information.

This report shows you where your visitors are located geographically, but it also shows that information relative to site usage, the number of goal conversions, and the e-commerce value of each visit. That information can then be used to target specific segments of your web site audience according to their location.

Figure 12-5: Map Overlay shows countries, regions, states, and cities of visitors.

There are several ways to dig deeper into the Map Overlay report. Of course, placing your pointer over any country will show you how many visits came from that country. But also, the actual map that you see is interactive, so if you click on any of the countries shown, you'll be taken to a deeper view of that country. For example, if you place your pointer over the Americas and see that you have visits from that section of the world, you can click on the Americas to be taken to the Continental Details. Clicking the map that appears in the Continental Details takes you to the Region Details. Another click takes you to Country Details, and another to State Details.

On the Map Overlay page, you have several options for drilling into your data as well. If you look below the map, there are links that let you choose detail level. So, instead of clicking on the map repeatedly, you can click the link to go to City Detail immediately.

One thing to keep in mind about the Map Overlay is that it lets you see more clearly where visitors to your site are located. However, you've got to take this information with a little skepticism. When you get as deep as the City Detail, there are dots that indicate visitor location. These dots could be located in the city where the visitor's ISP (Internet Service Provider) is located. Generally, it's pretty close to the same location, but in some instances, if a visitor lives in a rural area, the location could be off just a little.

Still, the graphic is valuable in helping you to understand where the majority of your visitors are located. For example, if your web site is very American-centric but the Map Overlay shows that a significant portion of your visitors are from Europe, you could be missing an untapped market. You'll also want to figure out what's drawing those European visitors to your site — but that's a topic for another chapter.

Visitor Segmentation

In finding additional information about your site visitors, you'll see there is also a drop-down menu that allows you to segment your visitors according to certain specifications. Your options on the Segment menu are:

- Source
- Medium
- Campaign
- Keywords
- Ad Content
- Visitor Type
- Landing Page
- Language
- Browser
- Operating System
- Screen Colors
- Screen Resolution
- Flash Version
- Java Support
- User-Defined

Each of these options takes you to a different report. For example, selecting **Source** from the drop-down menu takes you to the **All Traffic Sources** report.

It's still labeled Map Overlay, but the report is the same as the All Traffic Sources report. This allows you to quickly jump from a view of where in the world your visitors are from to a view of how in the world they made it to your site. It's all about usability. And maybe you need to know where visitors are from before knowing what language or browser they're using. The drop-down menu allows you to drill into the data collected by Google Analytics in a way that's meaningful to you.

In addition to the map and the drop-down menu, there's also a table that provides additional information about the Site Usage, Goal Conversions, and E-commerce aspect of your visitors, as shown in Figure 12-6. Each of these tabs enables you to look at the information about a specific continent, region, country, or city in the context of how that geographical region affects those areas of your data.

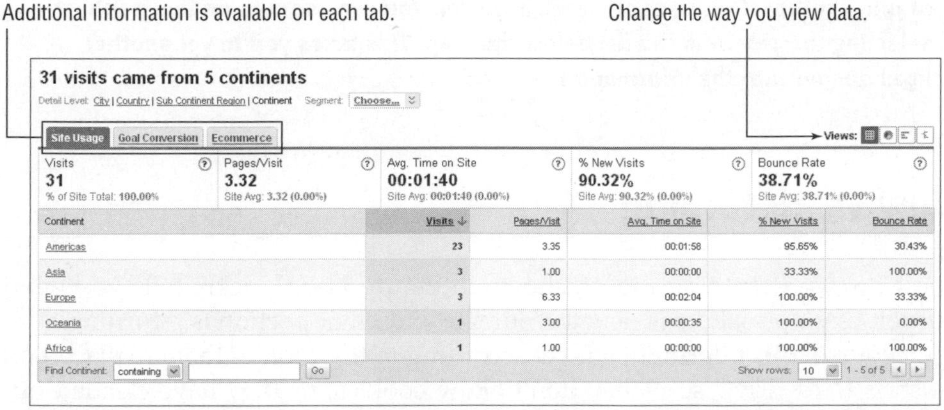

Additional information is available on each tab.   Change the way you view data.

Figure 12-6: Additional information about visits can be applied to geographical data.

One more aspect of these reports that you should know about is the capability for changing the way you view data. In Figure 12-6, the buttons that enable you to make that change are labeled. People understand data in different ways. If you're more a "picture" person, you'll find the graphing options help you to see better what your numbers mean. For example, if you're looking at a pie chart of your visitors by continent, you'll be able to tell very quickly which country was responsible for the most visitors to your site.

NOTE As with changing other aspects of the way you view data in Google Analytics, when you change the representation of data in the Map Overlay, it's a temporary change. When you navigate away from a report and then return, the default view will be what you see. There is no way to make the change to the data view permanent.

So you have the Map Overlay, and it shows you where in the world your visitors are located. How do you use it? Maybe you have a local computer repair business and your web site offers troubleshooting information designed to lead users to your physical location.

What happens if you look at your Map Overlay and find that the site is getting more visits from a nearby city than from the city where you're located? What you get is a clue that maybe there's an untapped market for your business in another location. So improve your targeting. Expand your marketing. Increase your business. Each task is relative to the location of your visitors.

TIP When you're looking at the City Detail of the Map Overlay, a few clusters of visitors are probably hard to distinguish. When several visitors from one location are counted, the spots that represent those visits can be piled on top of one another. There's good news, however. You can zoom in on the graphic by selecting the city from the list below the map. This takes you to yet another level deeper into the information.

New vs. Returning

The New vs. Returning report, shown in Figure 12-7, quickly tells you what portion of your visitors is new to your site and what portion is returning.

Of course, this information is set according to the cookies that are placed on a user's hard drive, so if they don't allow cookies, or they have cleaned out their cookies, that could impact the way the user is counted in each category of visitors.

This report shows you how the number of new and returning visitors to your site in the context of Site Usage, Goal Conversions, and E-commerce, just as the Map Overlay did. To see this information, click the appropriate tab in the table below the graphic.

So why do you need this information? Simply put, you need it to see how often your new and returning visitors reach your goal pages. If you offer a free report from your web site and have the download of that paper as one of your goals, you can track how often that happens. And if you find that only first-time visitors download that report, what does it tell you? Maybe that the report is drawing traffic to the site, but also that something else is pulling returning visitors back to the site. It could be another of the goals that you have established for the site, but it could be something entirely different. This report is the first stop along the way to finding those answers.

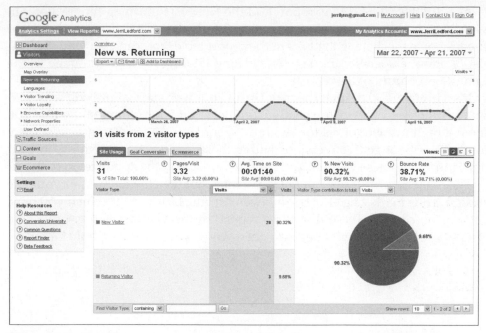

Figure 12-7: Use this report to separate new visitors from ones who visited earlier.

Languages

The Language report, shown in Figure 12-8, is a quick glance at the set language for your site visitors.

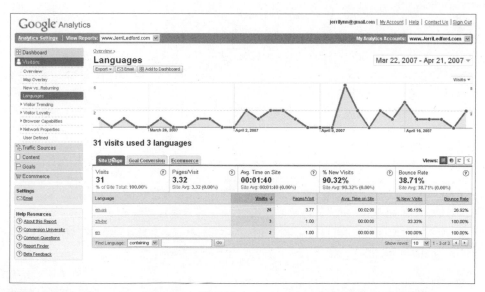

Figure 12-8: The Language report allows you to see the set language of visitors.

As with the Map Overlay report and the New vs. Returning report, you can view this information in the context of Site Usage, Goal Conversions, and E-commerce by clicking the tabs in the report table. You can also view the statistics about a specific language by clicking the link for that language in the Language column of the report.

It's a pretty good bet that the majority of your web site visitors will have language preferences set to your native tongue, but if your figures show that you have a high number of visitors with different language preferences *and* there are a majority of goal conversions within those languages, something on your site is drawing these visitors. You need to find a way to capitalize on that.

The visitors to your site can tell you a lot about the effectiveness of your site design, your marketing efforts, and even organic factors over which you have little or no control. These first three reports in the Visitors section of Google Analytics should help you begin to get to know your visitors a little better.

CHAPTER 13

Visitor Trending

Visitor Trending is a fancy way to say "what did my site visitors do while they were on my site." The new Visitor Trending report section in Google Analytics takes some of the most commonly used trending reports and places them all in one section. With these reports, you can quickly see how many visitors you had to your site, how many were first-time visitors, how many pages those visitors looked at, how long they spent on your site, and how many visitors came to a single page on your site and then left immediately.

The information provided in these reports is a first step toward seeing how effective your web site is at keeping people engaged. The longer a visitor is engaged on your site, the more likely that visitor is to reach one of your conversion goals. For example, if one of the goals for your site is to have first-time visitors sign up for your newsletter, then the trending information in these reports will tell you how your first-time visitors might reach that goal.

Visits

The first report in the Trending report section is the Visits report, shown in Figure 13-1.This report includes the number of visits that you've had to your site. That means not only new visitors, but returning visitors, as well.

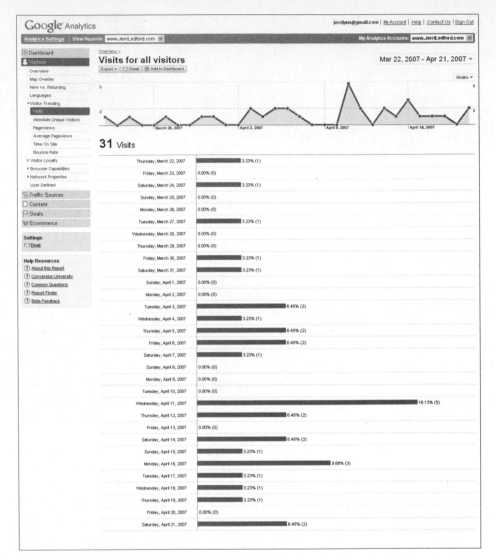

Figure 13-1: The Visits report is for all visitors, new or returning.

The Daily Visitors report shows you bar graphs that represent the number of visitors to your site on a given day. By default, you're shown a month's worth of visits, and this includes all the visitors to your site, whether they're "absolute unique" or returning visitors.

This is a plain-vanilla report. There isn't any hidden functionality in the report. It's designed to give you a quick overview of the traffic on your site for the defined time period. There isn't even an option to change the way the data is displayed. But that doesn't make this report less valuable.

In truth, this report lets you see very quickly how effective your marketing efforts are. You won't find any additional information, but at a glance you can see how many people came to your site. If you need a site-usage figure on the fly, this is the report that provides it.

Absolute Unique Visitors

Before we get too deep into the Absolute Unique Visitors report, it's necessary to understand how visitors are classified for trending purposes. By Google's standards there are two types of visitors to your site: absolute unique visitors, and returning visitors.

Absolute unique visitors are people who have never been to the site before, right? Not exactly. There are certain qualifications that make visitors absolutely unique. For example, did you know that a person can visit your site this month as an absolute unique visitor and then return to the site next month and also be an absolute unique visitor? It can happen.

It's one of those situations in which things may not always be as they seem — like stepping on the scale first thing in the morning. It seems that you weigh about two pounds less first thing in the morning than you do by lunchtime. Surely you're not putting on two pounds in four hours, right? Don't worry. You're not. But first thing in the morning, your body is deprived of liquid and may be slightly dehydrated. So, naturally, you're going to weigh less when you first get out of bed than you will at lunchtime after you've had several drinks and probably even some food, too.

That's the problem with measurements of any kind. The only time you can be absolutely certain that a measurement is accurate from one time to another is to completely understand and recreate the circumstances under which you take the measurement the second time. Fortunately, Google Analytics makes it possible for you to recreate those measurements easily.

An absolute unique visitor is a person who visits your web site for the first time during a stipulated period of time. This means that people can visit your site once this month and be counted as absolute unique visitors, but when they return other times during the month, they are counted as returning visitors, not absolute unique visitors.

However — and here's where it gets hinky — when these same visitors return to your site for the first time the next month, they are counted as absolute unique visitors again, but only one time for that month.

The one-month time frame isn't anchored in concrete. In fact, it may be a week or every hour, depending on how you set the date ranges for your reports. The time frame you determine will designate how often your returning visitors are counted as absolute unique visitors.

Then there are return visitors, who form a pretty self-explanatory category. They've been here before in the time period and decided it was worth coming back.

You may be wondering how Google Analytics knows the frequency with which a visitor comes to your site. It's possible to use two small pieces of technology to determine this. The first is your IP address. Every computer has an IP address; it's like your street address on the web. Just as a street address designates your house, your IP address designates your computer — the physical "where" of your location.

Another tool, and the one that Google (and every other company on the web) uses to keep up with visitor comings and goings on sites, is called a cookie. A cookie is a small piece of information placed on a visitor's computer; it contains information about the visitor relevant to the site that places the cookie.

Think about the last time you logged on to Amazon.com. If you've ever used Amazon, you were probably prompted to create an account that included a user name and password. The next time you returned to Amazon, did you happen to notice that near the top of the page, as shown in Figure 13-2, you were greeted by name and even directed to a store designed specifically to recommend items similar to those you've purchased in the past? That's what cookies do for you. They make it possible for companies to know that you've visited before and even to know some information about those past visits to help them serve you with better, more targeted content.

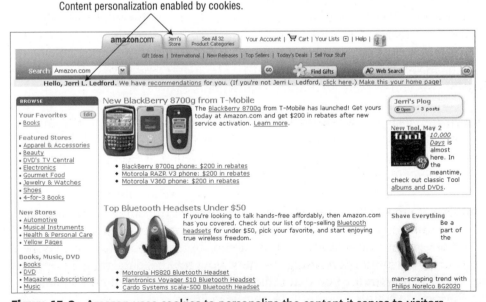

Figure 13-2: Amazon uses cookies to personalize the content it serves to visitors.

All of this is to say that a cookie makes it possible for Google Analytics to know whether a visitor is an absolute unique visitor or a returning visitor. And that information helps you understand how many and how often visitors return to your site. This information in turn can be used to optimize your site content for those categories (or to achieve those categories) of visitors.

To further expand on how Google measures absolute unique visitors, think back to Chapter 2. There we talked about how AWStats counts unique visitors — what Google calls absolute unique visitors — and what the inaccuracies in the process were.

Google Analytics measures absolute unique visitors in a slightly different way, which has its own benefits and drawbacks. When a new visitor comes to your site, Google Analytics places a cookie on that visitor's browser profile. Every time that user returns, Google Analytics reads the cookie it set the first time and knows whether the user is an absolute unique visitor or a return visitor.

This is both more and less accurate than what AWStats does, which is count unique IP addresses. On the whole, Google Analytics' strategy is more accurate, but there are still some caveats:

- **More accurate:** If two (or more) people use the same computer but different user accounts (for example, if they have different browser profiles, which means different favorites and cookies among other differentiators), Google Analytics counts two people because a cookie is placed in each account's profile. AWStats, on the other hand, counts only one person because the computer only has one IP address no matter who is using it on which browser profile.

- **Just as accurate (although the results in both are still misleading):** If several people share a user account on a single computer (lots of families still do this), Google Analytics will count one person because there is only one user profile in the browser. AWStats also counts one person in this situation.

NOTE If one person has more than one account on more than one computer (rather than the same account on more than one computer), then both GA and AWStats count as many unique visitors as there are computers. In other words, three computers are equal to three absolute unique visitors.

- **Less accurate:** If a person visits the site from more than one browser (on the same or on another computer), then a tracking cookie is set in each browser, and Google Analytics counts one absolute unique visitor for each browser used. AWStats counts only one IP address, no matter how many different browsers were used, and thus counts only one unique visitor.

NOTE If a user turns off all cookies settings (and many do for privacy reasons), then Google Analytics cannot track them at all. These users look like new, absolute unique visitors every time they visit the site.

It does get a little hinky, but these are pretty good guidelines for understanding how Google counts visitors as absolute unique visitors, or as returning visitors. And now that we understand the difference between absolute unique visitors and returning visitors, it's time to look a little closer at the concept. The Absolute Unique Visitors report, shown in Figure 13-3, shows additional information about these site visitors.

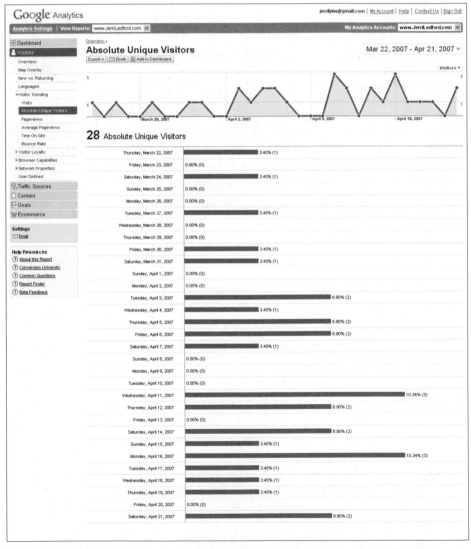

Figure 13-3: This report shows how many site visitors are absolute unique visitors.

The Absolute Unique Visitors report, much like the Visits report, is quite simple. It shows you exactly how many of your visitors are absolute unique visitors, but no additional drill-down information is available in this report.

Still, you can use this information to view how effective your marketing efforts are at driving absolute unique visitors to your web site. If you were tweaking an existing marketing campaign to drive more of these visitors to your site, this information would help you decide how future iterations of that marketing campaign could be changed or enhanced to get more absolute unique visitors, as well as more returning ones.

Page Views

There may be a distinct difference between the number of visitors to your site and the number of page views on your site. A visit is counted when a person first navigates onto your site, whether it's by clicking a link that leads there or by typing your URL directly into the address bar of a web browser.

The number of page views on your site is how many pages a visitor actually clicked when visiting your site. For example, if one person visits your web site, that counts as one visit. However, while visiting, that person might look at five different pages on your site. Those are page views.

The Page Views report, shown in Figure 13-4, shows you how many pages your visitors viewed while they were on your site.

What the Page Views Report doesn't show, however, is how many pages were viewed by each visitor. It's a subtle distinction, but an important one. The next report, Average Page Views, gives you that information.

In this report, all you see is the number of pages that were viewed by all visitors, per day. So, for example, if you're looking at page views over a month (as shown in Figure 13-4) then each day is represented by a bar in the graph. However, if you're looking at a single day or a week, then you still see the number of page views per day.

This general look at page views isn't really useful as a marketing tool. Although the numbers for page views can seem impressive, the truth is that this number is a collection of all the visitors to your site and all the pages those visitors looked at. So, while it gives you an accurate indicator of how much traffic your site receives (which helps you to plan for and manage the resources needed to support those visits), it doesn't tell you anything about how accurate your marketing efforts are.

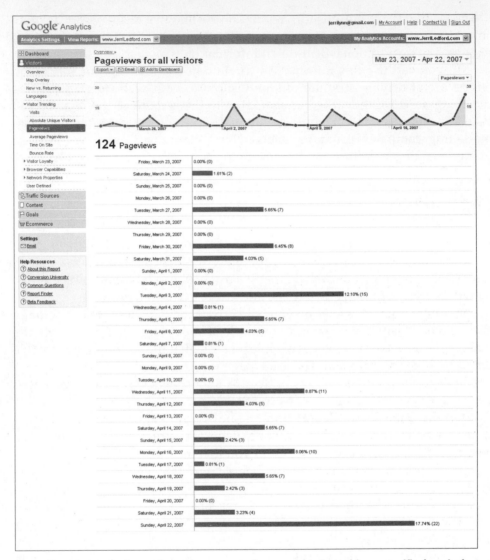

Figure 13-4: Page Views shows how many pages were viewed in a specified period.

Average Page Views

The Average Page Views report is a little different than the Page Views report. This report, shown in Figure 13-5, shows you an average of how many pages were viewed per visit.

This number is calculated by adding all of the pages viewed in a given day and then dividing that result by the number of visitors on that day. What that means is that this report doesn't show you how many *actual* pages each visitor went to. Instead, it shows the average number of pages each visitor viewed on a given day.

Now, even though this information isn't exact, per visitor, it's still useful. One of the benefits of having this information is that it tells you how your users are interacting with your site. If, for example, you have a high average number of page views on your site immediately after a content update, then you know that users are paying attention to that site.

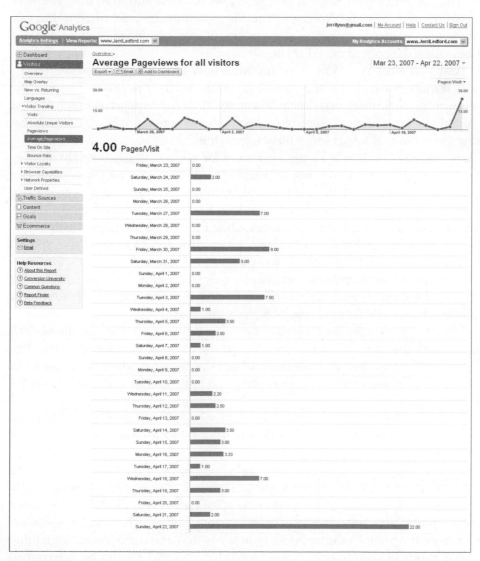

Figure 13-5: Average Page Views shows the average number of pages per visitor.

So, more accurately, this is a measure of web site quality. A higher number of page views is a direct reflection of the quality of the content on your site. Users tend to view more pages when the content on those pages is relevant to the reason they visited your site.

Time on Site

The Time on Site report, shown in Figure 13-6, is a little different measurement of visit quality than the Average Page Views report. Instead of showing you how many pages your visitors stopped on, this report shows you an average of how long they spent on your site.

I hear you already: "Why does it matter how long a visitor spends on my site?" It matters because if they aren't on your site, they're probably spending their time on a different one. Because you want them to spend as much of their available Internet time as possible on your site, you need to have content that draws them in and keeps them busy for a while.

How long is "a while"? That's a question for which there is no right answer. The time that a person spends on each of your web site pages depends on numerous things: what the user is looking for, what your page has to offer, how quickly users read/scan pages and find additional information to navigate to, and how often the phone rings while they're on the page. Really.

Here's a situation for you. On Monday, a visitor comes to your site, spends about 10 minutes surfing through the various pages, and then leaves. On Tuesday, that same user returns but spends only eight minutes because on Monday he saw all the pages and his return visit today is to hit some of the dynamic content on your site (think blog, podcast, or new articles).

Then on Wednesday, he returns again. This time he's in the middle of surfing through the same dynamic content, but the phone rings. Rather than closing out of the page, he takes the call and 20 minutes later when the call is over, he goes back to your site to finish reading the blog post he'd started when the phone rang.

Now you have this strange blip on your length-of-visit graph. It shows that one day, your average time on site is considerably higher than other days. Woohoo!

Just don't get too excited because unless it happens on a consistent basis, chances are that it's just a blip. On the other hand, if something is consistently drawing multiple users to your site who spend an unusually high amount of time surfing your pages, you may have a factor upon which you can capitalize.

If the number shows the opposite, you know that you need to add something to your pages to keep users there longer. What you add should be determined by what your users need. And that's a topic best left for a web-design book.

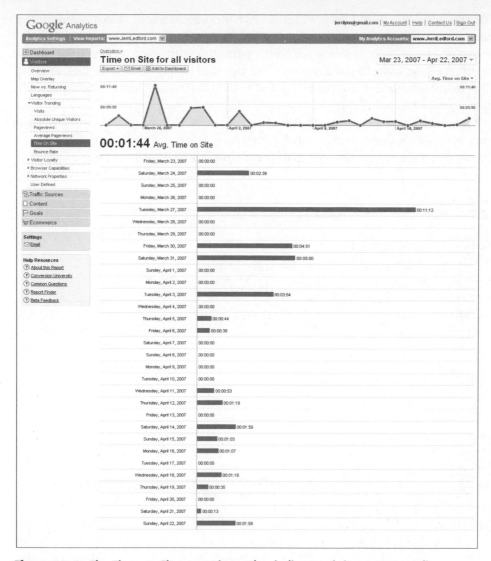

Figure 13-6: The Time on Site report is another indicator of site-content quality.

Bounce Rate

One more report that you'll find useful in this section of the Visits category is the Bounce Rate report, shown in Figure 13-7.

A bounce is when a visitor arrives on a page and immediately leaves. In essence, a bounce means, "Did not visit another page. Did not collect $200."

For the purposes of this report (and only this report), a visit, a visitor, and a page view are pretty much all the same thing.

Bounce rates can show how effective pages on your site are. For example, in Figure 13-7, you see that the average bounce rate for all visitors is 35.4 percent. This means that more than one-third of visitors to the site left immediately. It's not a great ratio.

The goods news is that at least some of those people found exactly what they wanted on that first page and then left. That's not a bad thing. Giving visitors what they are looking for is monumentally important.

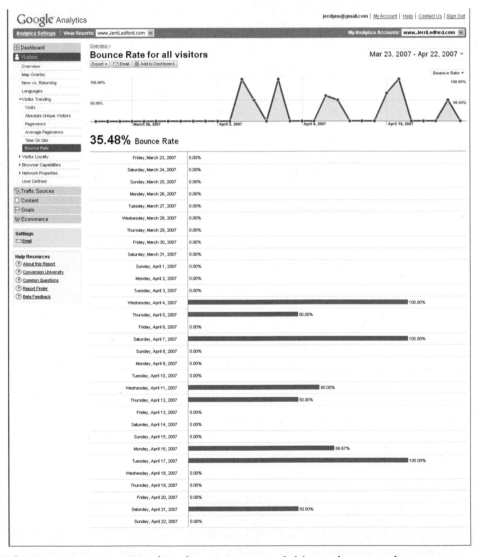

Figure 13-7: Bounce Rate data show percentage of visitors who saw only one page.

However, each page on your site should have at least one specific goal — to lure visitors deeper into the site. In the grand scheme of things, as promotions go, having more than 60 percent of those who respond to the promotion take the next step is pretty darn good.

Visitors come into a site, and some of them leave immediately. Coupled with additional information, such as sales info or goal conversion, it would be reasonable to deduce the effectiveness of your site or the ad bringing in those visitors. Both those observations require action from a business standpoint.

It's important to remember that you can't look at Google Analytics' metrics in isolation from other information about your business. As capable as Google Analytics is, it's still a medium-tier product. It won't function like a high-end (read "expensive") analytics package. You're going to have to use your head when applying outside data — such as actual sales — to Analytics' metrics. Analytics won't do everything for you.

Visitor Loyalty

Visitor loyalty — it is one of the most sought after aspects of drawing visitors to your web site. And it's not easy to accomplish. The Internet makes it really easy for users to pop into your site and then take off to find another if what they are looking for isn't immediately apparent on your site.

It's not at all like the "real world" where you might go into a store looking for something only to find that what you're looking for is a little more expensive, or the store doesn't carry the exact brand. Because you had to drive to the store, get out of your car, and find whatever it was you were looking for, you're less likely to take off and go to another store if the exact product you're looking for isn't available. It's just a pain to repeat that process all over again.

On the Internet, however, moving on is as simple as clicking a button. And users will move on for all kinds of reasons. If you have a web site that is slow to load, visitors go to the next web site on their list. If a user finds your site through a product or information search and what they were looking for isn't right there as soon as they click into your site, they'll move on. Any number of things can prompt a user to find another site.

It is also hugely expensive to continue drawing new customers to your site. If, however, you can build a core of loyal users — that would be users you know will return and will regularly be the source of a goal conversion for you — then you don't have to put quite as much time, effort, or money into drawing new visitors.

Yes, enticing new visitors to come to your site is a constant for every web site. However, if you are always searching for new visitors and not serving return visitors, then you'll invest far more into your efforts than the site that had a sizable group of regular users.

The reports in the Visitor Loyalty section help you to see how effective your efforts at creating loyal visitors really are. Each of these four reports is a quick, easy to read graphic that shows you exactly what you're looking for and nothing more. There is no hidden functionality or deeper data to view in any of these reports. What you see is all there is. But that doesn't make these reports less valuable. The are just more efficient.

Loyalty

How often do visitors return to your site? Is it once? Two hundred times? You can't know without some kind of indicator, and that's what you get with the Visitor Loyalty report, shown in Figure 14-1.

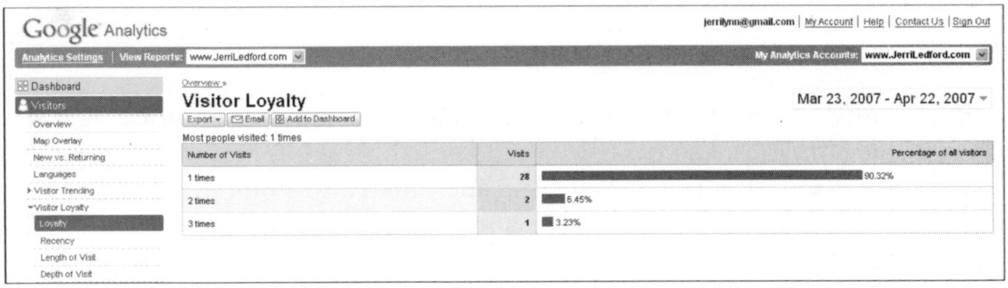

Figure 14-1: The Visitor Loyalty report shows you how often visitors return to your site.

"What's it all mean?" the reader wails in frustration. The histogram — bar graph — shows you, exactly how many times your site visitors return to your site. In the case of Figure 14-1, the maximum times a visitor has returned to the example site is three. However, if you have daily visitors to your site (assuming they come only one time per day), you could have visitors that return 31 times in a given month. It's even possible that they will return more.

The information contained here is used to gauge how loyal your site visitors are. If you find that you have a low number of returning visitors, it could indicate that you need to add something more to your web site to draw visitors back on a regular basis. Using time-shifted content, such as newsletters, blogs, and podcasts, is a great way to increase visitor loyalty.

Recency

A number that goes hand in hand with visitors' return visits to your site is how often they return — the recency of their visits. Do visitors come back every two days? Once a year? Knowing when visitors return to your site helps you understand what's driving them to return.

The Recency report is shown in Figure 14-2. The graph shows the visitor from zero days through more than 366 — over a year. So at a glance you can tell if visitors come one time each year for your annual sale or if they return for your daily podcast review.

Visitor behavior reveals a lot about the effectiveness of your web site. Graphics such as visitor loyalty and visit recency show you when (or if) your site visitors return and give you cues as to what works to drive traffic or returning traffic to your site. What you do with that information will determine how successful your site is in the long term.

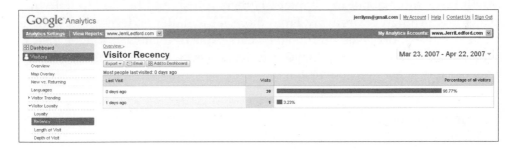

Figure 14-2: The Recency report shows you how often visitors return to your site.

Length of Visit

Knowing how long a visitor spends on your site is one way that you can determine how effective your site content is. The Length of Visit report, shown in Figure 14-3, shows you how long Visitors spent on your site, broken down by seconds.

Looking at the length of a visit gives you valuable clues to your users' habits. For example, if most of your visits fall in the 0- to 10-second range (as the report in Figure 14-3 shows), then you know that there is a problem with your site. Maybe the site is classified wrong, maybe your content is not enticing enough, or maybe there is some other reason entirely. Whatever the case, your site is not effective at holding visitors.

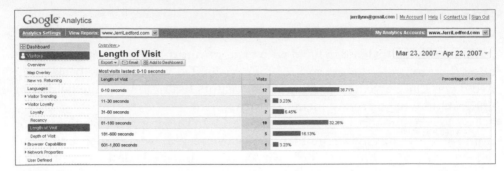

Figure 14-3: Time visitors spend on your site is detailed in the Length of Visit report.

In fact, if visitors are leaving within the first 10 seconds of a visit, then you know that those users are bouncing off your site just a quickly as they get there. It might take some investigative skills, but if you pay attention to the length of visit in combination with the most frequent landing pages (which you'll learn more about in Chapter 21) then you should be able to tell what pages are turning visitors away. From there, it's a matter of design and content to turn those short visits into longer visits. And ultimately, a longer visit is what you're striving for. The longer a visitor stays on your site, the more likely they are to reach a goal conversion.

Depth of Visit

Depth of Visit is a quick little report designed to show you one thing — how many pages users visited during their brief stop on your web site. It's like travelers who stop at a roadside store during a journey. One traveler might make a pit stop in the restroom, then swing by the soda cooler, stop at the chip display, and finally end up at the register to make a purchase. A different traveler might dash into the restroom and then leave without making a purchase. A third could come in only to purchase a soda and never even approach the restroom.

There's a lot to be learned about people's habits by studying their stops along a journey, even if their journey is a virtual one through your web site.

The Depth of Visit report, shown in Figure 14-4, shows you just how many stops your visitors make as they pass through your site.

Functionally, this information might seem a little obscure. Why in the world would you want to know how many pages your visitors viewed? Well, in short, the more pages viewed, the better. But if you look at this information and you find that your visitors are more the "get in and get out" types, you know that there's nothing compelling those readers to dig deeper into your content. So how can you change that?

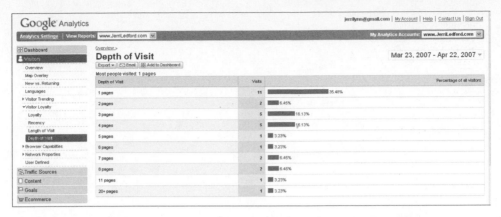

Figure 14-4: The Depth of Visit report shows how many pages your visitors go to.

It will take some experimentation. What drives your visitors? What would catch their attention and make them spend longer on the site? As an example, let's consider the (completely fictional) site BusyMommy.com. A visitor coming to this site is obviously very busy. The visitor is likely female, and she has children — probably young children — vying for her attention. So when she stops by your site, she's looking for something specific. And she doesn't want to spend too much time looking for it.

But if Busy Mommy finds what she wants and it leads her to something else that she didn't know she needed, she might spend a few extra seconds on your site or visit an additional page or two. Your content, of course, has to be very compelling and has to entice her to dig deeper into your site.

Now, this report won't tell you how to create that content, but it will tell you if you're reaching your audience in the way you want. If visitors are hitting one page and leaving and your site consists of hundreds of pages, there's some problem you should be worrying over. If your site is only a few dozen pages long, and visitors are hitting most of them, you know that you're appealing to those users. All you need to do is figure out how to capitalize on that.

CHAPTER 15

Browser Capabilities

Web design parameters are the different factors that affect the way users see your web site. And those parameters can have a huge impact on the number of visitors who come onto your site and bounce right back off or who stick around, browsing and reading the content that you've provided.

One goal of your site should be to make visitors stick around for a little while — at least until they reach one of the goals that you've set for your site. But if your site is hard to use, doesn't render well, or frustrates users for any reason, they will leave. The reports in the Browser Capabilities section of Google Analytics help you to see how different aspects of your site design and structure could affect how your visitors see, and use, your web site.

Browser

Web site design affects how the site renders in different browsers. For example, some web sites are best viewed with an Internet Explorer browser. If you try to view those sites using a non–Internet Explorer browser, such as Firefox, Opera, or Safari, very often the page won't display properly. Sometimes it's graphics that won't show up. Other times the graphics show up but the text behaves badly.

To prevent an issue with having a site that's not designed well for all of the users who visit, the Browsers report, shown in Figure 15-1, shows what browsers most frequently accessed your web site in a given time frame. This enables you to see at a glance how your visitors viewed your site.

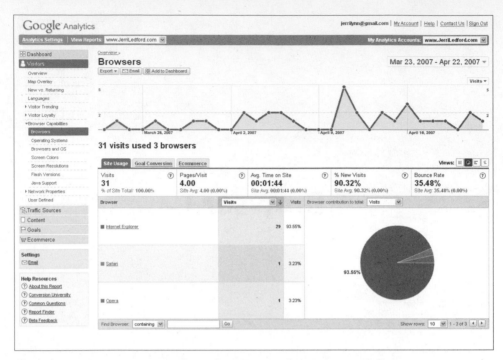

Figure 15-1: Browsers report shows browsers used to access your site.

NOTE It's worth mentioning that sometimes designing your site with the intention of including every browser out there (or even just more than one of them) can be a very bad idea. When you look at the Browsers report in Google Analytics, you might find that 99 percent of your visitors access your site with Internet Explorer. The other 1 percent might use Firefox. If that's the case, you have to ask, "Is it worth it to expend time and money to ensure the site is visible to that 1 percent of visitors who are not using Internet Explorer?" In many cases, the answer is: It's not worth it. If that's the case, then leaving your site alone is the best plan of action.

The usual tools are also there to help. You'll find tabs for Site Usage, Goal Conversions, and E-commerce. The really interesting part of this report, however, is that you can see the version of the browser your site visitors are using. Click the name of any browser, and you'll be taken to the specific browser analytics page, where there are links to the browser versions that accessed your site. Clicking those links takes you to the detail page for the browser version, as shown in Figure 15-2.

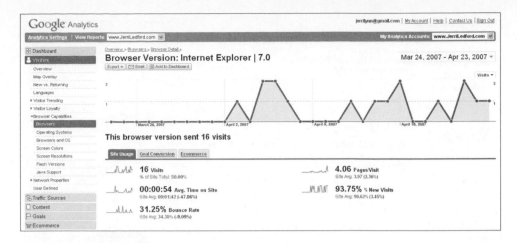

Figure 15-2: The Browser Version Detail shows the final level of browser data.

Browser, Browser Type, and Browser Version detail pages show the same type of information. The Site Usage, Goal Conversions, and E-commerce tabs enable you to see the number of visitors in the context of those elements. And the graph at the top of the page shows you the number of visitors per day for that browser, browser type, and browser version. The only place you really get any variation is the Browser Version detail page. That's as far into the data as you can go, so you won't find links to any additional information and there is no pie graph showing you a comparison between browsers or versions.

Operating System

More often than not, web sites are designed to work well with only the dominant operating system. But not having the capability to work with older operating systems may not be good business. For example, if you support Windows Vista only, then users who are working from Windows XP might be left out in the cold, especially if there are downloadable media files in the mix. If you don't have AWStats, or if the boss doesn't believe anything that doesn't come from the lips of corporate America, Google Analytics can come to the rescue. The Operating System report shown in Figure 15-3, shows which operating systems sent visitors to your site, and how many visitors used each type of operating system listed.

As with the Browser Version report, you can click any listed platform to drill down deeper into what version of that operating system visitors use.

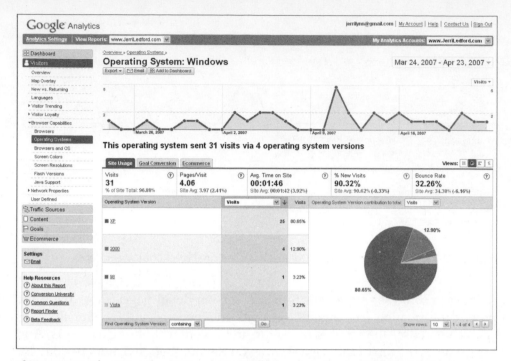

Figure 15-3: The Operating System report tells the operating systems that visitors use.

One interesting capability in all of these reports is the ability to compare date ranges. Remember back in Chapter 11 when you read through the information on date ranges? That information applies to all the reports available in Google Analytics. So you can compare the different operating systems used in two time periods. The resulting report, shown in Figure 15-4, allows you to see how operating systems change over time. This is especially helpful when there is a major change in operating systems such as the release of Microsoft Vista. Using this data, you know how quickly you need to make any changes necessary to ensure the new operating system works well with your web site design.

Browser and Operating System

Visitors don't come to your site using a browser that is independent of an operating system. Nor do they come using an operating system that's independent of a browser. And very often, the operating system that a browser is running on affects the way the browser behaves. So Google Analytics makes it easy for you to figure out what combination of platforms and browsers are used most often to access your web site.

The Browsers and OS report, shown in Figure 15-5, shows you the combination of web browser and operating system used most often to access your web site.

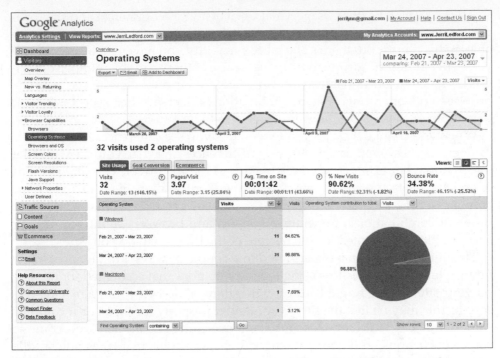

Figure 15-4: Compare date ranges to see how operating systems change over time.

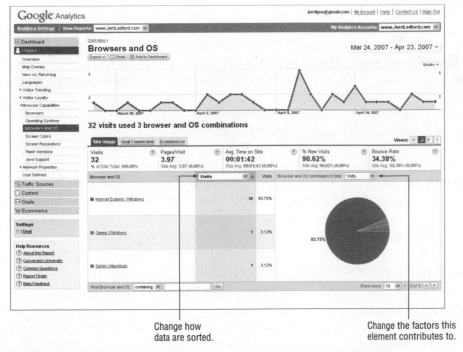

Change how
data are sorted.

Change the factors this
element contributes to.

Figure 15-5: The Browsers & OS report shows combinations visitors use.

All the same tabs (Site Usage, Goal Conversion, E-commerce) and the drill-down capabilities that you've seen in the other reports in this section are available in this report. But there's one more capability you haven't really looked at yet — the ability to sort the data by categories other than the number of visitors to the site. Additionally, you can change your data view to see how the browser and operating system combinations affected other aspects of your data. Both of these capabilities are labeled in Figure 15-5.

When you change the data you're viewing, you see differences. These subtle differences, however, can mean huge differences in what you do with that information. For example, if you're looking at these browser/OS combinations sorted by visits, but then you change the Contribution view to reflect the amount of time each user spent on your site, you might learn that while three different combinations of operating systems and browsers could access your site, one alone accounted for 100 percent of the time spent on your site.

This information can be interpreted in a couple of ways, but the most likely interpretation is that visitors using the combinations that accounted for no time on your site bounced right back off when they landed on your page. One reason for this may be that the site didn't render properly for them, or it could be something else. Watching these numbers over time should help you come to some conclusions. And once you know there is a problem, it takes only a little time and effort to fix it.

Screen Colors

Anyone who has ever printed a color picture or ordered a colored garment over the Internet knows that colors on a screen are vastly different from colors in real life. What you might not realize, though, is how different colors look on different types of monitors.

Because some web sites have a very specific color scheme, it's essential to ensure that all the colors in the site are distinguishable. To help with that, the Screen Colors report, shown in Figure 15-6, shows what color-rendering standard most of the site's visitors are using.

This report breaks down the graphic viewing capabilities of your site visitors so that you can be certain they're actually seeing what you intend for them to. It also gives you access to the additional capabilities — tabs and different views of the data — that you've become familiar with in other reports.

If you're not targeting the right graphics capabilities with your web site, users could be seeing red when you want them to see fuchsia.

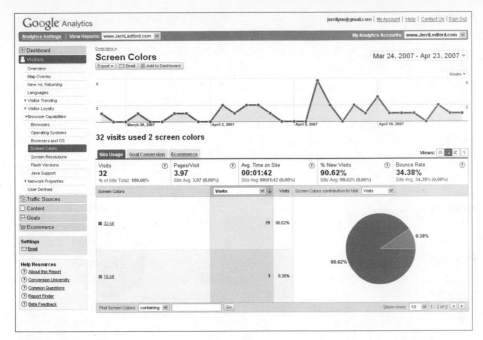

Figure 15-6: Screen Colors report shows what color-rendering standards visitors use.

Screen Resolution

How Jerri views a web site from her Windows-based laptop might be different from the way she views it on the 19-inch monitor of her desktop computer, and that's certain to be different from what Mary sees on her iBook. The screen and screen resolution that visitors use to view your site will make all the difference in the world in what they see.

To help you determine whether your site is displaying as well as it can for the majority of users, the Screen Resolutions report, shown in Figure 15-7, ranks visits according to screen resolution.

Users are ranked according to the resolution of the screen they are using, and you can click any resolution or use the calendar functions to dig deeper into the information or to view a different time representation. You can also switch between tabs to see how screen resolution affects your goal conversions or your e-commerce transactions.

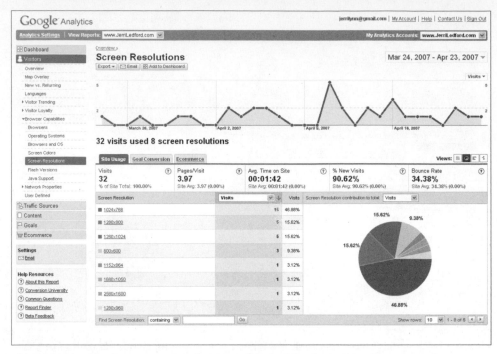

Figure 15-7: Use the Screen Resolutions report to view how visitors see your site.

Flash Version

Here's a news flash: Most web site visitors hate Flash (not because it's a bad technology but because it's very often used in advertising). This means that when visitors see a Flash graphic coming up on their page, they're a little reluctant to download a new version of Flash, just to be hit with an advertisement.

On the other hand, Flash openers are more acceptable (to Jerri at least; Mary still hates them), and can be very cool. But it's still a technology that must be used with care.

If you absolutely must have one of those exceptionally cool Flash splashes on your site (we know *you* would never use Flash advertisements), the Flash Version report, shown in Figure 15-8, will show you what version of Flash the majority of your users have installed.

Once you know what Flash version the majority of your users have, then you can use that version to create your Flash opener. That way, the fewest possible number of visitors will have to install a new version of Flash support. And you still get the super-cool opening page that will make your visitors go "Oohhh . . . Ahhhh!"

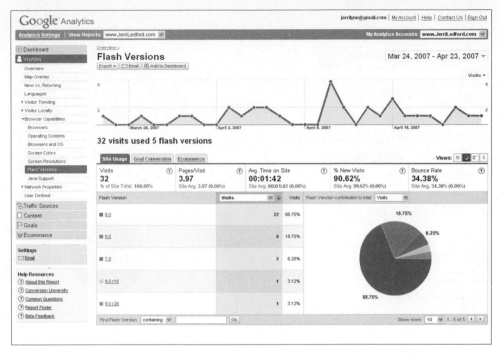

Figure 15-8: Flash Version report suggests what Flash version to use for openers.

Java Support

To Java or not to Java? That is the question. Okay, so maybe it's corny, but if you're considering putting a Java-enabled application on your web site, it's a question you could be asking yourself.

Web site visitors are a fickle bunch. Scores of studies have been done to show what users want and don't want from a web site. Among those reports are some that focus solely on Java, and the findings generally point to the fact that users who don't have a capability installed usually don't want to install it. So if you're putting Java on your site, you should probably make sure the majority of your users have Java-enabled browsers, unless you have a very good reason for doing otherwise.

The Java Enabled report is your way to tell. The report, shown in Figure 15-9, tells exactly how many visitors have Java capabilities and how many do not. With that knowledge in mind, you can make an informed decision about how valuable adding a Java application might be to your web site.

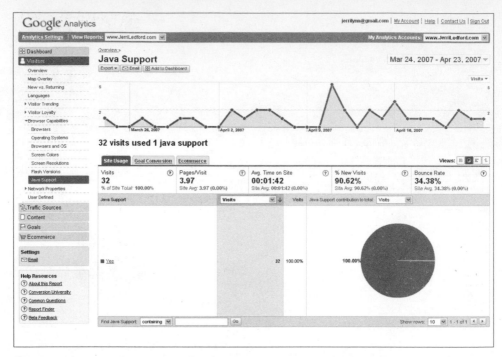

Figure 15-9: Learn how many of your visitors have Java support.

The remaining controls on this report are the same as previous reports, and you can drill into the information to see how the data breaks down for each category of visitors.

When you're building your web site, it often seems that the design and structure of the site is far less important than things like keyword placement and meta tagging. But the truth is, your design and structure are just as important. And if your site is not user-friendly, visitors are going to leave — quickly. Use the reports in this section to ensure that your site is as user-friendly as you can make it.

CHAPTER 16

Network Properties

Pick up any book about building web sites and it's pretty much guaranteed to have at least a few pages on usability. Usability is, simply, how usable your web site is to visitors. And as you saw in Chapter 15, there are a lot of usability factors that impact your web site traffic. But those are all factors directly related to the web site.

Usability doesn't end there, however. There are some elements of usability over which you have absolutely no control. Most notably, the network properties available to your site visitors can have a hug impact on the usability of your site. Factors such as network location, hostnames, and even connection speeds can change the usability quotient of your site. And that's exactly why it's important to monitor these factors.

The Network Properties section of Google Analytics shows you some of the important measurements that you might otherwise take for granted. The data collected for these reports aren't earth-shattering; however, the data will help you design your site so that it's accessible by as many visitors as possible.

Network Location

When you see the term "network location," you might think it refers just to the geographic location of a network. In this instance, you'd be wrong. The Network Location report, shown in Figure 16-1, is misleading because it actually tells you to what ISP (Internet service provider) or corporate network visitors to your site are connected.

What can possibly be gained by knowing the ISP or corporate network to which your users are connected? Here's a good example. In preparing this report, we noticed that among the list of networks in Mary's report is Emporia State University. By itself, that fact really doesn't mean anything. But when you consider that Emporia State University is in Kansas, you're getting a little closer to usable information. According to the report, 45 visitors (or 3.51 percent of the visitors) accessed the site from the Emporia State University network. Now, what can you do with that information?

Additional information about goal conversions can also be accessed by using the tabs in this report. So, in Mary's report, the goal-conversion information about Emporia State University indicated there were no goal conversions from these visitors. If there had been, however, Mary might want to pay more attention to that visitor segment and maybe even take advantage of it by placing an advertisement on the university's web site or in the school newsletter. In this case, however, the visits may have represented just a class assignment of some kind.

This is a simple example of how you can use this information. Look at your own statistics over time and think creatively about how you can use them to improve your business or solve a business problem.

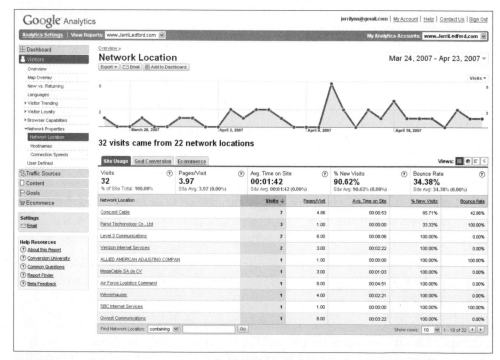

Figure 16-1: The Network Location report provides useful information about visitors.

It also helps to look deeper at the available data. On the Network Location report, you can click the name of any ISP to be taken to the specifics for that report. Once there, you can use the **Segment** drop-down menu to view further segmentation of your visitors. For example, in the report shown in Figure 16-2, the ISP is Panyi Technology Company, Ltd. However, if you use the segmentation capabilities to look at the countries those visitors come from, it reveals they're all from Taiwan. That could mean that a new market is opening to you in Taiwan. That's not really the case here, though. This time, it's likely just potential employers looking at Jerri's web site to see her resume and article clips.

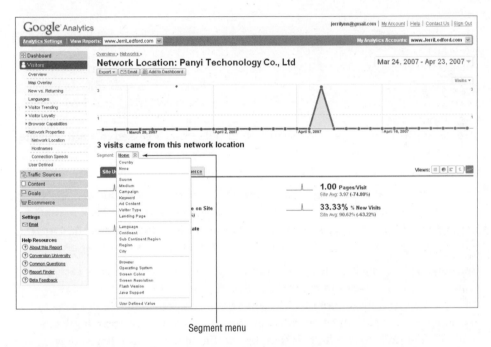

Figure 16-2: Use the Segment menu to access further segmentation data.

Hostnames

Some web site owners, like Mary, have multiple domains pointing to the same physical web space. If you park an old domain on your current site, separating old traffic from new could be difficult. But with Google Analytics, it's not. Analytics provides the Hostnames report, shown in Figure 16-3, to help you see which site got what traffic.

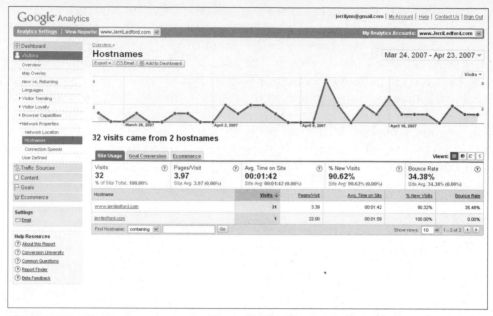

Figure 16-3: The Hostnames report shows which URLs users accessed to reach your site.

NOTE This report is one way to see if someone else is copying your web site's source code to build their own or to create a spoofed copy of your site. If a web site appears in this list that doesn't belong to you, it's possible that the site owner has copied your source code (and even your content) to use as his or her own.

Before you get all up in arms, make sure that it's not an ISP's proxy or cache, which, by law, is allowed to maintain copies of your pages. This is a place where it's worthwhile to note that because the proxy copies the whole page, including the Google Analytics code, page views that might escape a log-based analyzer like AWStats don't get lost in the shuffle. To Google Analytics, they look no different from page views served directly from your site.

With the Hostnames report, you can monitor the URL that users visit to access your site. Say, for example, that my actual web site is www.JerriLedford .com. But maybe my first web site was www.technologywriter.com. Users who have been visiting my site since it was www.technologywriter.com might still use that web address to access it. My Hostnames report, then, would break down my site visitors by those who typed www.JerriLedford.com and those who typed www.technologywriter.com.

That fact can help you to know how long you should hold on to the web site that is simply a referring site. If you find that your Hostnames report lists only one site, then the other might no longer be necessary.

Connection Speeds

Back in the late 1990s and early 2000s, there were scores of reports put together about web site usability. The concept behind such usability was to provide web sites that were easy for visitors to navigate. At the time, the studies looked at a variety of factors, including how long it took for a web page to load.

What was discovered was that Internet users are an impatient lot. We like to have our pages served up to us in less time than it takes to nuke a cup of coffee. Remember the days of going out for Chinese while a page loaded? These days, if a page takes more than a few seconds to appear, we're ready, willing, and able to move on.

Today, more and more users are connecting to the web via high-speed, broadband connections, but there are still some users who have dial-up connections, including the vast majority of non-American users (except in Korea). And those users don't want to deal with pages that take forever (in Internet time) to load. The Connection Speed report, shown in Figure 16-4, illustrates what speed your users connect to your site with. With this information, you know how complicated (or how simple) your web site can be and still draw users without testing their patience.

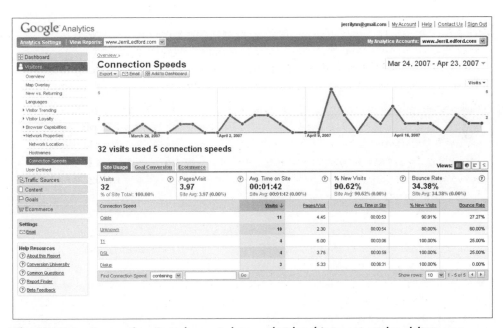

Figure 16-4: Connection Speed report shows what level Internet service visitors use.

Understand that there are various levels of Internet service from the slowest (which is dial-up Internet access) to the fastest (which would currently be cable). If your site visitors are all either dial-up users or broadband users, then you may only see two categories. However, you can also have other categories such as T1 and DSL. Both of these types of Internet service are faster than dial-up, yet slower than cable.

Simple things such as network location, hostnames, and connection speeds on the surface don't seem to be big factors for visitors to your web site. But in truth, these factors can have a major impact on the number of visits to your site. Knowing these details helps you to make your web site accessible to even more people.

User Defined

Dump a box of multicolored, different-shaped blocks on a table, and at some point someone will come along and separate them by color, shape, or both. It's human nature. We want to make sense of things, so we place everything in its own compartment.

This tendency to compartmentalize things serves other purposes, too. Think about working in your yard. If you reach down to pull a weed and spot something long and rounded, it's a pretty good bet you'll yank your hand back before you're even certain what you see.

That's the result of compartmentalization — also called segmentation. We give objects general classifications, like long, rounded, hairy, green, or fat, because that helps us know quickly where that object belongs. And it's not just objects. Basically everything can be classified as one thing or another.

Visitor segmentation works the same way, except it applies to your web site visitors. By segmenting visitors, first generally and then more specifically, you can determine how effective portions of your site are, what groups of visitors are the most valuable (or spend the most money), and which group of visitors provides the best return on investment.

Segmentation That's Customized

Google Analytics gives you a good standard selection for visitor segmentation. But as useful as the existing segmentation reports are, you'll probably want (or need) to segment site visitors in a way that's very specific to your business. In Google Analytics, the User Defined report, shown in Figure 17-1, enables you to segment your visitors according to differentiators that you define, and it shows you how those users measure up in conversions and e-commerce values.

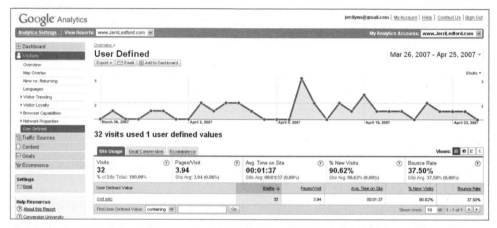

Figure 17-1: The User Defined report displays data from segmentation requirements.

When looking at Figure 17-1, you'll notice the only data there are labeled **not set**. In that report, a user-defined segmentation measurement hasn't been added, so Google Analytics is keeping up with all of the data, instead of just the type of data you tell it to. But adding a differentiator isn't all that difficult. It requires a snippet of Java-Script code placed on your web page below the tracking code that you've inserted so Google Analytics can collect visitor data from your site.

One measurement that you can use to segment your visitors is information from a form that visitors complete on your site. For example, if you push site visitors through a registration form when they enter a specific point on your site, you could include a drop-down menu in that form that allows users to select their specific job titles. That job title can then be used to track how registrants from each job category navigate through your site.

The User Defined segmentation in Google Analytics works by setting a cookie on a user's computer that points to a specific piece of data being monitored by a JavaScript function. So the first thing you need to do to set a user-defined variable is to add the Java Script code to your web site. The code should include the `utmSetVar()` function. It looks like this:

```
<script type="text/java_script">__utmSetVar('Marketing/PR');</script>
```

In this line of code, the script language should be replaced by the script that you're using. There's also a piece that reads (`'Marketing/PR'`). This is a variable and you should replace this portion of the code with the name of the variable that you want to track. So in our example of segmenting visitors by job title, your code might look like this:

```
<form onSubmit="__utmSetVar(this.mymenu.options ↵
[this.mymenu.selectedIndex].value);"> ↵
<select name=mymenu> ↵
<option value="Technical/Engineering"> ↵
Technical/Engineering</option>
<option value="Marketing/PR">Marketing/PR</option> ↵
<option value="Manufacturing">Manufacturing</option> ↵
<option value="General Management">General Management</option>
```

As you can see, each of the job titles that you've listed in your online form should be given a line in the code. That way, Analytics knows to track each of the separate job functions.

You can also track separately users who click certain links. The code for that segmentation might look like this:

```
<a href="link.html" onClick="__utmSetVar('Marketing /PR');">Click here
</a>
```

One other option you have is to track users according to a specific page that they visit. For example, if you have a visitor who stops by your Marketing/PR page, you can set a segmentation variable that will then track that visitor's movements through your site as a part of the Marketing/PR segment. Your code for this type of tracking might look something like this:

```
<body onLoad="javascript:__utmSetVar('Marketing/PR')">
```

What to Segment

One of the most difficult parts of using User Defined segmentation is knowing what to segment. The general segmentation settings included in Google Analytics seem (at first glance) to cover just about everything that you would need to know about your site visitors. And if you are looking at those segmentation categories in very broad terms, they might. But when you get into the normal daily workflow associated with your web site and the goals you have set for the site, then you begin to understand that there could well be other aspects of user demographics or behavior that might be important for you to understand.

For example, if your web site is a content site, then it might be important to you to learn how many of your users sign up for your newsletter every day. You can set up a user-defined report to show you this answer, and then you can further segment that data by using the provided segmentation reports.

Determining the right metric to monitor in user segmentation isn't always easy. A good rule, however, is that any User Defined segmentation that you create should apply to your specific business goals for your web site. Using a truly important measurement allows you to drill down into your data to see what emerges to drive meaningful action on your site. So when creating User Defined segmentation, the question you should be asking is, "Of what value to my business is this measurement?"

Visitor segmentation is all about figuring out how certain segments of your visitors behave in the context of that segmentation. There's a lot to be gained from segmenting your users. If you're segmenting by information included in a form, such as job titles, you can quickly learn how engineers use your site versus the way that IT managers use it. This is an easy way to learn quickly who the most profitable segments are among your site visitors.

All Reports: Traffic Sources

Understanding where your site visitors are coming from — not geographically, but from where on the web — can help you target users to bring even more traffic to your site. But to do that, you have to know basics such as how many of your visitors came directly to your site and how many were referred by outside lines, search engines, or advertisements.

The reports included in this part give you all of that information. Then you can use that information to draw (or drive) additional traffic to your site. And that's hugely important because the more people who see your site, the more likely you are to achieve the goal conversions you're trying to reach. (Remember that goal conversions mean that transactions are completed, whatever those transactions might be for you.)

CHAPTER 18

Traffic Sources

Where does your web site traffic come from? Do you know? Do you know why you should know?

Where your web site traffic comes from is one of the most basic analytics measurements, but that doesn't make it less valuable. It's important to know where your site traffic originates because this helps you to know where to target advertising dollars and marketing efforts.

Here's an example. Say you have a web site that's been around for a while. Every week you have an overview of your traffic sources sent to you from Google Analytics and after a while you begin to notice a pattern: Nearly 25 percent of your traffic is coming from one web site that you haven't done business with in years. So, you follow the links in the report and learn that what's driving that traffic is an old advertisement that you placed on a related web site about five years earlier.

Wait just a minute! A five-year-old advertisement that's not costing you a dime is pushing 25 percent of your site traffic? Now that's something you can work with. Maybe you decide to update the advertisement on the referring site. Maybe you choose to write an article and offer it to the site. Or maybe you purchase additional advertising on the site. Whatever action you take because of that information, you can rest assured that it will likely increase your site traffic. And the reason you can be so sure about that is that you have some very compelling evidence in the analytics that point to the value of a single ad.

This isn't really a "what if" situation. It's a situation that Jerri faced with her web site. When she began using Google Analytics, she learned that a link from a web site that she hadn't even visited in years was driving a sizable portion of her traffic. And that is what traffic sources can show you — patterns of visitors that you would never have guessed otherwise.

Traffic Sources Overview

When you click into the Traffic Sources reports, the first thing you see is the Traffic Sources Overview report, shown in Figure 18-1.

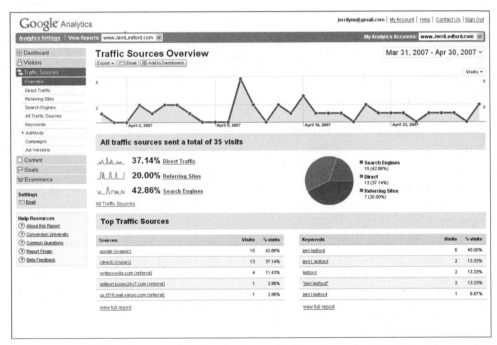

Figure 18-1: The Traffic Sources Overview is a quick snapshot of your site traffic.

The analytics contained on this report are all just quick overviews of the other reports in this section. However, you can click any of the links to be taken to a full view of that report. For example, at the bottom of the overview screen is a section labeled **Top Traffic Sources**. In this section, there is a list of the top sources and the top keywords. Click any one of the links in the source list and you'll be taken to a corresponding report for that link, whether it's a search engine, direct traffic, or referral traffic. Click any of the links in the keyword section and you'll be taken to the keyword report for that specific keyword (which is one level below the **Keyword** report).

The one frustration with these overview pages is that you cannot change them to reflect the metrics that are most important to you in a section. You can, however, export the Overview in PDF, XML, CSV, or TSV formats. To access this function, click the **Export** button right below the report title, as shown in Figure 18-2.

Export report to a file.

Figure 18-2: Export reports in various formats to share with management and colleagues.

When you click the **Export** button, the file options to which you can export the report appear. Select the file type, and the report is automatically opened in that application. So if you select PDF, the file opens in Adobe Reader. If you select CSV, the file opens in Excel (or your default spreadsheet application).

The purpose behind exporting reports is to share your analytics with others, without giving them access to your Google Analytics account. Export and save or print files to distribute to management and project or team leaders, or even to include as visual aids in a presentation.

NOTE The Export capability is available in all of the reports in Google Analytics, except the Site Overlay. You can export any report to share with others in the same manner shown above.

One other reminder about your reports. You can schedule automatic e-mail delivery of any report in Google Analytics (except the Site Overlay) by clicking the **Email** button below the report name. The exact steps for e-mailing a report were covered in Chapter 4, so they won't be repeated here, but remember this is an option that also enables you to share reports with others without granting access to your Google Analytics account.

Direct Traffic

Direct traffic is those visitors who come directly to your site by selecting your site address from a favorites list or by typing your URL directly into the address bar of their browser. The **Direct Traffic** report, shown in Figure 18-3, is a measurement of how many of your site visitors qualify as coming directly to your site and not through some outside source.

Figure 18-3: Direct Traffic shows how well the public knows your site or brand.

Direct traffic can be an indicator for a couple of factors about your web site. First, direct traffic can point to the popularity (or lack of popularity) of your brand. A brand is the image that users have of your company, which is associated with a general topic. For example, when you think of software, you probably automatically think Microsoft. And when you think of search capabilities, you probably think Google. That's because Microsoft and Google are more than just company names. They are also brands.

If your brand is well established, then when people think of a topic related to you, your name should come immediately to mind. And at that point, users who want to access your web site will first try typing www.*yourname*.com into the address bar of their web browsers. That's direct traffic.

Direct traffic can also indicate the effectiveness of your marketing or advertising efforts. If these efforts are reaching the right audience, then you're likely to see a boost in the number of direct-traffic visitors to your site.

Glancing at a Direct Traffic metric just once isn't going to give you a clear picture of the trending for direct traffic, however. This is a measurement that is best used over time. Ideally, you want your direct-traffic visitors to rise over time because you want to create a community of loyal users who come to your site directly because they are comfortable with your brand. However, you'll find there will be bumps — times when the direct traffic jumps considerably only to fall back to a more normal level. These bumps will tell you how you're doing in trying to increase direct-traffic numbers.

Referring Sites

Among the big questions about web sites are, "Where do users come from?" and "Who refers them?" Knowing where your traffic comes from makes it easier to target marketing efforts. It also lets you know if your current marketing efforts are working.

So, where does traffic come from? There's always the direct route. But then there are links that you've paid to have placed on other sites and links from banners, as well as newsletters, and other marketing efforts. And then you also have the people who stumble onto your site because they find it through a web search.

People come to your site from all manner of sources. To see what those sources are, there's the Referring Sites report, shown in Figure 18-4.

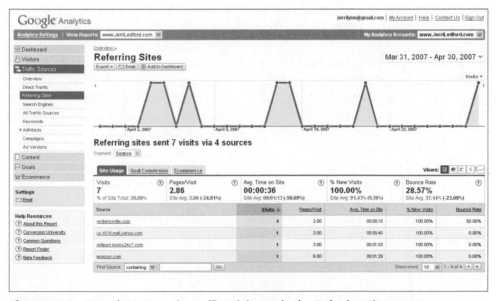

Figure 18-4: See where your site traffic originates in the Referring Sites report.

This report lays out the referral sites for your visitors and then illustrates how those visits translate into goal conversions and e-commerce data. Do the visitors who come from your newsletter buy more than the visitors who come from your AdWords campaigns? Or maybe the visitors who come from a high-end referral link spend more on average than visitors from a less costly referral link? The only way you'll ever know is to look at this report.

Of course, the report comes with all of the standard tools. Each link in the report takes you further into the detail about that referring site. And you can see how your data applies to goal conversions and e-commerce considerations by using the tabs. You can also further segment your data using the **Segment** drop-down menu.

As previously mentioned, you can use this report to help build on the potential that you might be missing, but even more important, the report also makes it obvious where something is not right. If you expect that products featured on your front page should generate more traffic or revenue than they actually do, you can easily see there's a problem that needs to be addressed.

Using this report, you can also see clearly how well your marketing and advertising efforts are generating revenue. You do need to tag the marketing links to persuade the report to track them, but by now you should be pretty comfortable with the process of tagging these links.

Search Engines

The topic of search engines — or more accurately search engine optimization — is highly important when it comes to creating traffic for your site. Some people spend virtually all their time learning which search engines bring the most traffic and how to target those search engines so they'll rank higher in search results.

It's no wonder there is a report that shows specific analytics for the search engines that refer visitors to your site. The Search Engines report, shown in Figure 18-5, lists the search engines that referred visitors to your site and how many visitors came from each search engine.

The default view for this report is all traffic. In other words, when you click on this report, you see all of the traffic that was pushed to your site by search engines, no matter whether the occurrences of that traffic were the result of organic search engine rankings or paid search engine ranking. However, you can change that view using the **paid** and **non-paid** links to look at only the segment of search engine traffic that was driving by paid rankings or by unpaid rakings.

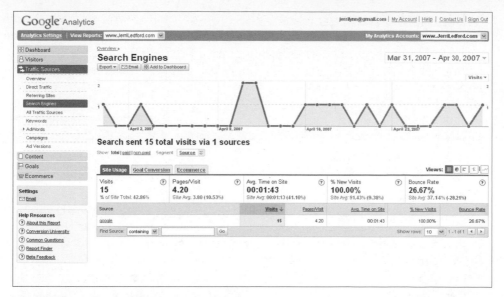

Figure 18-5: The Search Engines report shows how search engines affect site traffic.

This is an excellent way to tell how effective your organic ranking efforts are working, and how effective your paid listings are. Organic ranking efforts are design elements that you include in your site to ensure the site appears as high in search rankings as possible. For example, many people use keywords in the HTML of their site design to ensure that search engine crawlers will list the site correctly in search engine rankings. Even the links that you have on your site can have a bearing on the ranking that you get.

So, if you're looking at this report and your non-paid referrals are high, then you know that your organic ranking efforts are paying off (because, of course, organic means you're not paying for the ranking). If, on the other hand, your paid rankings are higher, then you can tell how effective those paid rankings are. If they're low, you might consider changing the rankings or even not using them at all. But if they're higher, then you know your targeting is right on.

Some people (sometimes called SEOs) spend all their time manipulating sites to take advantage of both paid and unpaid search rankings. You may not want to put that much time into it, but having a report that shows you how many site visitors were referred by search engines and whether those were organic or paid referrals can go a long way in helping determine if your efforts to draw visitors to your site through search engines are working or not.

All Traffic Sources

A way to tell how one type of traffic to your site compares to another type is to use the All Traffic Sources report, shown in Figure 18-6.

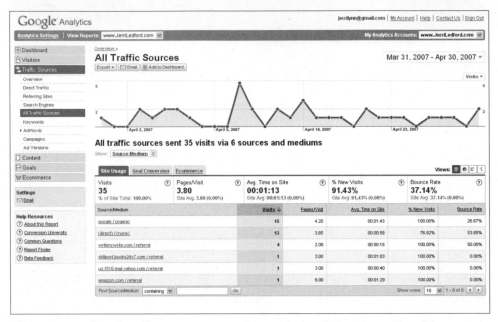

Figure 18-6: The All Traffic Sources report shows where all your site traffic originates.

This report shows you both the source of your traffic and the medium that pushed the measured traffic to your site. A source is the web site or search engine that leads users to your site. The medium is the type of marketing campaign that leads users to your site.

When you're looking at the All Traffic Sources report, you're viewing traffic by both source and medium. However, you can separate that traffic into those two categories by using the drop-down **Show** menu that's directly below the bold statement about the number of visitors from the number of sources and mediums.

When you choose the **Source** option in that menu, you're taken to a report that shows only the sources for your traffic, as shown in Figure 18-7. Using the tabs on this report, you can also look at those sources in the context of Goal Conversion (how many goal conversions did each source contribute) and E-commerce (how valuable were the visits from each source).

Figure 18-7: Learn what sources drive traffic to your web site in this report.

You can drill even deeper into the data to learn just what mediums were responsible for which source, as shown in Figure 18-8. All you have to do is click the link for one of the sources. The information that's included in the detail page will help you to understand how that particular source affected areas such as the average time users spent on your site and the number of pages per visit for that source.

This information can be very valuable when you're trying to draw new customers to your site, and even to keep track of what returning visitors are doing while they're visiting you. If the source or medium that draws users to your site is highly effective, you'll see that in these reports.

Of course, that doesn't really explain the medium. The medium is the type of marketing campaign that leads users to your site. If you're running a marketing campaign and you have your web pages tagged accordingly, then by using these reports you'll be able to tell quickly which campaigns are responsible for what percentage of site traffic, what percentage of goal conversions, and the e-commerce value of the visitors the campaign is pushing to the web site. All of this is valuable information. To help improve your site traffic and begin building a base of loyal users, this report will point you in the right direction. It also helps you to quickly discern which marketing efforts are effective for what types of sources.

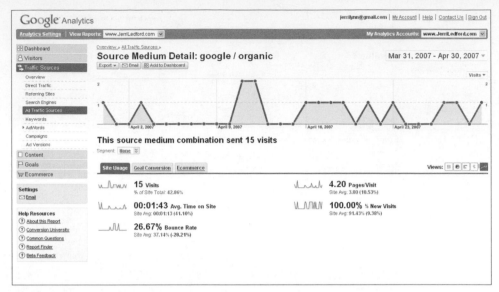

Figure 18-8: Source/Medium Detail report shows how these are connected.

> **NOTE** Source and Medium are two of the five dimensions of tracking marketing/advertising campaigns. The other three elements are: Term, Content, and Campaign. The term is the keyword or phrase users type into a search engine. Content is the version of an advertisement that users clicked through. And the Campaign differentiates product-specific promotions, such as "Free Day with 5 Day Rental" or "Buy One Get One Shoes." These campaign labels are tagged in your site/advertising code, as explained in Chapters 8 and 9.

Keywords

The Keyword report is similar in structure to the All Traffic Sources report. The report, shown in Figure 18-9, shows you the metrics for all keywords, both organic (or unpaid) and paid key words. And, as with the other reports, you have the option of viewing this information in the context of goal conversions and e-commerce value.

If you use the **Show** links, you can also change your view to analyze just paid or unpaid keyword results. And, of course, you also have the segment drop-down menu to further segment the keyword data by campaign details, geographical location, or technological capabilities.

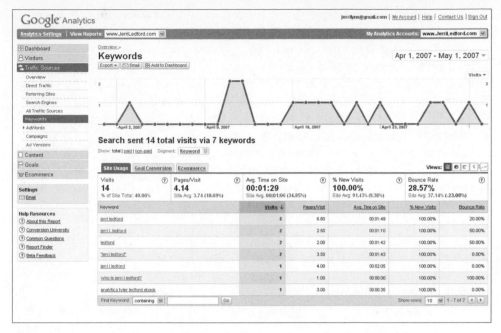

Figure 18-9: Keywords report shows what keywords are drawing visitors to a site.

But how do you use the information? To start with, use it to see what keywords are most effective at drawing visitors to your site. You may find, as you analyze the data, that an unpaid keyword is outperforming your paid keywords. Or you could find that a paid keyword is not performing at all. You can then use this information to tweak the keywords that you invest in.

You can also use it to find out where the highest number of goal conversions is coming from and the visit value for each keyword. A high number of conversions that results in low sales tells you that the visitors drawn by that particular keyword may not be as valuable as conversions that come from a different keyword that might have a higher visit value.

Don't look just at the most valuable keywords; look at the least valuable ones, too. These are keywords that indicate you either need to make changes to the advertisement driven by them or eliminate the keywords altogether.

Keywords are usually purchased through either a flat fee or a fee per click. But in the case of very popular keywords, you have the opportunity to bid on them within the confines of the daily budget that you've set. If you find that a keyword is performing poorly, you can remove that word from your list and return its cost to your budget. In turn, that additional budget can be used to purchase higher, more frequently converting keywords.

Another hint you may get from this report is what keywords (that you're not already using) you should consider including. If you find that a specific keyword or set of keywords seems to be performing well, you can test similar keywords to see how well they perform.

Finally, if you find that a keyword or set of keywords has activity but that this activity is lacking either conversions or visit value, you know that something within your site probably needs to change. Maybe you need to modify the pages that users land on when they are clicking a keyword.

For example, if you find that the keyword "pomegranate" has a lot of hits but the conversion rate is low, you should consider changing the page that this key word leads to. Maybe you have only one product on that page, or maybe that page just happens to have a strange navigational structure that makes it hard for the user to find other items on your site.

Try changing these aspects of your site — improve navigation, feature additional products, or entice visitors to click deeper into your site — and continue to monitor the keyword performance. Sometimes, something as simple as putting a recommendations bar on one side of the page will improve the length of time visitors spend on your site and the amount of money they spend while they're there.

The Keywords report is a useful tool for helping you fine-tune your keyword marketing efforts. Use the various aspects of the report to improve high-performing keywords and weed out the ones that are as worthless as two left shoes.

How can you use information about organic keywords that are generating conversions and high visit values on your site? Do you even know what those keywords are?

It's not enough to know that some keywords organically funnel visitors to your web site. You also have to know what they are. Then you need to find a way to use them.

The most obvious way to use these words is to convert them to paid keywords using a CPC (cost per click) program such as AdWords. But you don't necessarily have to spend money to get mileage from these keywords.

One of the ways to use this report is called search engine optimization (SEO). SEO is the concept and strategies used to optimize your web site for search engines. Remember how bots, spiders, and crawlers probe your site? Those programs are looking for keywords and metadata tags (which are like keywords on steroids) that can be used to classify your web site when users search for specific keywords.

If your Keywords report shows that certain organic keywords are frequently used to find your site and that these seem to result in a high number of goal conversions or a high-value visit, you should consider using those keywords in prominent places on your web site.

For example, you might find that three organic keywords are especially effective for a selected time period. These keywords can be "planted" in a web site to help draw users to the site. However, this is a bit of a tricky situation.

One of these keyword combinations could be several words long and it might be hard to work into the body of a web site. You can include the individual words in the text and the meta tags, but the exact combination might not always work. If you can't put them into the web site text, you can't take advantage of the traffic they are naturally generating. If, on the other hand, you can logically work them into the site, the chances are good that you'll be able to build on the traffic that your site is already generating.

The thing to remember when working these keywords into your site, however, is that you don't want to overdo it. Including the keyword or keywords on a page too many times could cause a search engine to view your page as keyword spam. When that happens, you can be delisted from the search engine; instead of gaining ranking, you could lose it altogether. It's a science that can be very hard to master.

But keyword optimization, when done right, can be a low-cost way to generate traffic — traffic that leads to goal conversions and increased visit values.

LEARN MORE ABOUT KEYWORD MARKETING

Keyword marketing is a very precise science. There are more nuances than can possibly be covered in a single book. But if you'd like to learn more about keyword marketing and how to use it to enhance your Internet business, here are a few titles that will get you started:

Beginner

■ *Pay Per Click Search Engine Marketing For Dummies* by Peter Kent. Wiley. ISBN: 0471754943.

■ *Pay-Per-Click Search Engine Marketing Handbook: Low Cost Strategies to Attracting New Customers Using Google, Yahoo & Other Search Engines* by Boris Mordkovich and Eugene Mordkovich. Lulu Press. ISBN: 1411628179.

Intermediate

■ *Search Engine Marketing, Inc.: Driving Search Traffic to Your Company's Web Site*. By Mike Moran and Bill Hunt. IBM Press. ISBN: 0131852922.

AdWords

If you have a web site, you know it's not all that difficult to get your site listed in search engines such as Google or Yahoo! For the most part, especially if your web site URL and title are the same, all you have to do is put the site up and wait. In many cases, within a few days a potential visitor can type the name of your web site into a search engine and it will appear in the search listings. Give it a little more time and you might even make it to the first page of the results.

That's the only easy part of search-engine marketing. If you have a service or product that you want to market by search engine, landing good placement in search-engine results is like catching electric eels by hand. Not only is it slippery and unpredictable, but if you do manage to catch it, there's a very good possibility that you're going to get a serious shock.

To help combat the difficulties of creating web pages that actually land on a relevant search-term result, an entire discipline of marketing is targeted at optimizing search-engine results. It's called Search-Engine Optimization. At the heart of this marketing strategy are keywords and keyword marketing.

Lumped together, this all adds up to search engine marketing — the art of gaining prominent placement in search engine results. And if you're trying to improve your search engine results, you're probably using some kind of keyword marketing.

Keeping up with the results of that marketing can be a difficult task that leaves you wishing you had a clone or maybe six of them. It's a difficult, time-consuming process. Or at least it *was*. Now that Google Analytics offers metrics for search engine marketing, all you really have to do is tag your keyword campaigns properly and Analytics will provide your tracking reports.

AdWords Campaigns

Google AdWords is a keyword marketing service offered by Google. The basics of AdWords are that you can bid on keywords to use in your advertising. The keywords are bid on by others, as well, and the person with the highest bid and the best quality rating is the one who gets the best placement for that keyword. So, for example, if you're bidding on the keyword Skating, then you're competing with every other person or company that also wants to use that keyword in search engine advertising.

The more people bidding on a keyword, the more expensive it is likely to be. Therefore, many web site owners try to use keywords that are completely relevant, but that might not be the same word that every other person in that industry is interested in. Once you've won the right to use a keyword, then advertisements for your business (you create these short, text advertisements) are displayed when someone searches for related content. How often your keyword advertisement is displayed determines how much traffic the keyword leads to your site.

The AdWords Campaign report shows how your AdWords campaigns perform. You probably remember from Chapter 8 how and why AdWords integrates with Google Analytics. This report is the proof of that integration, so to speak. When you click into the AdWords Campaigns report, you're taken to the **Site Usage** tab, as shown in Figure 19-1. From this tab, you can learn how your AdWords campaigns performed in terms of site visits — how many pages were visited, how long the visitor spent on each page on average, and how many visitors were new visitors or bounces.

The truly useful information in this report, however, comes from the **Clicks** tab. If you select that tab, then the report shown in Figure 19-2 is displayed.

This information includes:

- **Visits:** The number of visits to your site as the result of clicking through an AdWords advertisement.

- **Impressions:** The number of times your ad was shown to search engine users.

- **Clicks:** The number of times visitors clicked through an AdWords ad to get to your site.

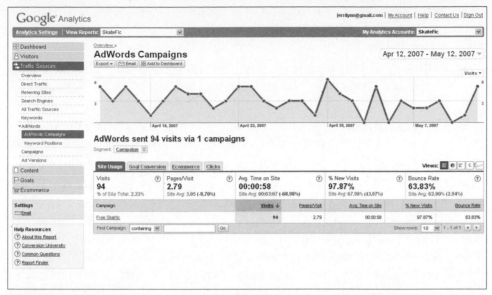

Figure 19-1: The AdWords Campaign report tells how campaigns perform.

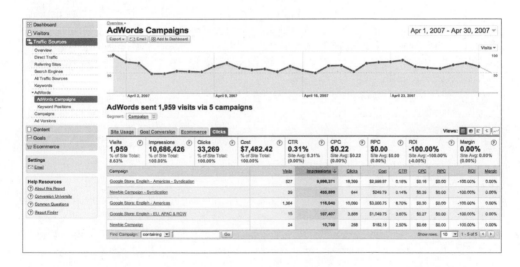

Figure 19-2: The most telling data about AdWords campaigns is on the Clicks tab.

- **Cost:** The cost of the AdWords clicks received.

- **CTR (Click-Through Rate):** The percentage of impressions that resulted in visitors clicking your AdWords ad.

- **CPC (Cost per Click):** The average cost of each click earned through an AdWords ad.

- **RPC (Revenue per Click):** The average revenue per click on AdWords ads. Revenue can be either the value of e-commerce sales or goal value as defined by you.

- **ROI (Return on Investment):** What are you making from your AdWords campaigns versus what you are spending on them? This measurement tells you.

- **Margin:** What percentage is your margin? In other words, how much are you making on your products when you consider how much you're spending on them?

Each AdWords campaign listed on this report is a link to a more detailed report about that specific campaign. For example, Mary has one AdWords campaign running — SkateFic. If you click the SkateFic link in the report, you're taken to the AdWords Ad Groups report, shown in Figure 19-3. This report shows you the same information that was shown in the AdWords Campaigns report; however, it is specific to a single AdWords campaign, rather than to all of the campaigns that you're running.

Within each AdWords campaign, it's possible to run more than one keyword or keyphrase. When you click into the AdWords Ad Groups report, you'll see a list of the keywords that are being used in that campaign. In Mary's AdWords campaign, SkateFic, she's using a single keyphrase, "free skatefic." If you click that phrase on the Ad Groups report, then you're taken a level deeper into the report, to learn more about that specific keyword, as shown in Figure 19-4.

Figure 19-3: The AdWords Ad Groups report shows specifics for a single campaign.

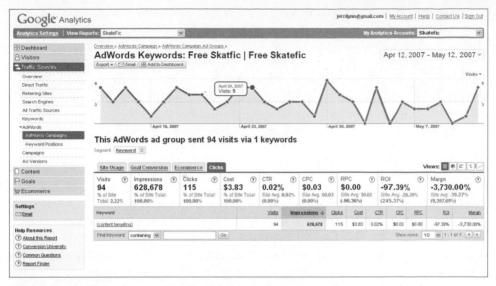

Figure 19-4: Click a keyword in the Ad Groups report to go deeper into the data.

Finally, you can click one level deeper into this data to the [content targeting] report. This report, shown in Figure 19-5, is another way to look at the data for that specific keyword.

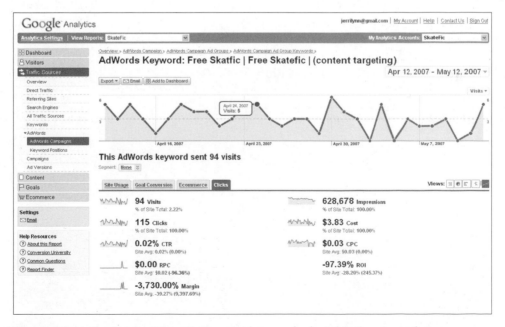

Figure 19-5: The [content targeting] report lets you look at data in yet another way.

So, what does all of this mean? What can you do with it? If you've used AdWords, then you already know how valuable this information is. If you haven't used AdWords before, this is a great time to try it. The information shown in these reports helps you to see quickly which of your AdWords campaigns are performing well, and which are not. You can then use the information to determine what campaigns need to be changed or discontinued and which ones might be worth investing more in.

Keyword Positions

How often have you wondered where your AdWords ads appear? Obviously you can't see every single time an ad is shown on the Google search results page, so you're left to wonder how often and where that ad is shown. Ads can appear in two places on the Google search results page — either the top of the page, above the search results, or on the side of the page, to the right of the advertisements. The Keyword Positions report shows you where, and how often, your keyword ads appear on the Google search results page, as shown in Figure 19-6.

The most useful part of this report is the actual graphical representation of where your keyword ads appear on the Google search results page. Each ad position is shown, with the position number and the number of times that your ad was placed in that position. Of course, if you don't have ad placements in one of the two positions, nothing is shown there. So, for example, Mary's keyword campaign did not generate any ad placements at the top of the Google search results page. As you can see in Figure 19-7, there are no indications of ads at all in the top position.

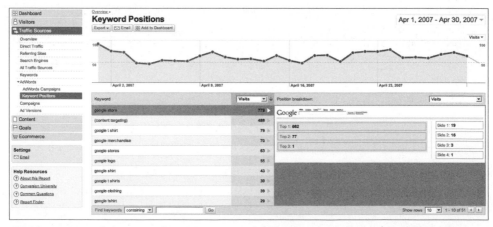

Figure 19-6: In the Keyword Positions report, you can see where your keyword ads appear.

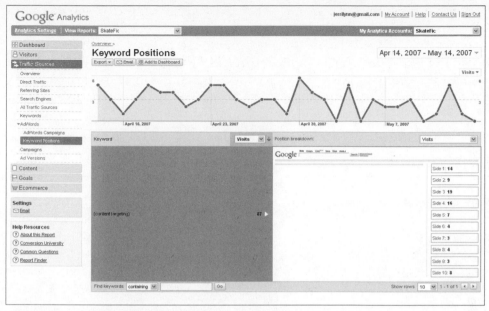

Figure 19-7: If ads don't appear, the ad-position spaces remain blank.

Once you can graphically *see* where your keyword advertisements appear on the Google search results page, then you can begin to correlate your keyword performance with the keyword placement. Do you want to know why your keyword doesn't draw more than 94 visits even though there were more than 600,000 impressions for that keyword? It *could* have something to do with the fact that your keyword ad appears only on the side of the page, and most of the time it's in a lower position on the page. Of course, that may not be the only reason your keywords aren't performing as well as expected, but it's certainly an indication that you might need to reconsider your keyword advertisements.

Again, none of the data collected in these reports are meant to be used alone. Sure, you can look at a single report and learn from it, but the truly useful information is in the combination of the analytics from several different reports.

CHAPTER 20

Additional Traffic Reports

Traffic, or visitors, to your web site is the most important element of the site. Sure, you can have great content. Or smooth transaction capabilities. You can even have the easiest site on the web to use. But if visitors don't come to your site, none of that means anything.

One way to draw people to your site is by using advertising campaigns. The most common way that many web site owners draw traffic is AdWords campaigns. But that's not the only way. Other advertising methods on the Internet can also be used to draw visitors, and you'll want to be able to track those ways.

The last two reports in the section — Campaigns and Ad Versions — help you track your AdWords and other types of advertising and marketing campaigns. These reports show you how well (or how poorly) your ads are performing. Unfortunately, they won't tell you how to fix that, but they could point you in the right direction.

Campaigns

Tracking the effectiveness of your marketing campaigns is just half the battle. The other half is understanding how the campaign affects the number of people who reach a defined goal on your web site. This is called goal conversion. And marketing is all about conversions.

The goal could be for a visitor to make a purchase, sign up for a newsletter, or even just link to the page. Whatever your desired marketing campaign results are, the number of conversions can be looked at in a variety of ways, and each conversion view tells you something more about the effectiveness of your marketing campaign.

If you're running only one marketing campaign, keeping up with the results of that campaign won't be too difficult. But it's more likely that you're running multiple paid (and free) campaigns. And keeping up with multiple campaigns might leave you feeling as if you've been chasing your tail — lots of work for very little return.

The Campaign report, shown in Figure 20-1, is a quick glance at how all your marketing campaigns are performing in terms of visits, pages per visit, average time on site, bounce percentage, and the percentage of new visitors.

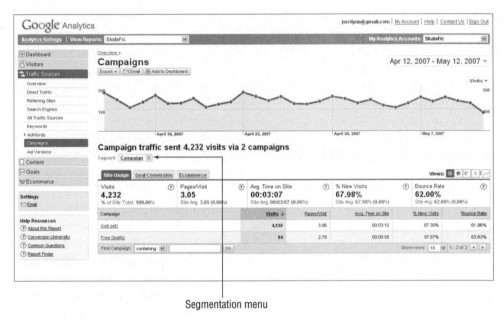

Segmentation menu

Figure 20-1: The Campaign report quickly shows how all your campaigns perform.

The Campaign report shows you your top-performing marketing campaigns, as long as they have been tagged for tracking by Google Analytics. Each of the lines in the table beneath the graph is dedicated to one marketing campaign that is either auto-tagged or that you have tagged for a specific campaign.

You may remember that Google tracks all instances of marketing campaigns — organic, referral, and direct. An organic campaign represents visits from an unpaid search engine; referral is the indicator used for visitors who clicked through an untagged marketing link; and direct indicates visitors who typed the URL for your site into the address bar of their web browser.

The tag [not set] may also appear in your list of campaigns. This indicates visitors who came to your site through all methods that are not specifically tagged. For example, organic and direct visitors are qualified as [not set] because there is no campaign tag associated with these visitors. Referral visitors, on the other hand, will usually come from an advertising campaign, and can be tracked by campaign if you tag the campaign properly.

So, in the report shown in Figure 20-1, Mary has only one advertising/marketing campaign set for SkateFic.com: Free Skatefic. All other visits to her site fall under the [not set] category because they are not associated with any advertising or marketing campaign.

Mary can quickly look at all these reports and see how many visits are related to each category and how those visits translate into goal conversions for each of the three goals she has set for the site. With this information, she can then adjust marketing campaigns to improve performance in an area where her campaigns aren't performing as well as she thinks they should.

If Mary were tracking more than one campaign, the information could also tell her which of her campaigns results in the highest visit value. This information can then be used to expand or shape future marketing campaigns.

A source is the web site or search engine that led users to your site. If you're using cost-per-click advertising from Yahoo! or Google's AdWords, then when a user clicks through one of your AdWords advertisements, the page (Yahoo! or Google) that refers the user to your site becomes a source of traffic for that site.

Each of the campaigns that's listed on the Campaigns report is a link to further information. If you click through one of those links, you're taken to the Campaign detail page, shown in Figure 20-2. This report shows the same information that is collected in the campaign report, only it is specific to the campaign to which it is assigned. So, instead of seeing the number of visits for all campaigns, you're seeing that information for a single campaign.

Stepping back one page to the Campaigns report, you should pay particular attention to the segmentation capabilities of this report. There are similar segmentation capabilities on all reports (though they do change slightly on some of the reports). However, they are extremely useful on this report because they give you even more detailed information about your advertising campaigns. The following sections detail some of the most important segments that you should consider examining.

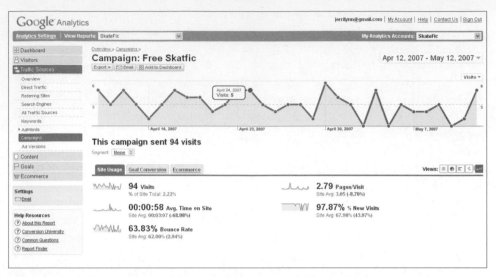

Figure 20-2: The Campaigns detail report shows a specific campaign.

Source

The Source segmentation shows you the top sources driving traffic to your site and how valuable those sources are in terms of conversion and visit value. The report, shown in Figure 20-3, is similar to other reports that you've seen. The source tracking is what sets this report apart.

Once you have segmented the campaign data by source, then you can further segment it by clicking the Goal Conversion or E-commerce tabs to see how each source translates to goal conversions or visit value.

Medium

You may remember that we have previously defined medium as the type of marketing campaign being tracked — e-mail campaigns, banner advertisements, and organic searches are just a few examples of what's considered a medium. The Medium Campaign segmentation shows you which of these types of marketing efforts is performing best by visits, or if you switch between the tabs, by Goal Conversions or E-commerce.

The Medium Campaign segmentation is shown in Figure 20-4 and is another of those reports that's similar in appearance to other reports but different in content.

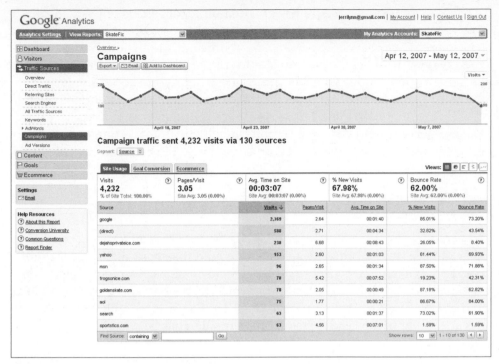

Figure 20-3: Source segmentation allows you to see what sources drive traffic.

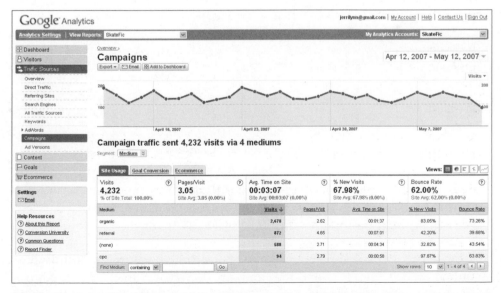

Figure 20-4: Medium segmentation enables you to see which ad medium performs best.

The key to using the Medium segmentation report effectively is to evaluate each marketing medium according to the number of goal conversions *and* the visit value if you have e-commerce capabilities. It's not enough to have goal conversions if you don't have the sales to support them. By switching between the tabs in this report, you can determine where you should increase your marketing investments to capitalize on the user's purchasing trends in relation to goal conversions. If you don't see any success (or only small success) in your goal conversions and visit values, you can tell which marketing mediums are not working, and that investment can be redirected to more successful efforts.

Ad Versions

Ad versions are different aspects, or slants, on the same advertising campaign. For example, many companies create one advertisement that differs slightly from region to region. Those are considered ad versions. Keeping up with those ad versions is essential to determining which works best and how to capitalize on that fact. The Ad Versions report, shown in Figure 20-5, ranks your site visitors according to how each version of a campaign has been tagged.

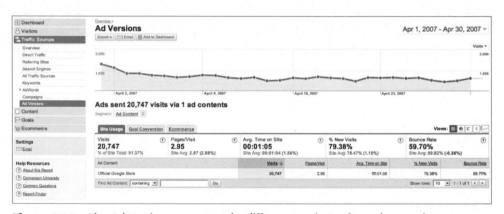

Figure 20-5: The Ad Versions report tracks different versions of an ad campaign.

SurePoint Lending, a subsidiary of First Residential Mortgage Network, is designed to excel in the very competitive market of online financial services. SurePoint is one of the top-rated financial services sites on the web, but it didn't get there by sheer luck.

Agency.com is the company in charge of ensuring that SurePoint ranks high in online financial services, and the company does that with Google Analytics. More specifically, the company does that by using Google Analytics to test ad versions for the keyword marketing campaign that drives traffic to the site.

Testing consists of comparing the results from hundreds of keywords, keyword landing pages, and content to learn which elements are most effective in driving qualified traffic to the site, leading in turn to high levels of conversions.

It's not a tool available only to companies such as First Residential Mortgage Network or Agency.com. You can use these same tools to create very similar results with your site. All you need to do is test your marketing efforts to learn which are most effective and then put that information to use increasing traffic and conversions. It's really not all that difficult.

A/B Testing

The first step in testing any marketing campaign, or group of marketing campaigns, is to compare one against another. (The A/B in the preceding title simply means comparing one thing with another.) This type of comparison has been going on for as long as there have been advertisements. Heck, you may have even started studying advertising way back in grade school when you were scrawling "Roses are red/Violets are blue/If I looked like Susie/I'd join the zoo" in a note, passing it around and waiting for results.

It wasn't nice, but it does illustrate the point. If it was a note not too many people saw, you were safe. If everybody saw it, Susie would be checking out handwriting and heading your way, fire in eye, brick in hand. Different ads perform at different levels in different places. And your online ads work in very much the same way. If one ad is performing better than another, you want to know it, and it's all right there in the Ad Versions report, in clearly defined detail.

On the other hand, you may be running only one ad. Or maybe you don't have any ads running. In that case, when you pull up your report, it will have little or no information included in it. To change this, you either need to begin running ads (such as keyword ads from AdWords or other types of ads that are properly tagged), or you need to tag your own ads properly.

In Chapter 8, we discussed tagging and gave you a little preview of how to go about doing it. You can flip back now if you need to. It's okay. Really. We'll wait.

Finished? Good. If you need more information on tagging your campaigns, you can find it in the Help section of Google Analytics by searching for "tagging."

So, exactly how do you use this Ad Versions report? Well, it starts with tagging your advertising campaigns (which is why you just flipped back for a refresher). For the comparison to work, you have to tag two different ad campaigns in different ways to distinguish them.

Specifically, what will change for each advertising campaign are the tag elements: `utm_source`, `utm_medium`, `utm_term`, `utm campaign`, and `utm_content`. Some but not all of these were mentioned in Chapter 8. And you don't have to use all of them — use only what applies to your specific needs. If you were tagging, say, to track your newsletter name, you might change `utm source` to `utm source=MyNewsletter`. If you wanted to tag keywords for a specific ad, you might make it `utm term=running+shoes`.

You might also need to use the `utm_campaign` tag to compare different marketing campaigns. For example, if you're using a 15-percent-off coupon in e-mail to drive traffic to your site and you also have a link in an industry newsletter, you can use the `utm_campaign` tag to compare the effectiveness of each campaign. That information can then be used to determine which campaign should have more capital investment based on the return on that investment.

Before you start muttering to yourself about the complexities of tagging, we have good news. Google Analytics provides a URL Builder tool, shown in Figure 20-6, that makes it easy to create the tagging URLs. To find the URL Builder tool, search Help once you've logged in to your Analytics account.

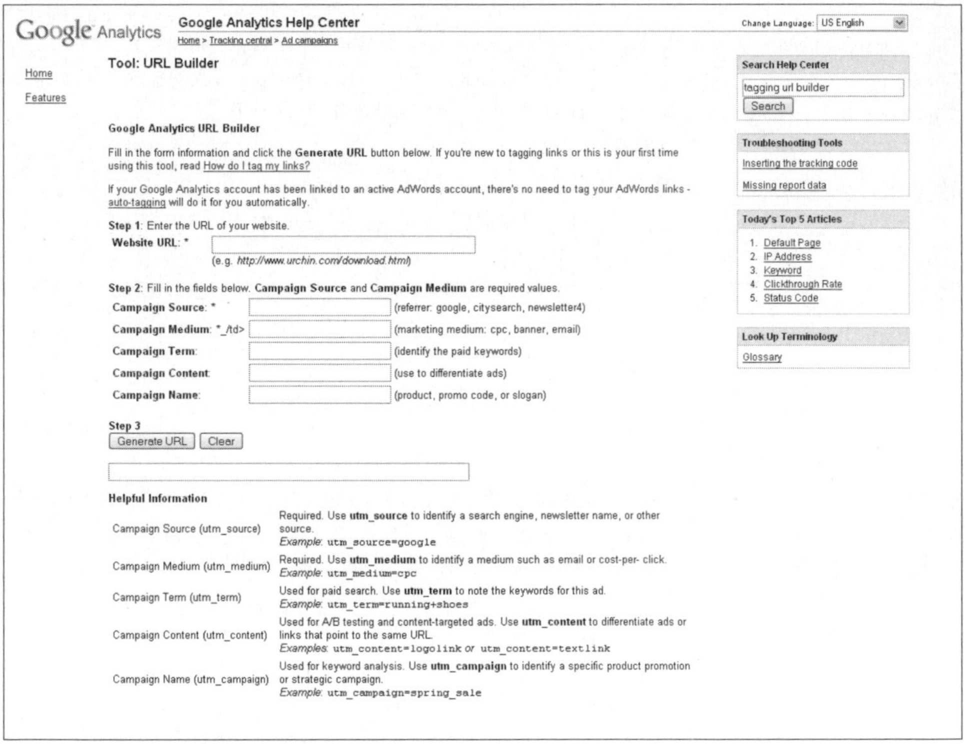

Figure 20-6: The URL Builder tool helps create tags for different campaigns.

Once you have the tag, all you have to do is insert it in your campaign. For example, if you're using two different types of links, you would generate a URL for each link and replace the direct URL (in a form such as `http://www.example.com`) with the tagged URL:

```
http://www.JerriLedford.com/?utm_source=Newsletter&utm_medium=li
nk&utm_content=textlink&utm_campaign=exampe_ad
```

NOTE Remember that AdWords automatically tags the source and medium of your keyword campaigns. However, you may want to add an `utm_term` addition to your keywords to track specific, paid keywords. This also can be done in the URL Builder tool.

One more note about tagging your ads. Remember that these tags are very sensitive. They translate *exactly* what you tell them to translate, so if you are inconsistent in naming your campaigns (Spring-Sale versus Spring_Sale), Analytics will read that as two different campaigns.

With the information that you garner from comparing one ad campaign to another (or from comparing different ads within the same campaign), you can analyze the performance of those campaigns or ads. That information, in turn, lets you know where to invest more or less of your advertising dollars, based on the results those campaigns generate.

Tracking ad versions isn't difficult, but it does require a little more effort than simply tracking your web site. Use the URL Builder tool, however, and you'll be tracking different advertising campaigns in no time at all.

All Reports: Content

One of the most important elements of any web site is the content on that site. And content optimization is no easy task. It requires an understanding of what content draws users and how they interact with that content.

To truly understand how content optimization affects your site, however, you need some metrics to tell you how each aspect of the content performs. Google provides some of the most commonly used metrics, such as Top Content and a Site Overlay that lets you see how each link on your site performs.

This section of the book also contains additional reports that illustrate important content metrics. In the pages that follow, we walk you through each of the content reports and tell you how to use them to improve your web site.

CHAPTER 21

Content Overview

How does the content on your web site affect your traffic patterns? Does it lead users to the site? Does it drive users to make a purchase, sign up for a newsletter, or fill out a form that you have on the site? Is there content on your site that performs better than you expect it to?

These are all questions that the reports in this section can answer. The content on your site — the content users land on when they come to your site — plays a big role in how long users stay and how much deeper into the site they go.

If you have an e-commerce site, there might be a natural driver that pushes users deeper into your site. Maybe users come to your site because you have a great price on laptop computers. But how is the content on your site going to direct users once they land there? If done well, you might be able to drive additional sales or create return users.

The only way you're going to know if your content is done well is to analyze the metrics associated with how users *use* your site. The reports in this section will show you exactly that. And what you do with that information determines just how useful it is for you.

Content Overview

The Content Overview report, like all of the overviews that you've seen to this point, is an overall look at your different content metrics. The report, shown in Figure 21-1, gives you a quick glance at the number of page views, unique views, and bounce rate. There's also information here on Top Content, which represents the most visited pages on your site.

In addition to the basic information that's included on this report, you can also click the links under page views and Top Content to dig deeper into these reports. The only report that's duplicated on this page is the **Site Overlay**, which you'll look at later in this chapter.

The links on the right side of the page (labeled in Figure 21-1) may be of special interest. These links take you deeper into the data that's available about your content and different segmentation views. Each report is unique and offers a different view of the content data that has been collected.

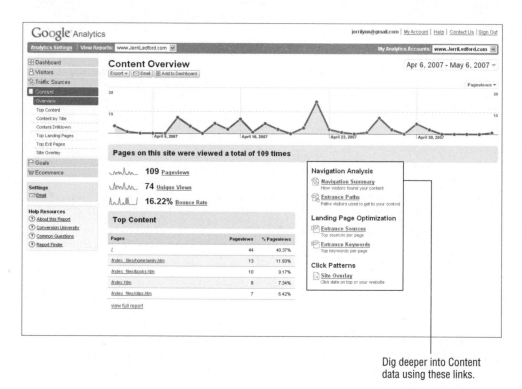

Dig deeper into Content data using these links.

Figure 21-1: The Content Overview shows the most important data on your content.

Navigation Summary

The Navigation Summary report, shown in Figure 21-2, shows you how often the given web page was an Entrance page, what pages were viewed *before* this page, how many visitors left your site from this page, and what pages were viewed *after* this page.

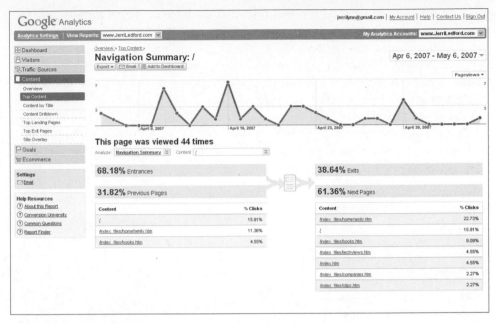

Figure 21-2: The Navigation Summary shows how the page fits into the path users took through your site.

By default, the page that is shown is your main web page (your index page or the page that ends with /). You can, however, change this to reflect the navigation summary of any page on your web site. Use the **Content** drop-down menu, shown in Figure 21-3, to select a different page on your site or to search for a page if it is not included in the drop-down menu.

You are also not limited to just navigation data. You can choose to view the data through other standard filters as well:

- Content Detail
- Entrance Paths
- Entrance Sources
- Entrance Keywords

These filters are available through the **Analyze** menu, shown in Figure 21-4, and they allow you to see different details for the pages of your web site.

Once you have these reports, this information can give you a picture of how your users come into, navigate through, and then leave your web site. It also provides additional detail about the way that users *use* your site. This all gives you a clearer picture of what works for your visitors. It will also point out, in no uncertain terms, which pages *don't* work.

Content drop-down menu

Figure 21-3: Examine navigation data for any page on the site using Content menu.

Analyze different data.

Figure 21-4: Use the Analyze menu to see navigation data that's filtered differently.

You can then use this information to further hone your page styles and content until you have pages that are successful throughout your site. Combining what you learn from analyzing this data with what you learn from analyzing other data (such as the e-commerce data or goals data) should give you a clear picture of how users use your web site.

Entrance Paths

An Entrance Path is quite literally the page on which a user enters your site. For example, most web sites have a high entrance path that starts at the page that ends with a slash (/) as in the following example: `http://www.JerriLedford .com/`. Another frequent entrance page is labeled `/index.html` (as in our example: `http://www.JerriLedford.com/index.html`). In both cases, this is where users jump on the page, and in both cases, it's usually because they type the web site address directly into the address bar of their web browser, though in some cases, the number of visits to these main pages can be attributed to search engine referrals.

The Entrance Path report, shown in Figure 21-5, illustrates where visitors come on to your site and where they end up. Each page listed can be selected to show information that is specific to that page.

This information helps you figure out where your visitors enter and exit your site, but it also does more. For example, if the majority of your visitors come into your main page (the page denoted by /) and also leave from that page, what does that tell you?

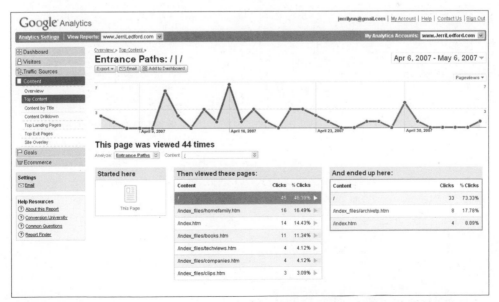

Figure 21-5: Use the Entrance Path report to find where visitors started and ended.

To me, it would say there are a high number of bounces on that main page, and that it needs to be made more reflective of the topic you want users to see. So if your site is showing as a search result for ice skates when you actually sell skating fiction, you need to make it much clearer that your site is about content related to skating, not about ice skates as products.

Entrance Sources

Entrance Sources differ from Entrance Paths in that sources are where the traffic comes from and paths are where the traffic lands. The Entrance Sources report, shown in Figure 21-6, shows what sources sent traffic to each page of your site. By default, the data for the main site page is displayed, but you can change that page using the **Content** drop-down menu.

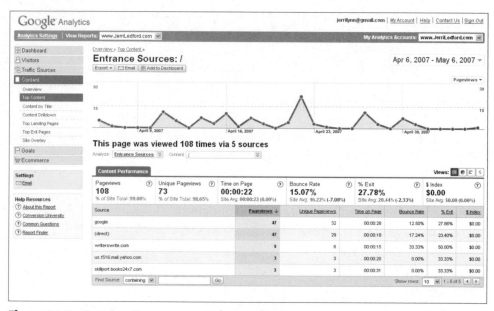

Figure 21-6: Entrance Sources report shows where users came to each page from.

This information is extremely valuable when you're running marketing campaigns that each point to a different landing page. When you know what those sources are, you can compare the sources shown on this report to find out how effective your marketing campaign is. Or how ineffective, as is sometimes the case.

Entrance Keywords

The Entrance Keywords report, shown in Figure 21-7, is similar to the Entrance Sources report, except that here you see which *keywords* led visitors to your site. This information is helpful when you're looking at the keywords that seem to work for your site. For example, if you find that the keywords included in the top positions on this site are organic keywords, then you know that you're unnecessarily spending money on paid keywords that aren't as effective as you need them to be.

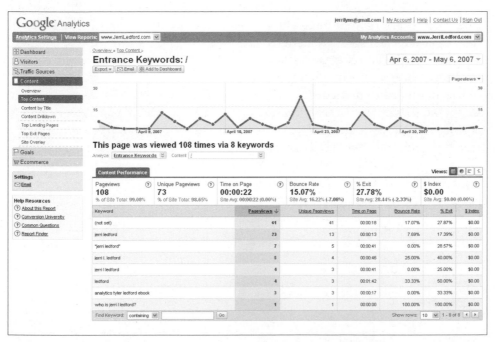

Figure 21-7: The Entrance Keywords report shows which words bring in the most traffic.

Site Overlay

The Site Overlay report is a report that shows you navigational information, directly on your web page. For now, it's enough for you to know that this report can give you detailed information about how users click through your content. For more detailed information about this report, including screenshots that show you what it looks like, keep reading. It's covered near the end of this chapter.

Top Content

In many cases, the top content on your site will be your front page — also called your index page. This is the first page that users who type your URL directly into the address bar on their web browsers will usually see. But that's not so in every case. If you're running a marketing campaign that pushes users to a page that's deeper in the site, *that* could be your top content. The only way to know for sure is to look at the Top Content report shown in Figure 21-8.

In this report, content pages are listed by the most frequent visits. You'll also find measurements for the number of page views for each page, the average time users spent on that page, the percentage of exits, and the value index of that page. This last measurement (the value index) helps you see what content is leading visitors to goal conversions, and this will come in handy later when you're tracking your funnel-navigation process.

Another measurement on this report to which you want to pay special attention is the percentage of exits for each page. If you have a page that seems to have an unusually high number of exits, the content on that page could be the reason visitors are leaving. If you can use this report to locate the pages where you're losing visitors, you can change or update the pages in an effort to improve "stickiness."

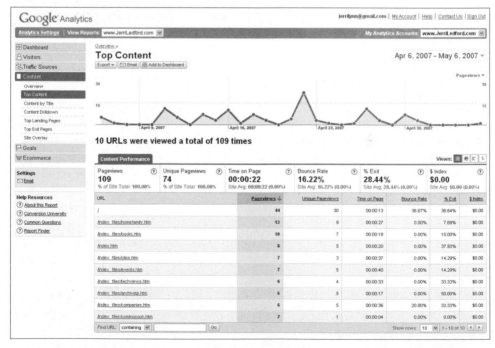

Figure 21-8: The Top Content report shows pages users came to directly most often.

You may also want to make note of the average time users spend on each page. There's no guideline that says users should spend X amount of time on each page, but obviously some pages (such as content pages) will require more time to view than others. You have to figure a baseline for your site using the measurements available to you. Then, if you decide that, on average, users should spend a minute and a half to two minutes on each page, and you find you have a page (or pages) on which users spend less than a minute, you know you should analyze the page to find out why users are clicking through (or worse, exiting at) that page.

Of course, each of these measurements alone is only valuable for that measurement. When you look at them as a whole, however, you begin to see a larger picture — such as how many users are exiting a page where they spend only 15 seconds or how many users are clicking through a page after two minutes to make a large purchase or complete some other goal you've established.

These traffic patterns give you insight into the minds of your users. Use them to improve goal conversions and sales through your site, and to funnel visitors to the pages that you consider most important in reaching those conversions or sales.

Content by Title

Another way to view the traffic to your site is with the Content by Title report. This report, shown in Figure 21-9, shows the value of your web pages by page title, using the same measurements as before: page views, unique views, average time spent on the page, bounce rate, percentage of exits that occur on that page, and the value of goal conversions that result from that page.

It's not at all unusual to see a page that not only has the highest number of page visits but also the highest number of exits. It's just naturally the way visitors tend to come and go from your site. However, if you happen to notice that a page with a low number of visits has the highest percentage of exits, you know that there's likely some kind of problem with that page and it needs to be changed or updated in some way.

The most important factor for you to know about this report is that page titles are determined by HTML titles. In the design of your page, there was probably some titling algorithm that set the HTML tagging and titling for the page. It's also possible that you set it manually. Either way, that's what is used to classify the page for this report. Here's the catch: If you happen to have multiple pages with the same HTML titles, those pages are going to be counted as a single page for measurement purposes. (It's possible to tinker with the HTML to separate them, but your skills have to be pretty high.)

Figure 21-9: The Content by Title report shows content metrics by title, not URL.

So while these measurements are useful, they can be a little deceiving in their presentation. However, as long as you remember that each of these measurements could feature more than one page, you should be able to use the information to determine where you need to change or improve your content.

Content Drilldown

How is your web site designed? Do you have pages that have subpages? Maybe you have a page on your site that includes articles about issues related to the products on your site. And from that page, there are links to past articles. Those past articles are probably located on subpages. So how do you know if those pages are of any value to your site at all?

Another consideration to keep in mind when looking at this report is the pages of dynamic content that might exist on your web site. When you think of dynamic content, you probably think of things such as articles or blogs — content that changes frequently. But that has nothing to do with dynamic content here. Most blogs are actually static pages — pages pre-built and stored in final form on the web server — that were created on submission of individual entries.

Dynamic content refers to pages where one file may be associated with multiple pages of content. Dynamic pages are built on-the-fly with a technology such as PHP, ASP, or Java Server Pages. These technologies use variables in the URL, called page-query terms, to dictate what content goes together to form the finished page. Site-search and catalogue functions are generally dynamic pages. Other sites implement dynamic pages for various other reasons.

Dynamic pages have unique challenges as far as tracking because what differentiates one dynamic page from another is not the file name. It's the query term or combination of terms.

The Content Drilldown report, shown in Figure 21-10, shows how each of your pages performs, whether that page is considered dynamic content or static content (which is content that rarely, if ever, changes).

For every page that you're shown in this report, there is a set of measurements that includes the unique views and pages, the average time spent on the page, the percent of visitors who exited from that page, and the value of pages that are commonly visited before a high-value conversion during that visit. The conversion could be a sale or another type of goal conversion, depending on how you have your conversion goals set up. You can also click each page title to see more detailed information about the visits to that page.

The purpose of this information is much the same as the purpose of the Top Content report. Use the information to determine which pages need to be changed or updated, and which pages work well as indicated by visits, goal conversions, and the value of those conversions.

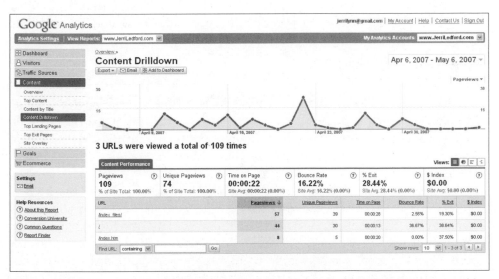

Figure 21-10: The Content Drilldown report shows how valuable subpages are.

Top Landing Pages

As we've discussed before, a bounce occurs when a visitor arrives on a page and immediately leaves. It differs from an exit, which refers just to the page from which the visitor left the site, possibly after visiting other pages. A bounce means "Did not visit another page. Did not collect $200." For the purposes of this report (and only this report), a visit, a visitor, and a page view are pretty much all the same thing (subject to the caveats about counting unique visitors and length-of-visit limitation discussed in Chapters 2 and 3).

The Top Landing Pages report, shown in Figure 21-11, illustrates how often visitors entered your page through a specific page and how often they bounced right back off your site from that page.

Bounce rates can show how effective a particular page is. For example, in Figure 21-11, the top landing page on the site, (which happens to be the main page) also has the most bounces.

The bad news is that nearly 37 percent of the visitors who arrive on this page also leave immediately. The goods news is at least some of those people were looking for the information on the front page of the web site. Having found what they wanted, they left. That's not a bad thing. Giving visitors what they're looking for is what a content site is supposed to do.

However, the main page also has another specific goal — to lure visitors deeper into the site. And the bounce rate reflected in this report shows that's not happening in about 37 percent of the cases. This could indicate that your site is classified wrong in search results, which could mean you need to retag the site, or it could mean that you need to reconsider how you see your site versus how visitors see it.

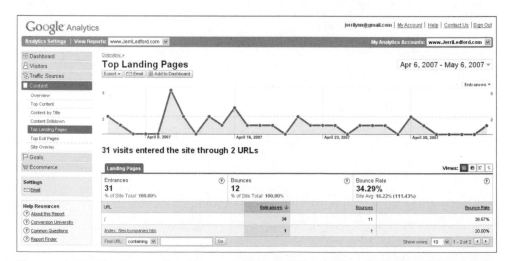

Figure 21-11: The Top Landing Pages report shows where visitors landed — and bounced.

If we haven't made this point enough, it's important to remember that you can't look at Google Analytics' metrics in isolation from other information about your business. As capable as Google Analytics is, it's still a medium-tier product. It won't function like a high-end (read "expensive") analytics package. You're going to have to use your head when applying data — such as bounce rates — to your site. Analytics won't do everything for you, and sometimes understanding what the metrics mean requires a little experimentation on your part.

Top Exit Pages

While knowing where visitors arrive is important, so is knowing where they're leaving from. You'll note that it's fairly common for your busiest pages overall to also be busiest from the entrances and exits standpoint. In Figure 21-12, you can see this effect.

Unlike the Entrance Pages, you can't assume that each page view on the Exits report is a visitor. A visitor could load the page, then wander off deeper into the site and eventually wander back. However, because you can assume each page view is a visit in the Entrance Pages report, you can do interesting things with the Exits report. You can isolate how many visits ended on a particular page when it's not the first and last page visited.

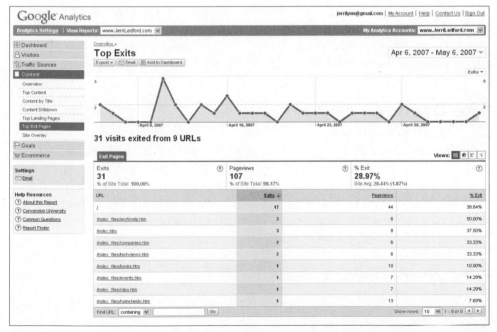

Figure 21-12: The Top Exit Pages report shows from which pages visitors leave most often.

For example, SkateFic's index page is ranked number two in exits and in bounces. Each entrance is a page view, so subtract Entrances from Pageviews for that line. So, if SkateFic has 3,575 page views and 2,086 entrances, the equation would look like this:

```
3575 - 2086 = 1489
```

What this tells you is how many page views came from visitors who had come in from other parts of the site. Now, assume that SkateFic has 1,243 bounces and 1,824 exits.

Technically speaking, bounces are exits, so subtract Bounces from Exits to remove duplicate exit counts.

```
1824 - 1243 = 581
```

This indicates how many of the visits entering from other parts of the site left once they hit this page. That in itself is an interesting metric, but it means more if you translate the two new figures to a percentage.

```
581/1489 = .39 or 39%
```

So overall, while 51 percent of page views mark the end of a visit and 60 percent of new visitors leave from here immediately, only 39 percent of visits that include other pages leave from here.

In English?

Once visitors get into the site, they are much less likely to leave from this page. For the home page (which SkateFic.com is), it may not mean much, but this kind of additional analysis can be helpful for other pages such as those involved in the sales process.

Site Overlay

Sometimes it's easier to understand a complex set of metrics if you draw a picture. That's exactly what the Site Overlay is. Each page of your web site has an overlay. On the overlay are small bar graphs for each link on the page. If you click the graphs, you get an overview of information for that link. But the point is that you can see at a glance how the various links on a single page are performing compared to one another.

Figure 21-13 shows the Site Overlay for Jerri's home page. As you can see, most of the small bars show little or no activity.

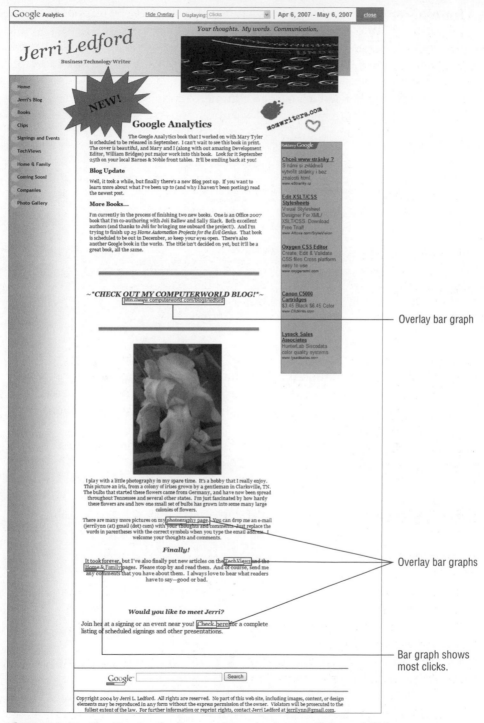

Figure 21-13: The Site Overlay Report shows how many clicks each link gets.

However, one of the bars, shown in Figure 21-14, seems to be responsible for a majority of the traffic. And when you hold your pointer over that bar, you get a quick view of some of the most important metrics for that link. That view includes a measure of the quality of those clicks — the value of the link based on average revenue generated per click. It will appear in all conditions where a click from the designated link led to goal or e-commerce conversion for the time range selected. The rate of conversion for this link is non-existent. So as you might expect, the quality rating for the clicks is pretty much nonexistent, too.

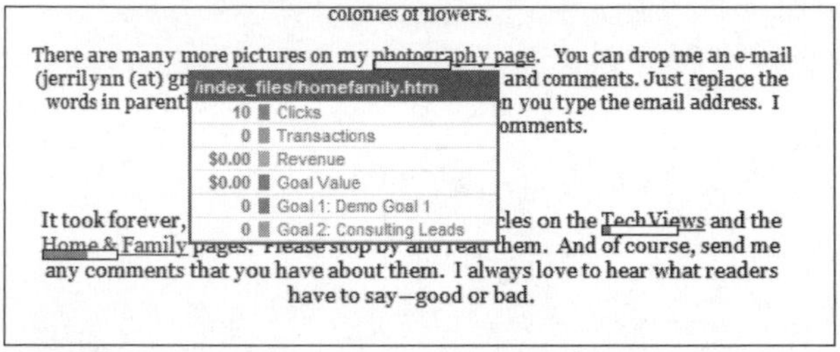

Figure 21-14: The quality of your links is displayed in the pop-up box.

At any rate, there are 414 clicks from this page on that link and the one to the same URL in the text menu at the bottom. About 11 percent of the traffic that comes to this page clicks that link, and during the visit some small percentage of those visitors completes goals two and three. There are no transactions from these clicks during this period.

The Average Score is zero as well. When a click results in a high-value conversion, such as a purchase, a lead, or a contact, the links in the chain to that conversion get points. Over the time period, those points add up and are averaged out to get the score. The higher the average score, the better the link is working toward achieving your conversion goals.

CAVEAT WEBMASTER: SITE OVERLAY IS ITCHY GLITCHY

At present, the Site Overlay has some glitches. Sometimes the small graphs overlap each other — and the all-important links you need to navigate the Site Overlay! The graphs also appear somewhat below and to the left of the link. If the link is a graphic, the graph for that link may overlap another graphic, making it somewhat tricky to see which link owns the graph.

Site Overlay doesn't always work the way you'd expect. And that includes the fact that it doesn't work with a variety of page technologies including:

- Javascript links
- CSS content
- Flash navigation
- Downloadable files (.pdf)
- Outbound links
- Frames
- Auto redirects
- Links using the deprecated `target= "_blank"` attribute

We also noticed some problems with the particular PHP templating scheme that SkateFic.com uses. It took about an hour to kludge in code to accommodate of requesting `/serials/tsts/index.p` the Site Overlay because instead of requesting `/index.php`, it was cURLing, or repeating, `/index.php/index.php`, and instead of `hp`, it wanted `/index.php/serials/tsts/index.php`. This caused all kinds of PHP warnings because a part of the page could not be found in the file structure.

Also, if two or more links go to the same URL, the information from those links will be aggregated. There are separate graphs for each link, but they all show the same aggregated information. This is because, short of tagging each link, there's no way to say which link on a page the user clicked.

Goals and goal setting in Analytics can be confusing. All of the information you've seen leading up to this point has been about goal conversions and how many are happening on your site. And back in Chapter 7 you learned about setting goals.

Now it's time to put those goals to work — to actually achieve the goal conversions that you've only considered at this point. This part of the book shows you just how important goal conversions are, and how users move from one point to another on their path to achieving goal conversions.

Ultimately, all your web site efforts are probably about goal conversions. And this part helps you understand the conversions that are happening on your site and how to achieve more conversions where possible.

CHAPTER 22

Goals Overview

Creating goals. Goal tracking. Goal conversions. Goals, Goals, Goals. You think you've heard enough about them already. But you haven't. There's more yet to add to the larger picture.

Goals and all the activities that go along with them are important to the success of your web site. It all comes down to what you want from that site. So in this chapter, we're going to look a little more at goals and what you can accomplish by using them. You may see a few things that you saw back in Chapter 7. And you'll see terms that have been used repeatedly throughout the book. But there's some new stuff here, too, so don't skip ahead. This is important information, and if you miss it you may find that your site doesn't work the way you want it to work.

Goals Overview

The Goals Overview report, shown in Figure 22-1, gives you a quick glance at some of the most important metrics in goal tracking and conversions.

> **NOTE** The Goals section of Google Analytics may prove elusive to you. If you don't see a Goals section in your report menu, it's because you have not yet set up your goals. Once you set up the first goal, the goals section becomes visible and available.

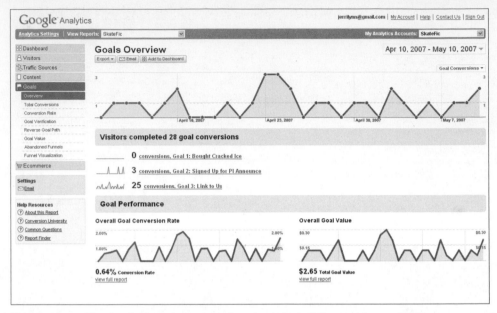

Figure 22-1: The Goals Overview report is a snapshot of the metrics available.

On this overview page, you'll find a graphical representation of the number of goal conversions that were completed by your visitors for each goal you have established for your site. You can have up to four goals for a profile (Google calls a web site a profile, and you can have more than one profile for each web site, so if you need more than four goals, you can set up another profile for your site).

Each goal on the report is a link to a Goal Detail report, as shown in Figure 22-2. This report provides information on the total conversions, conversion rate, and abandonment rate for each goal. Each of these metrics links to another report (Total Conversions, Conversion Rate, and Abandonment Rate), all of which will be covered in more depth later in this chapter.

You'll also notice there are links on the right side of the page that lead to further data analysis. Again, each of these links leads to another report, including the following:

- Languages
- Network Locations
- User Defined
- Browsers
- Operating Systems
- Browser and Operating Systems

Figure 22-2: The Goal Detail report adds details on conversions and abandonment.

- Screen Colors
- Screen Resolutions
- Java Support
- Flash
- Map Overlay
- Goal Funnel

The only one of these reports that has not yet been covered is the Goal Funnel report. It's covered in much more detail later in this chapter, however, so we won't go into it here. (If you want to flip back and review the other reports, you'll find them in Chapters 12, 15, 16, and 17.)

The Goal Overview also contains the Overall Goal Conversion Rate, which leads you to the Conversion Rate report. The Overall Goal Value leads to the Goal Value report.

The purpose of the Goals Overview is to give you a quick glance at some of the most accessed metrics associated with goals and conversion rates. That's not to say all of these metrics will necessarily be meaningful to you. Perhaps they are, but there are other metrics that are *more* meaningful. Unfortunately, as with the other Overview pages, this one cannot be altered to show the metrics you prefer to have shown.

Total Conversions

Conversions are the number of goals that have been reached by your site visitors. And those goals can be anything that you want them to be, whether they have a monetary value or not.

So what's the purpose of the Total Conversions report, shown in Figure 22-3?

It's nothing more than a quick glance at the number of conversions that you had for each goal during a given time period.

And why is it important?

If you're not getting goal conversions, there's a problem somewhere. Or if you're getting goal conversions but they're low, you can see this at a glance and then dig deeper into the information in later reports to find out why you aren't getting these conversions.

If you happen to be getting a very high number of goal conversions or an unbalanced number of goal conversions across all your goals, that's important information, too. Either of these cases should lead you to investigate what's working and, if necessary, what's not.

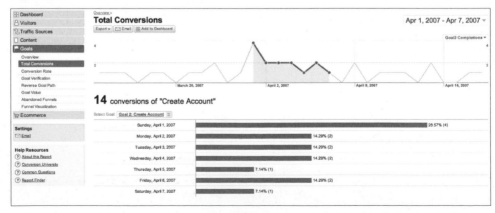

Figure 22-3: The Total Conversions report shows how many goal conversions occur each day.

As you investigate, the question becomes, "Are my conversion numbers good?" And if they're not, how do you increase those conversions?

There may not be an easy answer to those questions. How many conversions is enough? Obviously, you'd like every visitor who comes to your site to reach a conversion goal. But 100 percent conversion is probably unrealistic. So you have to decide what your target goal is. Then, if your numbers aren't showing the goal being met, it's time to try something different. Maybe users aren't finding the link to sign up. Or maybe the newsletter/announcement list isn't portrayed in a way that users think will interest them. This is where you need to decide what's enough and what needs to be done if what you have doesn't reach that criterion.

The problem with establishing goals (as you may remember from earlier goal discussions) is that it is not always easy to know what the right goal is. If you're looking at three different reports, you'll quickly see that not every goal is created equal. Some will naturally be more successful than others. However, if you find that you've created a goal that doesn't result in conversions, you know something is fundamentally wrong with that goal. Something needs to be changed. You're challenged with figuring out just what it is. Fortunately, some of the other reports in this section may help on that front.

Conversion Rate

In the Conversion Rate report, shown in Figure 22-4, each of your goal conversions in any given day — remember that you can have up to four goals per web site profile — is shown as a percentage. You can quickly see what percentage of your visitors is reaching the page that you've established for each goal.

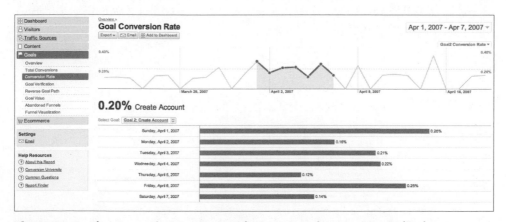

Figure 22-4: The Conversion Rate report shows conversion percentages by day.

You may notice that this report is very similar in appearance to the Total Conversions report. In fact, it contains much the same information, but presented differently. Where the Total Conversions report showed you the number of conversions for each goal, this report shows you the percentage of change in goals over the designated time frame.

The information is presented differently so you can see whether the number of goal conversions is increasing or decreasing without having to flip back and forth between different reports.

You even use the information in much the same way as the information from the Total Conversions report. However, here you can also use the information to see whether conversion for one of your goals is increasing or decreasing. If you can correlate that information with any changes that you've made during the specific time period shown, you can attribute those changes to the difference and either repair the damage you've done or use what you've learned to improve other goal conversions.

Goal Verification

When you set a goal for your site, it's possible to set a directory as the goal page. If you've ever done that, have you wondered how many goal conversions from that group of pages are actually attributable to each page? The Goal Verification report, shown in Figure 22-5, illustrates exactly which of those pages is responsible for goal conversions. It gives you a measurement for the goal pages viewed by users.

So how is this report useful? Well, in truth, it's not all that useful if your goal is on the front page of your web site. However, if you have a directory of pages as your goal (for example, you want people to reach a specific category of products, each with its own page), you will eventually want to know which of those pages within the directory led to the goal conversion. This is where you'll find that information.

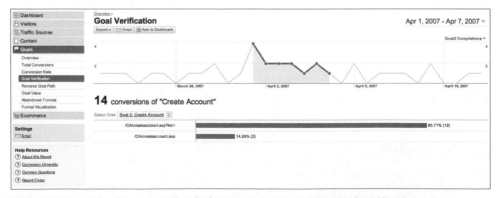

Figure 22-5: View the pages that led to a conversion in the Goal Verification report.

Once you have the information, you can use it to determine which pages within a directory are the most useful or most valuable. That information can, in turn, be used to gain more conversions from those pages or to improve conversions on other pages.

Reverse Goal Path

We've already established that not every visitor is going to use the same path that you've designated as a funnel to reach a goal conversion. And the path those users take can hold valuable clues as to how they navigate through your site. This is especially helpful if all users, even those who don't navigate through your funnel, reach a goal conversion through a specific page.

The Reverse Goal Path report, shown in Figure 22-6, shows you exactly how users reach your goal conversion pages.

You can also use this report to find out exactly what pages are required for a user to feel comfortable making a conversion.

The Reverse Goal Path is not limited to the defined funnel navigation that you laid out when you created your goals. That makes this report valuable for learning the movement patterns of your users and for further refining your funnel navigation.

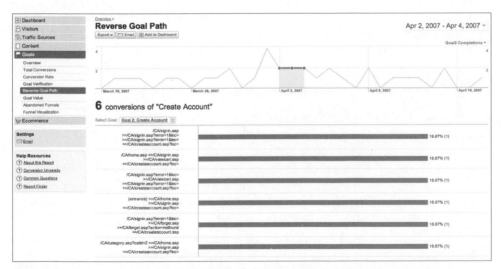

Figure 22-6: Reverse Goal Path shows how users reached goal conversion pages.

Goal Value

The Goal Value report, shown in Figure 22-7, illustrates the value of each of your goals, on a daily basis. Now if you run an e-commerce site, a goal value should be very easy to define. However, if you run a content site, you could find that defining a value for your goals might be a little harder. There was a description of how to come to a reasonable value for your goals in Chapter 9.

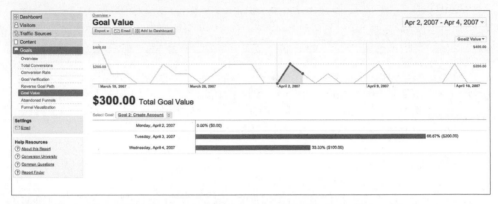

Figure 22-7: The Goal Value report shows value of goal conversions each day.

The goal value helps you to see how valuable your goal conversions are. If you have a goal conversion that's less valuable than you projected it would be, then you may need to consider redefining the goal, evaluating the navigation path, or changing the way the goal is marketed.

It's not an exact science if you have a content site, but at least it gives you a monetary value with which to work.

Abandoned Funnels

Funnel navigation is the process by which you gently nudge, or funnel, your site visitors to a conversion page. You might think of it as taking site visitors by the hand and leading them through the site, one page at a time. On each page, you give them a reason to want to go to the next, and then the next until they've reached the conversion page. At that point, the objective is to have built enough desire in the visitors that the process becomes a goal conversion. Unfortunately, users often abandon the process, a reaction that's called an abandoned funnel. The Abandoned Funnels report shows you exactly what percentage of people who start in a funnel navigation process abandon it. The report, shown in Figure 22-8, gives you a clear picture of how often your funnel process is ineffective.

When you view this report, one thing you need to remember is that a funnel is simply an indicator of how *you* think your visitors will navigate through your site to reach a specific goal. You can require that users hit certain pages, but even then not everyone thinks the same, so you could be missing out on conversions because you think differently than your users.

In short, this is a tool, nothing more. Use it to figure out where you're losing users along their journey to goal conversions. If you think that your users should hit a specific page as they make their way through purchasing a specific item, but they don't hit that page, view the pages they do hit and learn why their behavior is different from what you would expect it to be. That information will help you better understand your site users, and then you can create pages and content that specifically meet the needs of users.

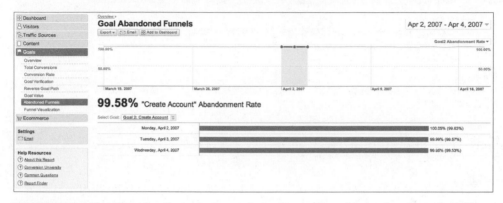

Figure 22-8: The Abandon Funnels report shows how often visitors abandon a funnel before conversion.

Funnel Visualization

Here's where things start to get a little bit interesting. Throughout these pages, you've seen information about defining a navigation funnel to lead users to a goal page. If you've been scratching your head and thinking, "How do I do this?" you're about to have your question answered.

First, however, let's recap a bit. A funnel is a page or group of pages that lead users to the page that you have established as a goal. So if one of your goals is for users to sign up for your newsletter, the pages that lead users to that goal would be the funnel.

There's a bit of philosophy to remember here. Water poured into a funnel has no choice of where to go. But visitors in your navigation funnel do have a choice, even if it's only to get irritated and leave your site. So the purpose of your funnel usually isn't to force visitors anywhere. Rather, it's to see in a more sophisticated way how they're moving around on your site and how you can make them more comfortable and ease their travel. And in the process maybe steer them a little toward your goals. Think of college-campus planners watching where students wear out the grass and then building sidewalks there.

When you first set up a goal for your site, you probably saw a page similar to the one in Figure 22-9. This is where you enter your goal information. But you may also notice that there's a segment of this page (it's indicated in Figure 22-9) titled Defined Funnel (optional). This is where you'll enter the navigation path for your funnel.

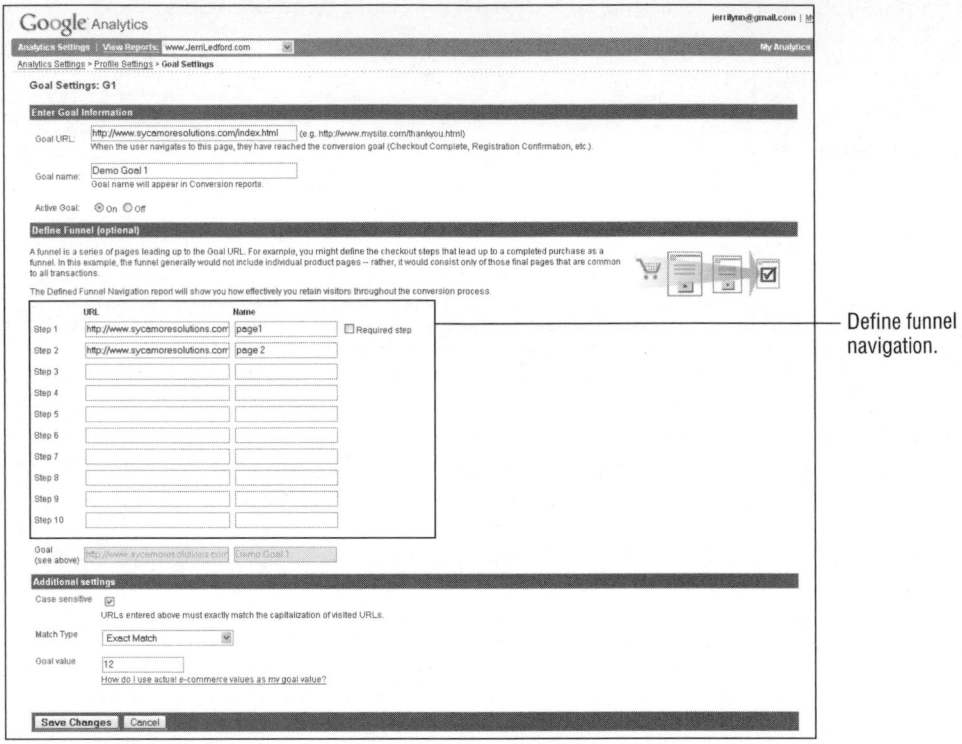

Figure 22-9: You can specify a funnel when you set up a goal for your site.

As you're entering this information, you have the option to make pages in the funnel navigation path required for the goal to be considered a conversion. Use these pages sparingly; otherwise, you'll end up with goal conversions that don't appear to be conversions because users didn't hit the required pages. However, if the user *must* go through a specific page to reach a goal conversion, you should include that as a required page.

Also, toward the bottom of the page where you're defining your funnel navigation, you'll see there is a text box for a goal value. If you have an e-commerce site, including this goal value is easy. What's the value of your product (or the product the user needs to purchase to reach a goal conversion)? That's your goal value.

But what if you don't operate an e-commerce site? Then can you enter a goal value? Of course you can. The fact that you're not selling a product doesn't mean your goals have no monetary value. If, for example, you're a consultant and your newsletter brings in new clients, the value of your newsletter goal conversion might be the value of one hour of your consulting time. You'll have to determine how much that goal conversion is worth, but once you do, you can place a specific monetary value on your goal conversions.

Now, back to this Funnel Visualization report. Once you've defined the funnel navigation for one (or all) of your goals, within a few days you can begin to generate the report. It might look something like the Defined Funnel Navigation report shown in Figure 22-10.

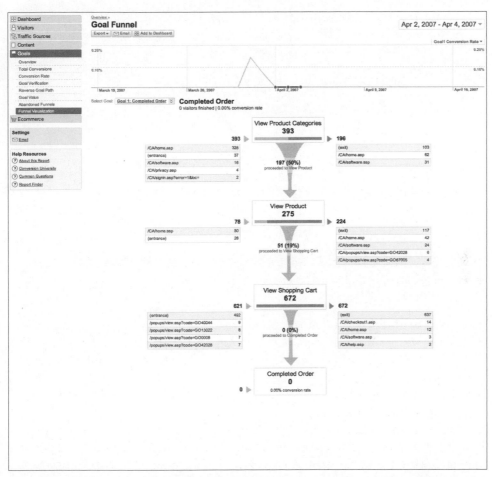

Figure 22-10: The Funnel Visualization report shows how visitors steer through a funnel.

The report illustrates where users enter the navigation process and how they follow the funnel until they either leave the funnel and eventually drop off the site or reach the goal conversion. In some cases, you'll see pages in the report that aren't part of your defined funnel navigation. This might mean you need to reevaluate your funnel navigation. The same is true if you tend to lose users along a specific portion of the funnel navigation, but that's covered more in the next section.

All Reports: E-Commerce

Transactions, revenue, product performance — all these are elements or factors in an e-commerce business. They're also measurements of how successful your e-commerce business is at driving sales.

These measurements are important in helping you track and monitor what works and what doesn't in your e-commerce infrastructure. How many visits does it take before a user makes a purchase? How much time do visitors spend on your site? And most important, how does this information fit with all of the other data that you've examined in Google Analytics?

Your e-commerce measurements can tell you. This section gives you a detailed look at the e-commerce reports included in Google Analytics. Each chapter explains different reports, how those reports function, and how you can use those reports to improve your web site and increase sales.

CHAPTER 23

E-Commerce

Commerce is defined as the buying and selling of goods. On a macroeconomic level, commerce could represent all of the sales within a city, state, or region, but we're not concerned with macroeconomics. Rather, we're concerned with microeconomics — the buying and selling of goods on a specific web site: *your* web site.

Even more specifically, you're probably concerned with how much you're selling from your web site. It's not enough just to know what you're selling, though. You also need to know how those sales happen because when you know, you can duplicate the process.

Google Analytics provides reports that help you understand the circumstances under which your products are sold. For example, do you sell more products on Monday than on any other day of the week? You can know for sure using the reports in this section.

ENABLING E-COMMERCE TRACKING

When you open Google Analytics, you may find that you don't have any e-commerce reports. Don't panic! You're not being denied anything. You just need to enable e-commerce tracking for your account. Follow these steps to do that:

1. Log into Google Analytics. You're taken to the Analytics Settings page.

2. From the list of Website Profiles, find the web site for which you would like to enable e-commerce and then click the edit link. You are taken to the Profile Settings page.

3. The first box on the Profile Settings pages is the Main Website Profile. Click Edit in the upper-right corner of this box to be taken to the Edit Profile Information page.

4. About half-way down the page, there's a setting for E-Commerce Website. Click the radio button next to Yes to enable e-commerce capabilities in Google Analytics.

Enabling e-commerce tracking will make the e-commerce reports available to you, but it won't automatically begin tracking e-commerce information. You also need to add tracking code to your web pages (in much the same way you tagged them for tracking with Google Analytics), or more specifically to your shopping-cart mechanisms. This means additional coding either through a server-side include or another template driver. Or, you can add the code to your HTML by hand.

In some cases, a shopping-cart provider will include a module that contains all of the tracking code needed for e-commerce tracking with Google Analytics (in other words, they do it for you). There are some cart providers (such as Yahoo! and PayPal) that do not, however. In that case, you can find the tracking code in Google's help files (www.google.com/support/googleanalytics/bin/answer.py?answer=55528&query=e-commerce+website&topic=&type). There's also additional information available on our blog at www.google-analytics-blog.com/.

E-Commerce Overview

The first report in the E-commerce section is the E-commerce Overview. You know the drill about overview reports — they're just a quick glance at the top metrics in the section. In the case of the E-commerce Overview, shown in Figure 23-1, the metrics you're viewing are a view of Conversion Rate, Sales, and Top Revenue sources.

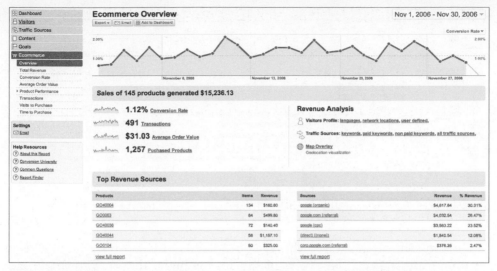

Figure 23-1: View basic e-commerce metrics on the E-commerce Overview report.

Each report section contains links that lead to other reports, where you can find more (and better segmented) data about that specific topic. For example, if you click the **Conversion Rate** link, you're taken to the **Conversion Rate** report (which is covered later in this chapter). And if you click the **Purchased Products** link, it takes you to the **Product Overview** report — as does the **Product** report at the bottom of the page.

The data in this report is your first step in understanding how income is generated on your site. Using this report, you can quickly see what your average order value is and what your top products are. This information can then be leverage to tweak advertising campaigns, or even to change the direction of an advertising campaign that's not showcasing a product well. Or it can be the catalyst to create an advertising campaign for a product that's doing better than expected. Of course, before you make all of those decisions based on this overview report, you might want to look a little closer at the more detailed reports that each section of it leads you to.

Total Revenue

Revenue and transactions are the basis of any commerce reporting. What are your sales, and how many transactions did it take to reach that sales level? The Total Revenue report, shown in Figure 23-2, illustrates the revenue part of that equation.

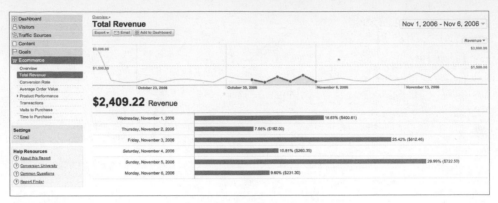

Figure 23-2: View revenues by day in the Total Revenue report.

The top chart in this report shows your total day-by-day revenue in a very graphic way. The chart lets you quickly see the highs and lows for the cycle that you're tracking. You can also compare date ranges in this report, which gives you the ability to see revenue increases or decreases over time. For example, one of the busiest months of the year for retailers is December. If you want to know how your December this year compares to that of last year, you can use the date ranges feature to quickly see the difference.

A little further down the page is a histogram that shows your transaction values by day, and the average value of those transactions. It, too, is very graphical, enabling you to quickly see where your highs and lows fall. Is one time of month better for sales than another? Or maybe a particular time of week or year is better, or whatever the case may be.

So how do you use this information? Aside from the obvious "quick-glance" format, which you can use to tell quickly where your revenue and transactions stand for the given time period, you can also use it to determine which day of the week the most revenue and transactions are generated.

Use this information over time to find patterns in user purchases and spending, or combine this information with other reports (such as the marketing reports) to learn what's driving customers to your site on a given day.

For example, if you send out a weekly newsletter, compare your revenue report to the Campaigns report for that particular time frame to find out if the newsletter is driving revenue and transactions on your site.

Conversion Rate

Conversion is the measure of how well you do at driving users to complete a transaction on your site. And transactions per visit is the name of this game. The Conversion Rate report, shown in Figure 23-3, illustrates the percentage of visitors that reach a conversion goal in a given day.

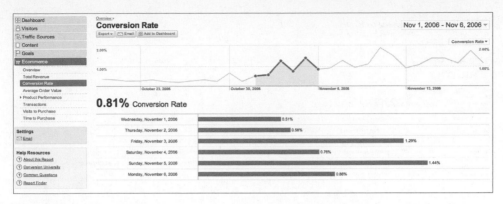

Figure 23-3: The Conversion Rate report tells how many visitors reach conversion goals.

Conversions can be defined in a number of ways. There is, of course, the exchange of money for goods. This is what most people commonly think about when setting conversion goals. You want visitors to buy your products.

However, not all web sites are about selling products, and even some that are have conversion goals that aren't specific to selling products. You can also consider a visitor's signing up for a newsletter, downloading a file, or completing a form as a transaction. It requires that you set that specific action as a transaction and give it a monetary value.

One last aspect of these reports: You also have the same capabilities that you had in the previous reports to change date ranges and compare by date ranges.

Average Order Value

Companies, such as McDonald's, understand the importance of average order value. Higher average order values translate into higher revenue. And even e-commerce sites need to keep track of this metric, especially if that site happens to be the type that changes products or layout on a regular basis.

The Average Order Value report, shown in Figure 23-4, shows you what the average value of transactions is on your site. Whether you have 50 sales or 500, the high-value transactions are interesting, the low-value transactions are depressing, but the average value tells the tale.

With this information, you can watch, over time, as changes in your site affect your revenue. The information is also useful for learning when you need to boost sales programs or increase resources and capabilities (if your average order values are consistently rising). What's more, if you implement a new marketing campaign, the Average Order Value is where you can see just how effective that campaign has been at increasing your order value.

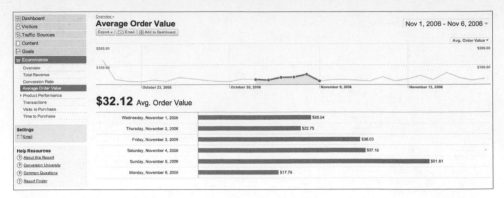

Figure 23-4: The Average Order Value report breaks down average order value over time.

This report really isn't any more detailed than the other reports in this section, but that doesn't mean the information isn't valuable to you. It simply means that you use this information, combined with the other facts that you can learn, about your web site, marketing campaigns, navigational structures, and even product information, to increase the sales efficiency of an e-commerce site or simply the exposure of a content site.

Ultimately, it's all about improvement. Right?

CHAPTER 24

Product Performance

Every item in every store you've ever been in has been strategically placed right where it is so that you'll see the item in a certain light or at a certain time in your visit. It's called product merchandising, and companies spend millions of dollars each year ensuring that product placement is just perfect because it really does matter when it comes to sales and revenue.

Several years ago there was a large craft company with several dozen sizable stores scattered around the southern United States. The company generated several billion dollars in revenue each year and spent millions on ensuring that products were placed within the stores in a way that was intuitive for customers. A large part of every employee's job was to make sure each department conformed to company standards for product placement.

Then a new CEO took over. One of his first orders of business was to change the layout of every store. The problem was that the CEO didn't understand how customers shopped in the stores, and customers were not happy with the new layout. They began shopping elsewhere, and within three years the company went belly-up. It probably wasn't only because the merchandising in the store was off, but that played a part in the overall demise of the stores.

If that CEO had looked at some of the measurements indicating how product merchandising affects revenue, he might have corrected his mistake before it was too late. Measurements like the ones in this chapter are essential to tracking the health of your product merchandising and how it affects revenue.

Google Analytics understands that it's all about the placement, and it supplies the tools you need to monitor the important merchandising metrics for your e-commerce business.

Product performance measurements give you insight into how well the product is being placed, priced, and displayed. In bricks-and-mortar stores, these are the all-important measurements. In e-commerce stores, it's a little trickier. You may need to play with your page placement to find the best place to display your products.

The Product Performance reports in this chapter are designed to help you see how well (or poorly) your products sell. The report shows the number of items sold, the total revenue, the average price, and the average order quantity for each product you sell online.

Additionally, you can click any product category to drill down to specific SKUs (Stock-Keeping Units) for more detailed information about sales.

These numbers are important because poorly performing products could indicate poor placement. If you find that an item that *should* perform well does not, consider moving the item to a different page on your web site or featuring the product more prominently on the front page of the site.

These measurements are also a good indicator of product-specific marketing that you may be conducting. If the marketing is driving sales, you should see an increase in sales for that specific product. If you do not, the marketing may not be performing effectively.

Product Overview

In previous chapters, we've defined *source* as the link or advertisement that leads visitors to your site. Now it's time to look at the purchases those visitors make once they come to your site. The Product Overview report, shown in Figure 24-1, illustrates sales for general categories of products and how much revenue those sales generated.

The report shows the number of items sold in what number of transactions — important information because the more items sold *per transaction* the higher sales tend to be. It also shows product revenue, which is the amount generated by all sales, as well as average price and average quantity. Using these numbers, you can gauge how effective your product selections are, how effective your marketing efforts are (especially if they are geared toward one specific product or category of products), and what kind of return you're making on your product investment.

Additional information about a category of products can be gained by clicking the name of a product category in the product list. This takes you to a product category detail, which includes SKUs that might fall under that product category, as shown in Figure 24-2.

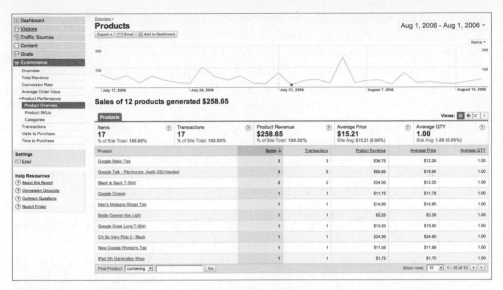

Figure 24-1: The Product Overview report shows sales and revenues over time.

Figure 24-2: Click the name of a product to drill down into additional data about it.

This information can be used to target your sales to your site visitors much more effectively. One way to do that would be to offer a discount coupon, available only to readers of your organization's newsletter. Another way might be to develop an article that features organization tips and recommends the product that's available on your web site. You could then offer the article, free of charge, to other newsletters sent to Internet users. The result should be increased sales from that specific audience.

With this information, as with much of the information supplied by Google Analytics, you can improve your marketing techniques and increase your sales. And just as with the other capabilities in Analytics, you don't necessarily have to have an e-commerce site to take advantage of these measurements. You just need to assign a value to the various goals you have in place. Then, when it all comes together, you still have access to all of the capabilities that Google Analytics has to offer.

Product SKUs

A product SKU is the number by which most retailers (and e-commerce dealers) track the products ordered versus the products sold. In the Product SKUs report, shown in Figure 24-3, the product SKUs that generate revenues for your site are shown along with information about the number of items, transactions, product revenues, average price, and average quantity.

The Product SKUs report enables you to quickly see which of your specific products are producing the most sales. But clicking an SKU number in the Product SKU list leads you to a drilldown report. This SKU detail report provides additional information specific to that SKU. For example, in the SKU report shown in Figure 24-4, you can quickly see how many items were sold in how many transactions, and what the average price of those items are.

Now, why would you want to know the average price? Maybe there has been a sale on that item. Or perhaps some customers have store-wide discount coupons. This report lets you see the average value of each item sold of that SKU. This helps you to keep track of how much you're earning on a product versus how much you've spent acquiring that product.

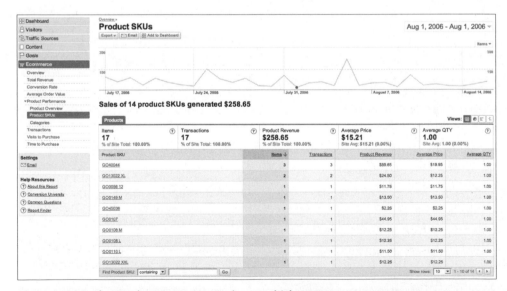

Figure 24-3: The Product SKUs report shows which SKUs generate revenue.

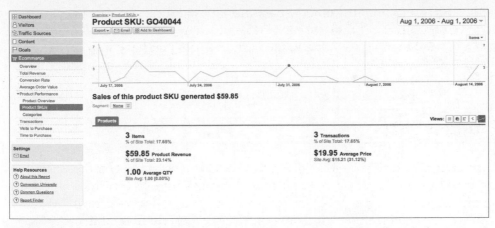

Figure 24-4: The SKU Detail report shows additional drilldown data for that SKU.

The data collected about product SKUs allows you to see, without doubt, which of your products sells best and which sells worst. With that kind of information, you can make adjustments to the amount and type of stock that you make available to site visitors, to capitalize on your return on investment (ROI).

If you're running a content site and don't have "products" to track, you can track content using the SKU report. However, it has to be downloadable content. The tracking won't work if you try to track the content pages. That's what Content reports are for. If you do have downloads on your site, however, you can label each one with a different SKU, and then track those SKUs just as you would track them for an e-commerce site.

Categories

Product categories are another helpful indicator of web site performance and product merchandising. For example, if you have two categories of products on your site — racing memorabilia and sports memorabilia — knowing which of the categories performs the best is essential to understanding how you should display those products.

If the racing memorabilia are selling better, you may decide to feature those products more prominently and increase articles about race car drivers or racing teams. If you really wanted to increase visitor interaction with the site, you could add a quiz or game related to racing.

The Products Categories report, shown in Figure 24-5, gives you the measurements that show which category of products on your site is generating the most revenue.

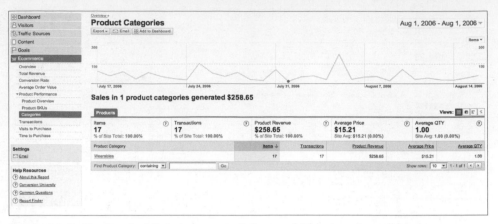

Figure 24-5: The Product Categories report shows which categories sell best.

The report shows the number of items sold, the total revenue, the average price, and the average order quantity for each product you sell online. You can also click the name of each category of products. This returns you to the Product Overview report you just saw.

The purpose of all of the reports in this section is to help you better manage the products that you offer on your site. Remember that you don't necessarily have to sell products to use these tracking tools. A little ingenuity will have you learning more about your non-product transactions before you know it.

CHAPTER 25

More E-Commerce Reports

There are so many elements that go into e-commerce. Not only do you need to watch the number of transactions that are completed on your site, but you also need to keep track of how those transactions take place, and also what's included in the transactions. Using these metrics, you can monitor thoroughly the effectiveness of your web site — everything from content to placement to product selection. You can also use these metrics to make educated guesses about products (or content, or services) that might be effective for your site in the future.

All the reports in this section seem minor when taken by themselves. When you combine these reports with additional information, however, you begin to put together a clear picture of how your site is performing and how that performance leads to conversions, transactions, and revenue. Then, if you need to follow up, having a complete list of transactions makes auditing easier and provides additional information on the transactions

Transactions

The first report in this section is the Transactions report. This report is exactly what it says, a transaction list. As shown in Figure 25-1, the report lists all of the transactions for your site within a given time frame.

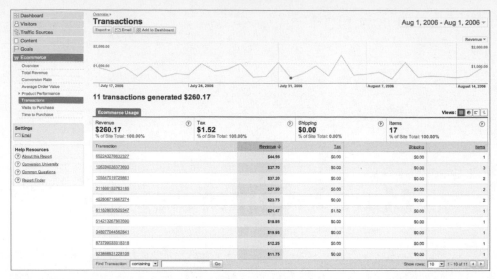

Figure 25-1: The Transactions report shows each transaction in a given time frame.

This information is most commonly used for auditing purposes, to ensure that actual transactions are represented properly in records and reports. It's a useful report if you want to see more details about the transactions that generate revenue.

This report has columns for tax, shipping, and the number of items in a transaction. This additional information gives you a method for monitoring changes in these categories. So if you find that the number of items in the average transaction is only two, you know you might need to recommend additional products using recommendation software or incentives to customers.

As with other reports in the new Google Analytics, clicking through a link, such as the link represented by each transaction number, takes you to a page on which you can view additional detail. In this case, clicking a transaction number takes you to the Transaction detail report, shown in Figure 25-2. This report shows exactly what products were purchased in the same transaction. The price and quantity of each item are also included. This information can be used in a variety of ways.

For example, if you're selling multiples of a single product during a majority of transactions, and this is unexpected, then you know this product has a special draw to your site visitors. Maybe it's just placed well on the site, maybe the content leading consumers to that product is especially well written, or perhaps you are the only e-commerce vendor on the web who has that item in stock (don't laugh, it happens). Whatever the case, you know that particular item is driving revenues, and that's a fact you can capitalize on, even if only for a short while.

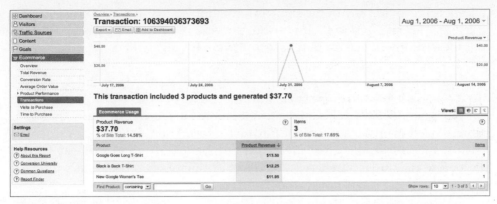

Figure 25-2: The Transaction detail report adds information about each transaction.

Visits to Purchase

The Visits to Purchase report, shown in Figure 25-3, shows you the number of visits that it took before a site visitor made a purchase.

In the Visits report, the measurement is the number of visits a user made to the site before making a purchase. So you're monitoring how many times they came to the site before being persuaded to buy.

This report might seem a little redundant, but it's not. How many of your visitors make a purchase the first time they visit your site? How many visitors come to your site five or more times before they make a purchase?

These measurements help you learn whether the content on your site is doing its job — making it easy for the visitor to make a decision. If your users have to return to your site numerous times before making a purchase, that probably means they were out comparing prices, reading reviews, or learning more about the product.

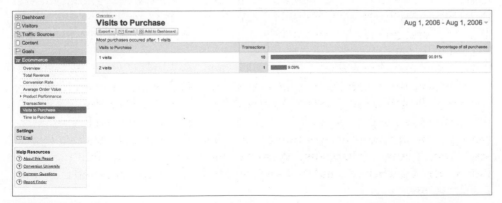

Figure 25-3: The Visits to Purchase report shows how many visits before a purchase.

Can you provide any of the same information so that the user doesn't have to leave your site to find it? If you can provide it, you have a greater chance that the visitor will make a purchase with you. It's all about convenience. And he who provides the most convenience wins.

Use this report to build more convenience into your site. It tells you how often visitors leave and come back; now all you have to do is change that. Web site designers should take into consideration all the information that consumers need to make a decision. Put that information at the customer's fingertips, and you're likely to decrease the number of times a visitor leaves your site before making a purchase, which in turn increases revenue. It's timeless economics. What's new now is the medium.

Time to Purchase

I know a person who spends a lot of time thinking about a shopping decision. He compares prices at all of the web sites that carry the product he seeks, he visits a page multiple times before making the decision to purchase, and he may even start the purchase several times and never complete it because he's indecisive about spending money, especially if he's looking for a high-ticket item.

This describes a large number of people in today's world. Money is tight for almost everyone, so we agonize over making purchases of all sizes. That's why you've designed your site to help your users make those purchasing decisions. If you have a good site, there might be reviews of the product included on the product page, or maybe there are articles about how the product could improve the user's life or workflow. It's even possible that you've included video testimonials from other users who have purchased the product and were happy with it.

The point here is that very often, users don't make a decision about buying a product on the first day. It's more likely they'll take several days to make the decision, but once it's made, the purchase is usually completed fairly quickly. Are your customers the instant-gratification types who want it right now, or are they more like the Thinking Man, stuck for a time in indecision?

The Time to Purchase report, shown in Figure 25-4, should answer that question for you. If you find that the majority of your users make purchases on their first visit, you know that whatever is drawing them to your site (it could be newsletter coupons, advertisements, or word of mouth) is working to complete the sale.

On the other hand, if your users seem to take several visits to make a purchase, how could you improve that? What information could you provide to the user to close the sale? This graph shows you which area you should concentrate on: driving more traffic or decreasing the time-to-purchase ratio.

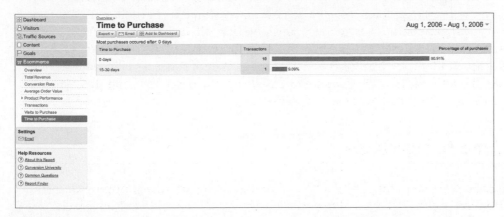

Figure 25-4: The Time to Purchase report tells how many visits precede a purchase.

Index

include filters
  in Filter Type drop-down menu, 74
  overview of, 90–91
indexes
  Google, 27
  spiders and, 28
Internet Explorer (IE)
  gathering stats about browser use, 33–34
  web site design affecting how a browser renders a
    site, 203–204
Internet service providers (ISP), 214
IP addresses
  AWStats countries list based on, 26–27
  AWStats hosts list based on, 27
  filters matching, 79
  predefined filters, 89
  unique visitors and, 187
ISP (Internet service providers), 214

J

Java Enabled report, browser capabilities, 211–212
JavaScript
  activating tracking and, 50–52
  user defined variable and, 221

K

keyphases, 242–243. *See also* keywords
Keyword Positions report, 244–245
keywords
  in AdWords campaigns, 242–243
  AWStats tables, 38
  bidding on to use in advertising, 240
  marketing and, 237
  positioning (Keyword Positions report), 244–245
  tracking keywords used in a campaign, 138
  traffic sources (Keywords report), 227
  where visitors came form (Entrance Keywords
    report), 265

L

Language report, Visitors Overview, 181–182
Linux OSs, user stats, 32–33
local business dashboards, 162–163
log analyzers
  AWStats (Advanced Web Statistics). *See* AWStats
    (Advanced Web Statistics)
  fudge factors in logging access, 16
  how they work, 10
  requests vs. actual page views, 18
long-term trends, metrics for, 24
lookup table filters
  in Filter Type drop-down menu, 75
  overview of, 93–94

M

Mac OSs, user stats, 32–33
manual tagging, 138
Map Overlay
  Standard Traffic Reports, 149–150
  Visitors Overview, 176–180
margin, AdWords ads and, 242
marketing. *See also* campaigns
  direct traffic reflecting effectiveness of, 228
  fine tuning with keywords, 236–237
  goal conversions and, 247–248
  keyword marketing, 239–240
  testing marketing campaigns, 253–255
  traffic (Referring Sites report), 230
marketing dashboards, 154–155

Medium detail, All Traffic Sources report, 233–234
Medium segmentation, campaign data, 250–252
Medium tag
  AdWords tag requirements, 117
  URLBuilder, 140
metrics
  analytics and, 5
  for goals, 104–105
  short-term and long-term trends, 24
  for site use, 259
  for user segmentation, 222
monetizing (valuing) goals. *See* goals, monetizing
  (valuing)
Monthly History, AWStats reports, 24
Mozilla, 33–34

N

navigating Google Analytics site, 53–57
Navigation Summary report, 260–263
needs analysis, 106–107
Netscape, 33–34
Network Location report, 213–215
Network Properties, 213–218
  connection speeds, 217–218
  hostnames, 215–216
  location, 213–215
  overview of, 213
New vs. Returning report, 180–181
newsgroups, "Connect to site from", 35
number of visits, AWStats summary, 19–20

O

objectives. *See also* goals
  defined, 103
  relationship to goals and specifics, 106
Opera, 203
Operating System report, 205–206
operating systems
  AWStats reports and, 32–35
  browser capabilities, 205–208

P

Page Views report, 189–190
pages (page views, page hits), AWStats summary,
  15–19
Pages-URL, AWStats reports, 30–32
passwords, signing up for Google Analytics and, 47
paths
  how users reach goal conversion (Reverse Goal
    Path report), 285
  viewing start and end points (Entrance Paths),
    263–264
Pending, tracking status, 64
permissions, setting user permissions, 69–70
predefined filters, 89
privacy, Google privacy policy, 49
Product Categories report, 303–304
Product Overview report, 300–302
product performance, 299–304
  overview of, 299–300
  Product Overview report, 300–302
  viewing which product category sells best
    (Product Categories report), 303–304
  viewing which products sell (Product SKUs
    report), 302–303
Product SKUs report, 302–303
Profile Settings page, 110
profiles. *See* web site profiles
purchases
  finding patterns in, 296